Contents

W9-BAK-996

Unit 1

NUMBER SENSE

Unit 2

ADDING WHOLE NUMBERS

Unit 3

SUBTRACTING WHOLE NUMBERS

To the Learner

The four books in the Steck-Vaughn series *Math Skills for the Workforce* are *Whole Numbers; Fractions; Decimals and Percents;* and *Measurement, Geometry, and Algebra.* They are written to help you understand and practice arithmetic skills, real-life applications, and problem-solving techniques.

This book contains features that will make it easier for you to work with whole numbers and to apply them to your daily life.

A Skills Inventory test appears at the beginning and end of the book.
- The first test shows you how much you already know.
- The final test can show you how much you have learned.

Each unit has several Mixed Reviews and a Unit Review.
- The Mixed Reviews give you a chance to practice the skills you have learned.
- The Unit Review helps you decide if you have mastered those skills.

There is also a glossary at the end of the book.
- Turn to the glossary to find the meanings of words that are new to you.
- Use the definitions and examples to help strengthen your understanding of terms used in mathematics.

The book contains answers and explanations for the problems.
- The answers let you check your work.
- The explanations take you through the steps used to solve the problems.

Whole Numbers Skills Inventory

Write each number in words.

1. 25 _____

2. 177 _____

3. 3,511 _____

Compare each set of numbers. Write > or <.

4. 60 ☐ 70   **5.** 25 ☐ 15   **6.** 41 ☐ 14   **7.** 89 ☐ 100

Write the value of the underlined digit in each number.

8. <u>1</u>2 _____   **9.** 2<u>7</u> _____   **10.** <u>1</u>42 _____   **11.** 2,<u>3</u>90 _____

Round each number to the nearest ten.

12. 62 _____   **13.** 671 _____   **14.** 1,355 _____

Round each number to the nearest hundred.

15. 417 _____   **16.** 7,874 _____   **17.** 33,765 _____

Round each number to the nearest thousand.

18. 8,650 _____   **19.** 45,099 _____   **20.** 234,508 _____

Add.

21.
$$\begin{array}{r} 5 \\ + 6 \\ \hline \end{array}$$

22. $3 + 9 + 8 =$

23.
$$\begin{array}{r} 37 \\ + 40 \\ \hline \end{array}$$

24. $8 + 71 + 20 =$

25.
$$\begin{array}{r} 330 \\ + 345 \\ \hline \end{array}$$

26.
$$\begin{array}{r} 5,311 \\ 660 \\ + \quad 28 \\ \hline \end{array}$$

27.
$$\begin{array}{r} 34 \\ + 57 \\ \hline \end{array}$$

28. $76 + 83 + 10 =$

29.
$$\begin{array}{r} 547 \\ + 367 \\ \hline \end{array}$$

30.
$$\begin{array}{r} 923 \\ 5,687 \\ 15 \\ + 1,236 \\ \hline \end{array}$$

31. $234,000 + 46,677 =$

32.
$$\begin{array}{r} 2,430,000 \\ 3,899 \\ + \quad 24,801 \\ \hline \end{array}$$

Subtract.

33.
13
− 6

34. 11 − 3 =

35.
56
− 32

36.
79
− 8

37. 38 − 32 =

38.
699
− 37

39.
8,427
− 307

40. 9,278 − 6,152 =

41.
37
− 28

42. 82 − 9 =

43.
40
− 7

44.
30
− 15

45.
843
− 695

46. 726 − 259 =

47. 5,300 − 1,486 =

48.
12,020
− 1,942

49.
130,000
− 99,469

Multiply.

50. 8 × 3 =

51.
52
× 2

52. 902 × 3 =

53.
3,020
× 4

54.
23
× 13

55. 530 × 32 =

56.
110
× 123

57.
502
× 438

58.
6,100
× 100

59. 2,409 × 1,000 =

60. 25 × 7 =

61.
389
× 4

62.
3,509
× 5

63. 15 × 38 =

64. 6,070 × 46 =

65.
297
× 163

66.
509
× 600

67.
1,270
× 302

7

Divide.

68.
$12 \div 6 =$

69.
$5\overline{)30}$

70.
$497 \div 7 =$

71.
$9\overline{)819}$

72.
$8\overline{)59}$

73.
$16 \div 3 =$

74.
$483 \div 5 =$

75.
$4\overline{)1,314}$

76.
$6\overline{)1,303}$

77.
$2\overline{)10,230}$

78.
$86\overline{)93}$

79.
$54\overline{)504}$

80.
$1,309 \div 17 =$

81.
$30\overline{)20,650}$

82.
$832\overline{)8,016}$

83.
$523\overline{)53,870}$

Below is a list of the problems in this Skills Inventory and the pages on which the skills are taught. If you missed any problems, turn to the pages listed and practice the skills. Then correct the problems you missed in the Skills Inventory.

Problem	Practice Page	Problem	Practice Page	Problem	Practice Page
Unit 1		*Unit 3*		58-59	101-102
1-3	10	33-34	55-58	60-61	105-106
4-7	13	35-37	60-61	62	107-108
8-11	18-19	38-40	62	63-64	110-111
12-14	20	41-42	66-67	65	112-113
15-17	21	43-44	68-69	66-67	114-115
18-20	22	45-46	72-73	*Unit 5*	
Unit 2		47-49	75-78	68-69	123-126
21	29-31	*Unit 4*		70-71	127-128
22	32	50	85-87	72-74	129-130
23-24	34-35	51	89-90	75	134-135
25	36	52-53	91	76-77	136-137
26	37	54	95	78-80	140-142
27-28	41-42	55	96	81	143
29	43	56-57	97-98	82	147-148
30	44			83	149-150
31	45				
32	48				

Unit 1 NUMBER SENSE

Numbers are everywhere. They are found on road signs, paychecks, gas pumps, book pages, and in advertisements. Number sense can help you find a better buy at the store, understand your paycheck, and figure out how many miles it is from one place to another.

In this unit, you will learn about numbers — what they mean, how they are formed, and how to compare them. You will also learn some of the language used in mathematics.

Getting Ready

You should be familiar with the skills on this page and the next before you begin this unit. To check your answers, turn to page 173.

 A number line shows the order of whole numbers. As you move to the right along the number line, the numbers get larger.

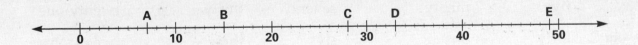

Each mark on this number line represents a whole number.

Write the number that each letter represents.

1. A ___7___   2. B _____   3. C _____   4. D _____   5. E _____

Getting Ready

 Numbers can be written as words.

Write each number in words. You can use the list below to check your spelling.

0 zero	1 _____
2 _____	3 _____
4 _____	5 _____
6 _____	7 _____
8 _____	9 _____
10 _____	11 _____
12 _____	13 _____
14 _____	15 _____
16 _____	17 _____
18 _____	19 _____
20 _____	21 twenty-one
22 _____	23 _____
24 _____	25 _____
30 _____	40 _____
50 _____	60 _____
70 _____	80 _____
90 _____	100 _____
1,000 _____	

eight	five	ninety	seventy	thirty	twenty-one
eighteen	forty	one	six	three	twenty-three
eighty	four	one hundred	sixteen	twelve	twenty-two
eleven	fourteen	one thousand	sixty	twenty	two
fifteen	nine	seven	ten	twenty-five	zero
fifty	nineteen	seventeen	thirteen	twenty-four	

Number Patterns

You can create number patterns by counting forward or backward by a certain number. For example, when you count forward by 1, you create a pattern. Each number is one more than the number before it. To find the next number in the pattern below, count 1 more.

4, 5, 6, __7__
rule: count 1 more

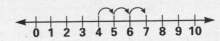

When you count backward by 3, you also create a pattern. Each number is 3 less than the number before it. To find the next number in the pattern below, count 3 less.

10, 7, 4, __1__
rule: count 3 less

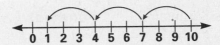

Use These Steps

Find the rule for the pattern 6, 4, 2, _____. Then write the missing number.

1. Look at each number in the pattern 6, 4, 2.

2. Write the rule for the pattern.

   rule: count 2 less

3. Use the rule to find the missing number.

   6, 4, 2, __0__

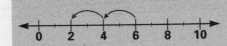

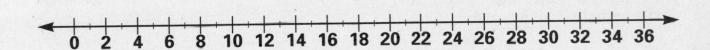

Find the rule for each pattern. Then write the missing number.

1. 5, 8, 11, __14__

rule: __count 3 more__

2. 5, 10, 15, _____

rule: _____

3. 8, 12, 16, _____

rule: _____

4. 13, 11, 9, __7__

rule: __count 2 less__

5. 9, 6, 3, _____

rule: _____

6. 17, 14, 11, _____

rule: _____

7. 18, 22, 26, _____

rule: _____

8. 27, 25, 23, _____

rule: _____

9. 33, 26, 19, _____

rule: _____

10. 4, 10, 16, _____

rule: _____

11. 24, 19, 14, _____

rule: _____

12. 10, 7, 4, _____

rule: _____

Number Groups

Our number system is based on tens. We can write two-digit numbers as groups of tens and ones. We can write three-digit numbers as groups of hundreds, tens, and ones.

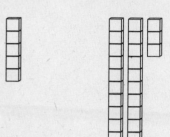
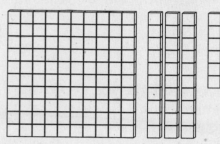

5 ones = 5   2 tens 3 ones = 23   1 hundred   3 tens   6 ones = 136

Use These Steps

Write 104 as groups of hundreds, tens, and ones.

1. Look at the digit on the left. Write the number of hundreds that this digit shows.

104

__1__ hundreds

2. Look at the digit in the center. Write the number of tens that this digit shows.

104

__0__ tens

3. Look at the digit on the right. Write the number of ones that this digit shows.

104

__4__ ones

Write each digit in the correct group.

1. 2 __2__ ones

2. 6 ___ ones

3. 15 __1__ tens __5__ ones

4. 89 ___ tens ___ ones

5. 10 ___ tens ___ ones

6. 20 ___ tens ___ ones

7. 50 ___ tens ___ ones

8. 90 ___ tens ___ ones

9. 254 __2__ hundreds __5__ tens __4__ ones

10. 971 ___ hundreds ___ tens ___ ones

11. 855 ___ hundreds ___ tens ___ ones

12. 482 ___ hundreds ___ tens ___ ones

13. 106 ___ hundreds ___ tens ___ ones

14. 605 ___ hundreds ___ tens ___ ones

15. 408 ___ hundreds ___ tens ___ ones

16. 302 ___ hundreds ___ tens ___ ones

17. 500 ___ hundreds ___ tens ___ ones

18. 100 ___ hundreds ___ tens ___ ones

19. 700 ___ hundreds ___ tens ___ ones

20. 600 ___ hundreds ___ tens ___ ones

Comparing Numbers

A number line can be used to compare numbers. Remember, as you move to the right, the numbers get larger.

This number line shows whole numbers from 10 to 40.

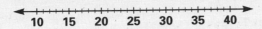

The symbol > means *greater than*.   25 > 20
The symbol < means *less than*.   15 < 20

Use These Steps

Compare 23 and 32.

1. Find 23 and 32 on this part of the number line.

2. Decide which number is farther right. It is the greater number. The number that is farther left is the lesser number.

3. Use the symbols to show *greater than* or *less than*.

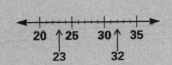

32 is greater than 23
or
23 is less than 32

32 > 23
or
23 < 32

Compare each set of numbers. Write > or <.

1. 50 > 40   2. 10 < 20   3. 80 ☐ 10   4. 70 ☐ 30

5. 25 ☐ 30   6. 51 ☐ 40   7. 10 ☐ 29   8. 30 ☐ 42

9. 100 ☐ 96   10. 52 ☐ 34   11. 48 ☐ 54   12. 64 ☐ 68

13. 79 ☐ 82   14. 63 ☐ 83   15. 91 ☐ 81   16. 22 ☐ 33

17. 41 ☐ 22   18. 33 ☐ 35   19. 100 ☐ 10   20. 89 ☐ 99

21. 42 ☐ 24   22. 89 ☐ 98   23. 19 ☐ 91   24. 0 ☐ 10

13

Number Meaning

Every number is made up of other numbers. You can use several combinations of numbers to express a given number. For example, to pay for a shirt that costs $12, you could use 1 five-dollar bill and 7 one-dollar bills. You could also use 1 ten-dollar bill and 2 one-dollar bills. The number line below shows both combinations.

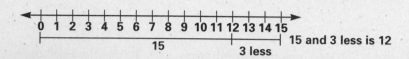

You could also express 12 by counting backwards from a number greater than 12. 15 and 3 less is 12.

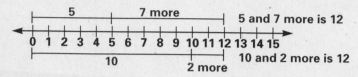

Use These Steps

Write the number 9 two different ways.

1. Choose a number less than 9. Try 5. Count forward to 9 from 5.

2. Choose a number greater than 9. Try 10. Count backward to 9 from 10.

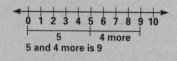

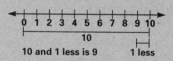

Use the number line to write each number two different ways.

1. 5

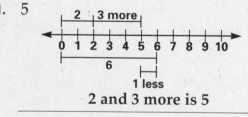

2 and 3 more is 5

_____

6 and 1 less is 5

_____

2. 8

_____

_____

3. 10

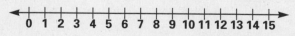

_____

_____

4. 14

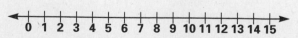

_____

_____

Application

You use numbers when you measure things. For example, you measure weight in numbers of ounces and pounds, and cost in numbers of dollars and cents.

The groups below show measurements we use every day. The sign = means *equals*.

12 inches	= 1 foot
3 feet	= 1 yard
5,280 feet	= 1 mile

16 ounces	= 1 pound
2,000 pounds	= 1 ton

100 cents	= 1 dollar

60 seconds	= 1 minute
60 minutes	= 1 hour
24 hours	= 1 day
365 days	= 1 year

Circle the letter of the most likely measurement.

1. the weight of an office chair
   a. 18 pounds
   b. 18 ounces

2. the weight of a hammer
   a. 10 pounds
   b. 10 ounces

3. the height of a telephone pole
   a. 30 feet
   b. 30 inches

4. the time a meeting takes
   a. 45 minutes
   b. 45 seconds

5. the length of a room
   a. 12 inches
   b. 12 feet

6. the time it takes to paint a building
   a. 3 days
   b. 3 years

7. the time it takes to drive to work
   a. 1 day
   b. 1 hour

8. the cost of a pencil
   a. 2 cents
   b. 2 dollars

9. the weight of a delivery van
   a. 2 tons
   b. 2 pounds

10. the length of a store aisle
    a. 100 yards
    b. 100 miles

11. the cost of a 3-ring binder
    a. 6 cents
    b. 6 dollars

12. the time it takes to cut someone's hair
    a. 20 hours
    b. 20 minutes

15

Find the rule for each pattern. Then write the missing number.

```
◄───┼──┼──┼──┼──┼──┼──┼──┼──┼──┼──┼──┼───►
    0  5  10 15 20 25 30 35 40 45 50 55
```

1. 8, 6, 4, _____   **2.** 18, 15, 12, _____   **3.** 11, 16, 21, _____

rule: _____   rule: _____   rule: _____

4. 7, 14, 21, _____   **5.** 24, 18, 12, _____   **6.** 51, 44, 37, _____

rule: _____   rule: _____   rule: _____

Write each digit in the correct group.

7. 4 ____ ones   **8.** 28 ____ tens ____ ones

9. 134 ____ hundreds ____ tens ____ ones   **10.** 614 ____ hundreds ____ tens ____ ones

Compare each set of numbers. Write > or <.

11. 25 _____ 31   **12.** 42 _____ 22   **13.** 37 _____ 41

14. 20 _____ 50   **15.** 44 _____ 39   **16.** 51 _____ 15

Use the number lines to write each number two different ways.

17. 4

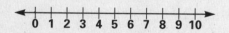

_____

_____

18. 7

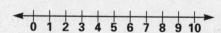

_____

_____

19. 11

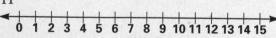

_____

_____

20. 13

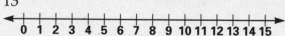

_____

_____

Circle the letter of the most likely measurement.

21. the weight of an apple
   a. 10 pounds
   b. 10 ounces

22. the cost of a car
   a. ten thousand dollars
   b. ten dollars

Application

In any workplace, such as the Baywater Bus Company, the employees need to know how to compare numbers to do their jobs well.

Solve.

1. John's bus route is 36 miles long. Mary's bus route is 32 miles long. Which bus driver has the shorter bus route, John or Mary?

   Answer _____

2. Yesterday Rosa sold 34 bus tickets from Baywater to Brookfield. Today she sold 43 tickets. Did she sell more tickets yesterday or today?

   Answer _____

3. There were sixty-eight passengers on the 8:00 A.M. bus and seventy-seven passengers on the 10:00 A.M. bus. Were there more passengers on the 8:00 A.M. bus or the 10:00 A.M. bus?

   Answer _____

4. Mary has been driving a bus for Baywater for 25 years. John has been driving for Baywater for 29 years. Who has been driving longer for the bus company?

   Answer _____

5. Last Sunday the temperature outside the bus station reached a high of 102°. This Sunday the temperature reached 92°. On which Sunday was the temperature higher, last Sunday or this Sunday?

   Answer _____

6. One day the trip by bus from Baywater to Taylor took 45 minutes. The return trip took 56 minutes. Which trip took longer, from Baywater to Taylor or from Taylor to Baywater?

   Answer _____

7. John loaded two boxes on his bus, a large box weighing 17 pounds and a small box weighing 24 pounds. Which box weighed more, the large box or the small box?

   Answer _____

8. On Monday, Rosa collected $300 in bus ticket sales and $250 in shipping fees. Did Rosa collect more for tickets or for shipping fees?

   Answer _____

Place Value to the Hundreds Place

The value of a digit in a number depends on its place. For example, you know that 25 is a group of 2 tens and 5 ones. In 25, the value of the 2 is 20, and the value of the 5 is 5.

The place value chart shows the digits in the number 25 in their correct groups.

Use These Steps

Write the value of each digit in the number 590.

1. Write each digit in its correct place in the chart below.

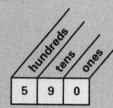

hundreds	tens	ones
5	9	0

2. Write each digit in the correct number group. Then write the value of the digit.

5 hundreds = 500
9 tens = 90
0 ones = 0

Write each number in the chart. Then write each digit in the correct number group, and write the value of the digit.

1. 67

   6 tens = 60
   7 ones = 7

2. 92

   _____ tens = _____
   _____ ones = _____

3. 125

   1 hundreds = 100
   2 tens = 20
   5 ones = 5

4. 490

   _____ hundreds = _____
   _____ tens = _____
   _____ ones = _____

	hundreds	tens	ones
1.		6	7
2.			
3.			
4.			

Write the value of the underlined digit in each number.

5. 5̲7 50
6. 3̲6 _____
7. 9̲8 _____
8. 1̲35 _____

9. 37̲9 _____
10. 854̲ _____
11. 2̲05 _____
12. 3̲00 _____

13. 57̲0 _____
14. 499̲ _____
15. 68̲7 _____
16. 70̲4 _____

18

Place Value to the Thousands Place

A place value chart can also show thousands. The number 4,189 is a group of 4 thousands, 1 hundred, 8 tens, and 9 ones.

Commas are used to separate digits into groups of three. This makes large numbers easier to read.

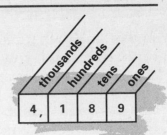

Use These Steps

Write the value of each digit in the number 7,036.

1. Write each digit in its correct place in the chart below.

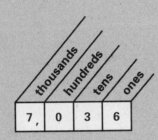

2. Write each digit beside the correct number group. Then write the value of the digit.

_7_ thousands = _7,000_

_0_ hundreds = _000_

_3_ tens = _30_

_6_ ones = _6_

Write each number in the chart. Then write each digit in the correct number group, and write the value of the digit.

1. 2,437

_2_ thousands = _2,000_

_4_ hundreds = _400_

_3_ tens = _30_

_7_ ones = _7_

2. 3,013

_____ thousands = _____

_____ hundreds = _____

_____ tens = _____

_____ ones = _____

	thousands	hundreds	tens	ones
1.	2,	4	3	7
2.				
3.				
4.				

3. 4,608

_____ thousands = _____

_____ hundreds = _____

_____ tens = _____

_____ ones = _____

4. 5,520

_____ thousands = _____

_____ hundreds = _____

_____ tens = _____

_____ ones = _____

Write the value of the underlined digit in each number.

5. 5̲67 _500_

6. 6̲9̲0 _____

7. 70̲3̲ _____

8. 1,3̲3̲4 _____

9. 3̲,701 _____

10. 8̲,006 _____

11. 6,4̲00 _____

12. 5,632̲ _____

13. 9,95̲5̲ _____

19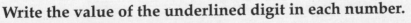

Rounding to the Nearest Ten

In working with numbers, sometimes you do not need to use an exact number. Instead, you need to know *about how many*, rather than *exactly how many*. To find *about how many*, use rounding.

You can use a number line to round a given number. To round a number to the nearest ten, find a number in the tens place that is closer to that number. That is the number you round to.

If the digit in the ones place in the number you're rounding is less than 5, round down to the nearest ten. If the digit in the ones place is 5 (is halfway between two tens) or is greater than 5, round up to the higher number in the tens place.

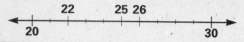

22 is closer to 20 than to 30   22 rounds down to 20
25 is halfway between 20 and 30   25 rounds up to 30
26 is closer to 30 than to 20   26 rounds up to 30

You can round a number without using a number line.
Follow the steps below.

Use These Steps

Round 37 to the nearest ten.

1. Look at the digit in the ones place. Is it less than 5, exactly 5, or greater than 5?

    3 <u>7</u>

    7 > 5

2. Since the digit in the ones place is greater than 5, round up to the nearest ten.

    37 rounds up to 40

Round each number to the nearest ten.

1. 45 _____50_____

2. 58 _____

3. 54 _____

4. 52 _____

5. 71 _____

6. 55 _____

7. 886 ____890____

8. 911 _____

9. 448 _____

10. 794 _____

11. 385 _____

12. 176 _____

13. 9,554 ___9,550___

14. 1,406 _____

15. 6,501 _____

16. 2,004 _____

17. 8,765 _____

18. 1,979 _____

19. 44 _____

20. 224 _____

21. 903 _____

22. 1,889 _____

23. 75 _____

24. 9,989 _____

Rounding to the Nearest Hundred

To round a number to the nearest hundred, find a number in the hundreds place that is closer to that number. That is the number you round to.

If the digit in the tens place in the number you're rounding is less than 5, round down to the nearest hundred. If the digit in the tens place is 5 or is greater than 5, round up to the higher number in the hundreds place.

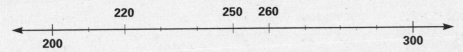

220 is closer to 200 than to 300   220 rounds down to 200
250 is halfway between 200 and 300   250 rounds up to 300
260 is closer to 300 than to 200   250 rounds up to 300

You can round a number without using a number line. Follow the steps below.

Use These Steps

Round 370 to the nearest hundred.

1. Look at the digit in the tens place. Is it less than 5, exactly 5, or greater than 5?

   3 <u>7</u> 0

   7 > 5

2. Since the digit in the tens place is greater than 5, round up to the nearest hundred.

   370 rounds up to 400

Round each number to the nearest hundred.

1. 410   __400__
2. 540   _____
3. 650   _____

4. 649   _____
5. 733   _____
6. 421   _____

7. 1,550   __1,600__
8. 2,640   _____
9. 4,680   _____

10. 1,242   _____
11. 1,101   _____
12. 2,142   _____

13. 16,660   __16,700__
14. 24,441   _____
15. 92,621   _____

16. 18,492   _____
17. 10,401   _____
18. 13,899   _____

19. 780   _____
20. 50,149   _____
21. 9,790   _____

22. 2,560   _____
23. 33,842   _____
24. 569   _____

Rounding to the Nearest Thousand

To round a number to the nearest thousand, find a number in the thousands place that is closer to that number. That is the number you round to.

If the digit in the hundreds place in the number you're rounding is less than 5, round down to the nearest thousand. If the digit in the hundreds place is 5 or is greater than 5, round up to the higher number in the thousands place.

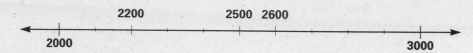

2,200 is closer to 2,000 than to 3,000   2,200 rounds down to 2,000
2,500 is halfway between 2,000 and 3,000   2,500 rounds up to 3,000
2,600 is closer to 3,000 than to 2,000   2,600 rounds up to 3,000

You can round a number without using a number line. Follow the steps below.

Use These Steps

Round 3,700 to the nearest thousand.

1. Look at the digit in the hundreds place. Is it less than 5, exactly 5, or greater than 5?

   3,_7_ 00

   7 > 5

2. Since the digit in the hundreds place is greater than 5, round up to the nearest thousand.

   3,700 rounds up to 4,000

Round each number to the nearest thousand.

1.	7,300	7,000	**2.**	5,500	_____	**3.**	4,100	_____
4.	4,490	_____	**5.**	6,210	_____	**6.**	4,530	_____
7.	18,081	18,000	**8.**	97,999	_____	**9.**	36,561	_____
10.	21,801	_____	**11.**	13,569	_____	**12.**	92,489	_____
13.	111,591	112,000	**14.**	213,649	_____	**15.**	139,492	_____
16.	264,949	_____	**17.**	955,611	_____	**18.**	231,499	_____
19.	8,700	_____	**20.**	149,300	_____	**21.**	47,499	_____
22.	561,180	_____	**23.**	86,399	_____	**24.**	6,790	_____

Problem Solving: Using a Table

The table to the right shows the 1980 and 1990 populations of five cities. Some of these cities had more people in 1990 than they had in 1980. Some of them had fewer people. Use the table to answer the questions below.

Example Which city had the largest population in 1980?

▶ **Step 1.** Look at the populations in the column for 1980.

▶ **Step 2.** Compare the values of the digits on the left in each number. If the digits are the same, compare the next digits.

$\underline{1}2,965$
$\underline{2}3,312$
$\underline{1}1,573$
$\underline{2}4,599$
$\underline{2}2,207$

▶ **Step 3.** Find the largest number. Write the name of the city that had the largest population in 1980.

Benton

	1980	1990
Pattonville	12,965	13,012
Shoreline	23,312	23,501
Eagle City	11,573	11,416
Benton	24,599	24,467
Hillview	22,207	22,299

Population Figures for Five Cities

Solve.

1. Which city had the smallest population in 1980?

2. Which cities had more people in 1990 than in 1980?

Answer _____

Answer _____

3. Which cities had fewer people in 1990 than in 1980?

4. Which city had the larger population in 1990: Pattonville or Shoreline?

Answer _____

Answer _____

5. Which city had the smaller population in 1990: Eagle City or Pattonville?

Answer _____

6. Which city had the largest population in 1990?

Answer _____

7. Was the population of Benton smaller in 1980 or in 1990?

Answer _____

8. Which city had the smallest population in 1990?

Answer _____

9. Which city had the smaller population in 1980: Hillview or Shoreline?

Answer _____

10. Was the population of Shoreline larger in 1990 or in 1980?

Answer _____

11. Write the name and population of each city in the table below. Then for each year, round the populations to the nearest thousand.

City	1980 Population	Nearest Thousand	1990 Population	Nearest Thousand

Unit 1 *Review*

Write each number in words.

1. 25 _____

2. 41 _____

3. 987 _____

4. 603 _____

5. 1,001 _____

6. 6,852 _____

Find the rule for each pattern. Then write the missing number.

7. 35, 45, 55, _____   8. 18, 20, 22, _____   9. 3, 6, 9, _____

    rule: _____   rule: _____   rule: _____

10. 15, 13, 11, _____   11. 20, 30, 40, _____   12. 14, 12, 10, _____

    rule: _____   rule: _____   rule: _____

Compare each set of numbers. Write > or <.

13. 20 ☐ 19   14. 44 ☐ 72   15. 11 ☐ 10   16. 38 ☐ 98

17. 90 ☐ 70   18. 64 ☐ 40   19. 44 ☐ 33   20. 22 ☐ 26

Use the number lines to write each number two different ways.

21. 6

0 1 2 3 4 5 6 7 8 9 10

_____

_____

22. 2

0 1 2 3 4 5 6 7 8 9 10

_____

_____

23. 12

0 1 2 3 4 5 6 7 8 9 10 11 12 13 14 15

_____

_____

24. 9

0 1 2 3 4 5 6 7 8 9 10 11 12 13 14 15

_____

_____

Circle the letter of the most likely measurement.

25. the length of a desk
    a. 4 feet
    b. 4 yards

26. the height of a flagpole
    a. 20 miles
    b. 20 feet

27. the weight of a pair of glasses
    a. 1 pound
    b. 1 ounce

28. the cost of a can of soda
    a. 60 cents
    b. 60 dollars

Write the value of the underlined digit in each number.

29. 1̲73 _____   **30.** 4,52̲2 _____   **31.** 9̲07 _____

32. 8̲,406 _____   **33.** 5,617̲ _____   **34.** 9,24̲0 _____

Round each number to the nearest ten.

35. 84 _____   **36.** 15 _____   **37.** 59 _____   **38.** 104 _____

39. 155 _____   **40.** 271 _____   **41.** 1,235 _____   **42.** 4,556 _____

Round each number to the nearest hundred.

43. 456 _____   **44.** 923 _____   **45.** 555 _____   **46.** 199 _____

47. 1,222 _____   **48.** 5,889 _____   **49.** 33,499 _____   **50.** 58,541 _____

Round each number to the nearest thousand.

51. 7,456 _____   **52.** 4,499 _____   **53.** 9,489 _____   **54.** 10,732 _____

55. 34,567 _____   **56.** 99,099 _____   **57.** 167,998 _____   **58.** 132,721 _____

Below is a list of the problems in this review and the pages on which the skills are taught. If you missed any problems, turn to the pages listed and practice the skills. Then correct the problems you missed in the Unit Review.

Unit 2 ADDING WHOLE NUMBERS

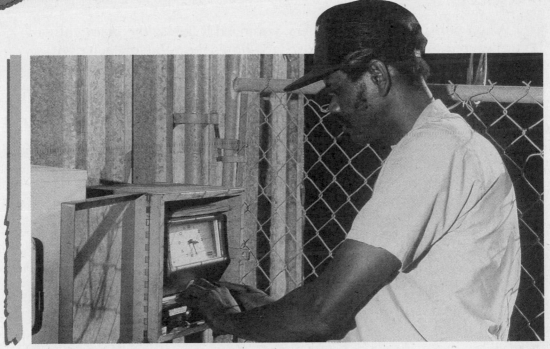

You add whole numbers when you count the number of hours you work in a week, the number of calories you eat in a day, or the number of miles you travel from one place to another.

In this unit, you will learn the addition facts and how to line up and add whole numbers. You will also learn how to estimate to find an approximate answer when an exact answer is not needed.

Getting Ready

You should be familiar with the skills on this page and the next before you begin this unit. To check your answers, turn to page 176.

 When you write out numbers, you need to know the place value of each digit.

number	place value
25	2 tens 5 ones
392	3 hundreds 9 tens 2 ones
1,200	1 thousand 2 hundreds 0 tens 0 ones

Write each digit in the correct group.

1. 37 ___3___ tens ___7___ ones

2. 550 _____ hundreds _____ tens _____ ones

3. 3,901 _____ thousands _____ hundreds _____ tens _____ ones

For review, see Unit 1, page 12.

When you add whole numbers, you need to know the place value of each digit. The place value chart shows the value of each digit.

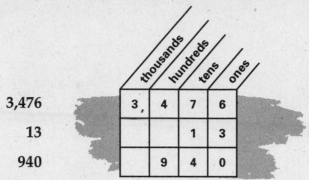

Write the value of the underlined digit in each number.

4. 2,161 __2,000__   **5.** 25 ____   **6.** 64<u>3</u> ____   **7.** <u>8</u>17 ____   **8.** 4,<u>2</u>00 ____

9. <u>5</u>6 ____   **10.** 50<u>9</u> ____   **11.** 1<u>0</u>2 ____   **12.** <u>9</u>,094 ____   **13.** 7<u>8</u> ____

For review, see Unit 1, pages 18-19.

 When you round whole numbers, you need to know the place value of each digit.

Round to the nearest ten: 15 rounds to   20
Round to the nearest hundred: 203 rounds to   200
Round to the nearest thousand: 7,960 rounds to 8,000

Round each number to the nearest ten.

14. 35 __40__   **15.** 122 ____   **16.** 309 ____   **17.** 2,449 ____

Round each number to the nearest hundred.

18. 135 __100__   **19.** 4,559 ____   **20.** 16,630 ____   **21.** 89 ____

Round each number to the nearest thousand.

22. 1,087 __1,000__   **23.** 15,987 ____   **24.** 234,191 ____   **25.** 999 ____

For review, see Unit 1, pages 20-22.

Addition Facts

To add larger numbers, you should first know the basic addition facts.
You will find it helpful to know the following facts by heart.

Add the following numbers to complete each row. Notice that the answers form a pattern.

1.

| $\begin{array}{r} 0 \\ +0 \\ \hline 0 \end{array}$ | $\begin{array}{r} 0 \\ +1 \\ \hline 1 \end{array}$ | $\begin{array}{r} 0 \\ +2 \\ \hline 2 \end{array}$ | $\begin{array}{r} 0 \\ +3 \\ \hline 3 \end{array}$ | $\begin{array}{r} 0 \\ +4 \\ \hline 4 \end{array}$ | $\begin{array}{r} 0 \\ +5 \\ \hline 5 \end{array}$ | $\begin{array}{r} 0 \\ +6 \\ \hline 6 \end{array}$ | $\begin{array}{r} 0 \\ +7 \\ \hline 7 \end{array}$ | $\begin{array}{r} 0 \\ +8 \\ \hline 8 \end{array}$ | $\begin{array}{r} 0 \\ +9 \\ \hline 9 \end{array}$ |

2.

| $\begin{array}{r} 1 \\ +0 \end{array}$ | $\begin{array}{r} 1 \\ +1 \end{array}$ | $\begin{array}{r} 1 \\ +2 \end{array}$ | $\begin{array}{r} 1 \\ +3 \end{array}$ | $\begin{array}{r} 1 \\ +4 \end{array}$ | $\begin{array}{r} 1 \\ +5 \end{array}$ | $\begin{array}{r} 1 \\ +6 \end{array}$ | $\begin{array}{r} 1 \\ +7 \end{array}$ | $\begin{array}{r} 1 \\ +8 \end{array}$ | $\begin{array}{r} 1 \\ +9 \end{array}$ |

3.

| $\begin{array}{r} 2 \\ +0 \end{array}$ | $\begin{array}{r} 2 \\ +1 \end{array}$ | $\begin{array}{r} 2 \\ +2 \end{array}$ | $\begin{array}{r} 2 \\ +3 \end{array}$ | $\begin{array}{r} 2 \\ +4 \end{array}$ | $\begin{array}{r} 2 \\ +5 \end{array}$ | $\begin{array}{r} 2 \\ +6 \end{array}$ | $\begin{array}{r} 2 \\ +7 \end{array}$ | $\begin{array}{r} 2 \\ +8 \end{array}$ | $\begin{array}{r} 2 \\ +9 \end{array}$ |

4.

| $\begin{array}{r} 3 \\ +0 \end{array}$ | $\begin{array}{r} 3 \\ +1 \end{array}$ | $\begin{array}{r} 3 \\ +2 \end{array}$ | $\begin{array}{r} 3 \\ +3 \end{array}$ | $\begin{array}{r} 3 \\ +4 \end{array}$ | $\begin{array}{r} 3 \\ +5 \end{array}$ | $\begin{array}{r} 3 \\ +6 \end{array}$ | $\begin{array}{r} 3 \\ +7 \end{array}$ | $\begin{array}{r} 3 \\ +8 \end{array}$ | $\begin{array}{r} 3 \\ +9 \end{array}$ |

5.

| $\begin{array}{r} 4 \\ +0 \end{array}$ | $\begin{array}{r} 4 \\ +1 \end{array}$ | $\begin{array}{r} 4 \\ +2 \end{array}$ | $\begin{array}{r} 4 \\ +3 \end{array}$ | $\begin{array}{r} 4 \\ +4 \end{array}$ | $\begin{array}{r} 4 \\ +5 \end{array}$ | $\begin{array}{r} 4 \\ +6 \end{array}$ | $\begin{array}{r} 4 \\ +7 \end{array}$ | $\begin{array}{r} 4 \\ +8 \end{array}$ | $\begin{array}{r} 4 \\ +9 \end{array}$ |

6.

| $\begin{array}{r} 5 \\ +0 \end{array}$ | $\begin{array}{r} 5 \\ +1 \end{array}$ | $\begin{array}{r} 5 \\ +2 \end{array}$ | $\begin{array}{r} 5 \\ +3 \end{array}$ | $\begin{array}{r} 5 \\ +4 \end{array}$ | $\begin{array}{r} 5 \\ +5 \end{array}$ | $\begin{array}{r} 5 \\ +6 \end{array}$ | $\begin{array}{r} 5 \\ +7 \end{array}$ | $\begin{array}{r} 5 \\ +8 \end{array}$ | $\begin{array}{r} 5 \\ +9 \end{array}$ |

7.

| $\begin{array}{r} 6 \\ +0 \end{array}$ | $\begin{array}{r} 6 \\ +1 \end{array}$ | $\begin{array}{r} 6 \\ +2 \end{array}$ | $\begin{array}{r} 6 \\ +3 \end{array}$ | $\begin{array}{r} 6 \\ +4 \end{array}$ | $\begin{array}{r} 6 \\ +5 \end{array}$ | $\begin{array}{r} 6 \\ +6 \end{array}$ | $\begin{array}{r} 6 \\ +7 \end{array}$ | $\begin{array}{r} 6 \\ +8 \end{array}$ | $\begin{array}{r} 6 \\ +9 \end{array}$ |

8.

| $\begin{array}{r} 7 \\ +0 \end{array}$ | $\begin{array}{r} 7 \\ +1 \end{array}$ | $\begin{array}{r} 7 \\ +2 \end{array}$ | $\begin{array}{r} 7 \\ +3 \end{array}$ | $\begin{array}{r} 7 \\ +4 \end{array}$ | $\begin{array}{r} 7 \\ +5 \end{array}$ | $\begin{array}{r} 7 \\ +6 \end{array}$ | $\begin{array}{r} 7 \\ +7 \end{array}$ | $\begin{array}{r} 7 \\ +8 \end{array}$ | $\begin{array}{r} 7 \\ +9 \end{array}$ |

9.

| $\begin{array}{r} 8 \\ +0 \end{array}$ | $\begin{array}{r} 8 \\ +1 \end{array}$ | $\begin{array}{r} 8 \\ +2 \end{array}$ | $\begin{array}{r} 8 \\ +3 \end{array}$ | $\begin{array}{r} 8 \\ +4 \end{array}$ | $\begin{array}{r} 8 \\ +5 \end{array}$ | $\begin{array}{r} 8 \\ +6 \end{array}$ | $\begin{array}{r} 8 \\ +7 \end{array}$ | $\begin{array}{r} 8 \\ +8 \end{array}$ | $\begin{array}{r} 8 \\ +9 \end{array}$ |

10.

| $\begin{array}{r} 9 \\ +0 \end{array}$ | $\begin{array}{r} 9 \\ +1 \end{array}$ | $\begin{array}{r} 9 \\ +2 \end{array}$ | $\begin{array}{r} 9 \\ +3 \end{array}$ | $\begin{array}{r} 9 \\ +4 \end{array}$ | $\begin{array}{r} 9 \\ +5 \end{array}$ | $\begin{array}{r} 9 \\ +6 \end{array}$ | $\begin{array}{r} 9 \\ +7 \end{array}$ | $\begin{array}{r} 9 \\ +8 \end{array}$ | $\begin{array}{r} 9 \\ +9 \end{array}$ |

Addition Facts Practice

Use the addition facts from page 29 to complete the table.

| **Example** | Find an empty box in the table. Look up the column to the top number. Then move left from the box to the number at the beginning of the row. Add these two numbers. Write the answer in the box. |

+	0	1	2	3	4	5	6	7	8	9
0	0	1	2	3	4	5				
1	1	2	3	4						
2	2	3	4							
3	3	4								
4	4									
5	5									
6										
7										
8										
9										

To use the table to complete addition facts, find one number at the top of a column, and the other number at the beginning of a row. The sum is the number in the box where the row and column meet.

Complete the following addition facts.

1. $3 + 6 = 9$

2. $3 + 9 =$

3. $4 + 8 =$

4. $0 + 2 =$

5. $6 + 7 =$

6. $9 + 2 =$

7. $6 + 6 =$

8. $8 + 6 =$

9. $1 + 1 =$

10. $7 + 3 =$

11. $4 + 9 =$

12. $5 + 6 =$

13. $2 + 7 =$

14. $5 + 9 =$

15. $8 + 1 =$

16. $3 + 2 =$

17. $9 + 7 =$

18. $5 + 5 =$

19. $9 + 9 =$

20. $6 + 4 =$

Addition Facts Practice

Addition problems can be written vertically or horizontally.

$$\begin{aligned} \text{addend} &\rightarrow 5 \\ \text{addend} &\rightarrow \underline{+\ 1} \\ \text{sum} &\rightarrow 6 \end{aligned} \quad \text{is the same as } 5 + 1 = 6$$

Fill in the boxes to complete the following addition facts. You can use the table on page 30 if you need help remembering the facts.

1. $8 + 6 = \boxed{14}$

2. $9 + 1 = \square$

3. $7 + 9 = \square$

4. $6 + 3 = \square$

5. $5 + \square = 6$

6. $3 + \square = 5$

7. $4 + \square = 10$

8. $7 + \square = 13$

9. $\square + 2 = 2$

10. $\square + 4 = 7$

11. $\square + 6 = 14$

12. $\square + 9 = 15$

13. $4 + 8 = \square$

14. $\square + 7 = 16$

15. $0 + \square = 0$

16. $8 + 3 = \square$

17. $2 + \square = 8$

18. $7 + 9 = \square$

19. $2 + \square = 3$

20. $0 + \square = 9$

21. $6 + 4 = \square$

22. $1 + \square = 6$

23. $8 + \square = 12$

24. $\square + 2 = 7$

Fill in the boxes with any numbers that make the sums. There may be more than one set of numbers that makes a true statement.

25. $\boxed{5} + \boxed{4} = 9$

26. $\square + \square = 15$

27. $\square + \square = 18$

28. $\square + \square = 12$

29. $\square + \square = 5$

30. $\square + \square = 13$

31. $\square + \square = 7$

32. $\square + \square = 4$

33. $\square + \square = 16$

34. $\square + \square = 10$

35. $\square + \square = 14$

36. $\square + \square = 11$

37. $\square + \square = 17$

38. $\square + \square = 8$

39. $\square + \square = 6$

40. $\square + \square = 3$

Column Addition

You can use the addition facts to add three or more numbers in a column.

Use These Steps

Add 4
     3
   +2

1. Be sure that the digits are lined up in a column.

   4
   3
 +2

2. Add the first two digits.

   4   $4 + 3 = 7$
   3
 +2

3. Add the last digit to the sum of the first two digits.

   4
   3
 +2 $2 + 7 = 9$
   9

Add.

1.
  4
  4
+3
11

2.
  6
  2
+2

3.
  3
  1
+5

4.
  8
  1
+1

5.
  5
  2
+6

6.
  4
  1
+6

7.
$9 + 0 + 2 =$
  9
  0
+2
11

8.
$3 + 2 + 1 =$

9.
$6 + 3 + 3 =$

10.
$4 + 7 + 2 =$

11.
$5 + 6 + 1 + 6 =$
  5
  6
  1
+6
18

12.
$7 + 3 + 9 + 2 =$

13.
$0 + 5 + 8 + 4 =$

14.
$3 + 5 + 7 + 6 =$

15. Roy worked for 4 hours on Friday, 6 hours on Saturday, and 5 hours on Sunday. How many total hours did he work during these three days?

16. Jean works part time as an accountant. Last month she prepared taxes for 3 clients one week, 6 clients the next week, 4 clients the next week, and 5 clients the week after that. How many clients did Jean prepare taxes for in all?

Answer_____

Answer_____

Application

You can use addition to make decisions when you buy items at the store.

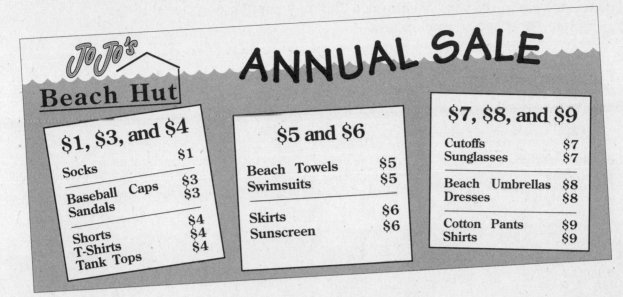

Use the prices in the advertisement to find the answer to each problem. Circle the letter beside the correct answer.

1. Harry wants to buy a beach umbrella and a T-shirt at Jojo's annual sale. He has $15 to spend.

   a. He has exactly the right amount of money.
   b. He does not have enough money.
   c. He will get change back when he buys both items.

2. Dolores has $10 to spend at Jojo's. She could buy a beach towel and

   a. a skirt.
   b. sandals.
   c. cutoffs.

3. If Jasmine buys sunglasses, a beach towel, and sandals, the total bill will be

   a. more than $10.
   b. exactly $10.
   c. less than $10.

4. Carl bought cotton pants and a shirt. Kai bought a baseball cap, a tank top, socks, and a beach umbrella.

   a. Carl spent more money than Kai.
   b. Kai spent more money than Carl.
   c. They spent the same amount of money.

5. Chris has $20 to spend. He wants to buy sunglasses and a shirt. He also has enough money to buy

   a. a beach umbrella.
   b. cutoffs.
   c. sandals.

6. Sue bought a tank top and sunglasses at the sale. For the same amount of money, she could have bought

   a. a dress and shorts.
   b. a skirt and a beach towel.
   c. a swimsuit and a beach umbrella.

Adding Two-Digit Numbers

You can use the addition facts to add two-digit numbers. Just be sure to put your answers in the correct columns. You may want to use the table you completed on page 30 to help you.

Use These Steps

Add   37
      + 21

1. Be sure that the ones and the tens are lined up.

```
3 7
+ 2 1
```

2. Add the ones. 7 + 1 = 8 ones. Put the 8 ones in the ones column.

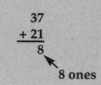

```
 37
+21
  8
```
8 ones

3. Add the tens. 3 + 2 = 5 tens. Put the 5 tens in the tens column.

```
 37
+21
 58
```
5 tens

Add.

1.
```
  50
+ 34
  84
```

2.
```
  65
+ 12
```

3.
```
  41
+ 58
```

4.
```
  36
+ 31
```

5.
```
  72
+ 20
```

6.
```
  33
+ 15
```

7.
```
  90
+  6
  96
```

8.
```
  45
+  3
```

9.
```
  17
+  1
```

10.
```
  54
+  4
```

11.
```
  38
+  1
```

12.
```
  16
+  2
```

13.
```
  76
+ 23
```

14.
```
  81
+ 10
```

15.
```
  49
+ 40
```

16.
```
  60
+  4
```

17.
```
  37
+  1
```

18.
```
  52
+ 15
```

19.
```
  71
+ 16
```

20.
```
  25
+  4
```

21.
```
  30
+  5
```

22.
```
  66
+ 22
```

23.
```
  48
+ 30
```

24.
```
  31
+ 14
```

25.
```
  80
+  1
```

26.
```
  47
+ 22
```

27.
```
  58
+ 21
```

28.
```
  50
+  8
```

29.
```
  61
+ 34
```

30.
```
  72
+  5
```

Adding Two-Digit Numbers

To add numbers that are not lined up, first put the digits in columns.
Line up the digits that have the same place value.

$$50 + 25$$

```
 tens ones
   5   0
 + 2   5
   7   5
```

Use These Steps

Add 60 + 12 + 4

1. Write the digits in columns so that the digits with the same place values are lined up.

```
  60
  12
+  4
```

2. Add the ones.
0 + 2 + 4 = 6 ones.

```
  60
  12
+  4
   6
```
← 6 ones

3. Add the tens.
6 + 1 = 7 tens.

```
  60
  12
+  4
  76
```
↘ 7 tens

Add.

1.
$$42 + 27 =$$
```
  42
+ 27
  69
```

2.
$$15 + 13 =$$

3.
$$51 + 44 =$$

4.
$$70 + 14 =$$

5.
```
  56
+ 12
```

6.
```
  33
+ 16
```

7.
```
  50
+ 27
```

8.
```
  34
+ 10
```

9.
```
  25
+ 24
```

10.
$$42 + 20 + 16 =$$
```
  42
  20
+ 16
  78
```

11.
$$32 + 24 + 11 =$$

12.
$$30 + 12 + 6 =$$

13.
$$28 + 11 + 30 =$$

14. Marta booked 10 vacation packages to Mexico one week, 5 the next week, and 4 the week after that. How many vacations to Mexico did she book in all?

15. John bought a notebook for $1 and a box of diskettes for $12 at Arnie's Discount Store. How much did he spend all together?

Answer_____

Answer_____

Adding Three-Digit Numbers

To add three-digit numbers, first be sure that the digits with the same place values are lined up in the ones, tens, and hundreds columns. Add only the digits that have the same place value. Be sure to put your answers in the correct columns.

Use These Steps

Add 360
    36
 + 3

1. Be sure that the digits are lined up.

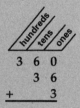

```
hundreds tens ones
   3   6   0
       3   6
 +         3
```

2. Add each column, starting with the digits in the ones place.

```
  360        360        360
   36         36         36
 +  3       +  3       +  3
    9         99        399
```

     9 ones   9 tens   3 hundreds

Add.

1.
```
  106
+  23
  129
```

2.
```
  794
+ 105
```

3.
```
   32
+ 142
```

4.
```
  181
+ 816
```

5.
```
  431
+   4
```

6.
```
  670
+ 129
```

7.
```
   36
+ 502
```

8.
```
    1
+ 378
```

9.
```
  322
+  76
```

10.
```
  210
+   8
```

11.
```
  203
  222
+ 164
  589
```

12.
```
  622
  100
+ 177
```

13.
```
  340
   23
+   5
```

14.
```
   64
  520
+  13
```

15.
```
  200
  120
+  47
```

16.
```
    3
  220
  100
+ 146
  469
```

17.
```
  201
  383
   10
+ 301
```

18.
```
  212
  311
  203
+ 162
```

19.
```
  320
  200
  211
+   7
```

20.
```
   60
  201
  400
+  23
```

Adding Larger Numbers

To add numbers that are not lined up, first put the digits in columns.
Add only the digits with the same place values. Be sure to put your
answers in the correct columns.

Use These Steps

Add   1,006 + 41 + 2

1. Line up the digits in columns.

```
  1 , 0   0   6
        4   1
+           2
_____
```

2. Add the digits in each column, starting with the ones
place.

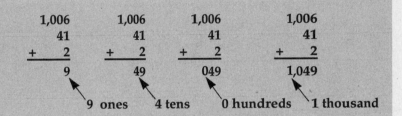

```
  1,006      1,006      1,006      1,006
    41         41         41         41
+    2       +   2      +    2      +    2
____         ____       ____       _____
   9          49         049       1,049
```

9 ones   4 tens   0 hundreds   1 thousand

Add.

1.
$1,246 + 343 =$
```
  1,246
+  343
_____
  1,589
```

2.
$3,300 + 500 =$

3.
$4,973 + 1,022 =$

4.
$6,811 + 25 + 100 =$

5.
$742 + 3 + 1,010 =$

6.
$2,422 + 163 + 4 =$

7.
$7,041 + 10 + 3 =$

8.
$3,006 + 2,021 + 340 =$

9.
$34 + 200 + 2,335 =$

10.
$5,143 + 736 + 100 =$

11.
$9,240 + 420 + 307 =$

12.
$2,040 + 712 + 5,133 =$

Problem Solving: Using Rounding and Estimating

Many people and businesses make a monthly budget. They add up their expenses for one or more months. Then they estimate how much money they will spend in the coming months. A budget keeps them from spending more money than they make.

You do not need exact numbers to prepare a budget. You can use rounded numbers to add the numbers faster.

Example At the end of last month, Terry wrote down his expenses. He spent $63, $75, $39, and $51 on food. About how much should he plan to spend on food next month?

▶ **Step 1.** Round each amount to the nearest ten.

$63 rounds to $60
$75 rounds to $80
$39 rounds to $40
$51 rounds to $50

▶ **Step 2.** Add the rounded amounts.

$ 60
$ 80
$ 40
$ 50
─────
$230

Terry should plan to spend about $230 on food.

Week	Food	Clothes	Bus Fare	Other
1	$63	0	$5	$13
2	$75	$13	$7	$22
3	$39	$22	$12	$37
4	$51	$49	$19	$9

Round each amount to the nearest ten. Then add.

1. Terry spent $13, $22, and $49 for clothes. About how much should he plan to spend for clothes next month?

2. He spent $5, $7, $12, and $19 on bus fare. About how much should he plan to spend for bus fare next month?

Answer _____

Answer _____

3. Terry spent $13, $22, $37, and $9 on other expenses. About how much should he plan to spend for these expenses next month?

Answer _____

4. Does Terry spend more money on clothes or on bus fare?

Answer _____

5. Does Terry spend more money on food or on his other expenses?

Answer _____

6. Rent and utilities cost Terry about $500 per month. About how much did he spend all together last month on rent and utilities, food, and bus fare?

Answer _____

7. Terry's income is about $1,000 each month. He will be getting a $75 raise next month. About how much will his income be next month?

Answer _____

8. Terry saves about $50 each month. He can save $18 more each month when he gets his raise. About how much can he save each month after his raise?

Answer _____

9. Terry wants to buy a stereo with his savings. The stereo he wants to buy costs $239, plus $18 tax. About how much all together does the stereo cost?

Answer _____

10. Terry has saved $250. Does he have enough money to buy the stereo?

Answer _____

Mixed Review

Write the value of the underlined digit in each number.

1. 35 _____
2. 78 _____
3. 99 _____

4. 356 _____
5. 750 _____
6. 900 _____

7. 1,247 _____
8. 5,775 _____
9. 9,043 _____

Round each number to the nearest ten.

10. 56 _____
11. 44 _____
12. 75 _____

13. 145 _____
14. 978 _____
15. 817 _____

16. 2,467 _____
17. 5,306 _____
18. 4,985 _____

Add.

19.	20.	21.	22.	23.	24.
23 + 45	31 + 3	30 + 48	65 4 + 20	33 56 + 10	48 50 + 1

25. 46 + 20 =

26. 52 + 22 =

27. 30 + 39 + 10 =

28. 54 + 31 + 12 =

29.	30.	31.	32.
4,641 223 + 11	3,010 632 + 1,225	1,025 133 7,520 + 1,300	220 3,210 4,200 + 2,259

33. 4,752 + 36 + 10 =

34. 7,930 + 2,012 + 21 =

35. 4 + 250 + 9,325 =

Adding Two-Digit Numbers with Renaming

When you add digits in the ones column, the sum can sometimes be 10 or more. When this happens, rename by carrying to the tens column or the place to the left.

Use These Steps

Add   15 + 39

1. Line up the digits in columns.

```
tens ones
  1   5
+ 3   9
```

2. Add the ones. 5 + 9 = 14 ones. Rename 14 ones as 1 ten and 4 ones. Write 4 ones in the ones column. Carry the 1 ten to the tens column.

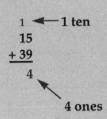

```
  1  ←— 1 ten
  15
+ 39
   4
```
       ↖ 4 ones

3. Add the tens, plus the carried 1. 1 + 1 + 3 = 5 tens. Write 5 tens in the tens column.

```
  1
  15
+ 39
  54
```
       ↖ 5 tens

Add.

1. 39 + 3 =

```
  1
  39
+  3
  42
```

2. 27 + 27 =

3. 65 + 25 =

4. 87 + 3 =

5.
```
  47
+ 33
```

6.
```
  56
+  9
```

7.
```
  62
+ 18
```

8.
```
  19
+ 73
```

9.
```
  25
+  5
```

10.
```
  33
  26
+ 11
```

11.
```
  49
  28
+ 20
```

12.
```
  35
  21
+ 19
```

13.
```
  14
  38
+ 40
```

14.
```
  54
  18
+ 23
```

15. 36 + 48 + 1 =

16. 8 + 4 + 32 =

17. 6 + 13 + 64 =

18. 6 + 12 + 15 =

19. 3 + 18 + 22 =

20. 45 + 18 + 13 =

Adding Two-Digit Numbers with Renaming

When you add digits in the tens column, the sum can sometimes be 10 or more. When this happens, rename by carrying to the hundreds column or the place to the left.

Use These Steps

Add 96 + 38

1. Line up the digits in columns. Add the ones. 6 + 8 = 14 ones. Rename. Write 4 in the ones column. Carry the 1 ten to the tens column.

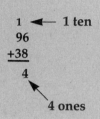

```
  1  ← 1 ten
 96
+38
  4
      ↖ 4 ones
```

2. Add the tens. 1 + 9 + 3 = 13 tens. Write 3 in the tens column.

```
  1
 96
+38
 34
   ↖ 3 tens
```

3. Write 1 in the hundreds column.

```
  1
 96
+38
134
   ↖ 1 hundred
```

Add.

1.
```
  1
 68
+47
115
```

2.
```
 74
+29
```

3.
```
 81
+39
```

4.
```
 93
+78
```

5.
```
 48
+96
```

6. 49 + 94 =

7. 38 + 91 =

8. 54 + 88 =

9. 55 + 97 =

10. 77 + 89 =

11.
```
 17
 99
+58
```

12.
```
 43
 19
+62
```

13.
```
 28
 93
+79
```

14.
```
 84
 47
+67
```

15.
```
 16
 98
+43
```

16. 45 + 23 + 55 =

17. 77 + 56 + 6 =

18. 76 + 1 + 19 =

Adding Three-Digit Numbers with Renaming

When you add three-digit numbers, you may need to rename two or more times.

Use These Steps

Add 372 + 499

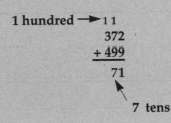

1. Line up the digits in columns. Add the ones. 2 + 9 = 11 ones. Write 1 in the ones column. Carry 1 ten.

```
  1  ←—1 ten
 372
+499
   1
```
↑ 1 one

2. Add the tens. 1 + 7 + 9 = 17 tens. Write 7 in the tens column. Carry 1 hundred.

```
1 hundred →11
          372
         +499
           71
```
↑ 7 tens

3. Add the hundreds. 1 + 3 + 4 = 8 hundreds. Write 8 in the hundreds column.

```
  11
 372
+499
 871
```
↑ 8 hundreds

Add.

1.
```
  11
 349
+552
 901
```

2.
```
 878
+ 25
```

3.
```
 563
+449
```

4.
```
 981
+ 39
```

5.
```
 613
+387
```

6. 39 + 877 =

7. 886 + 29 =

8. 640 + 466 =

9. 72 + 379 =

10.
```
  11
 433
 297
+462
1,192
```

11.
```
 331
 828
+433
```

12.
```
 849
 908
+884
```

13.
```
 119
 488
+281
```

14.
```
 670
 821
+943
```

15. 561 + 849 + 999 =

16. 189 + 248 + 577 =

17. 251 + 629 + 125 =

18. 159 + 623 + 851 =

43

Adding Larger Numbers with Renaming

When you add the thousands column, you may need to rename by carrying to the next column or place to the left.

Add.

1.
```
  1 11
  1,938
+   289
  2,227
```

2.
```
  2,579
+   164
```

3.
```
   769
+  433
```

4.
```
   821
+  399
```

5.
```
  3,352
+   190
```

6. 4,882 + 595 =

7. 1,379 + 845 =

8. 8,950 + 959 =

9. 8,987 + 7,134 =

10.
```
  6,826
  3,891
+ 8,717
```

11.
```
  8,686
  2,982
+ 6,531
```

12.
```
  9,997
  3,987
+ 4,003
```

13.
```
  14,970
   8,206
+  7,334
```

14.
```
  19,986
  11,861
+ 19,374
```

15. 3,567 + 14,556 + 435 =

16. 45,679 + 23,440 + 2,400 =

Adding Zeros

Zero plus any number equals that number. Remember to add carried numbers.

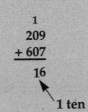

Use These Steps

Add   209 + 607

1. Line up the digits in columns. Add the ones.
   9 + 7 = 16 ones.

   ```
     1  ←— 1 ten
    209
   + 607
   ─────
      6
   ```
   ↑ 6 ones

2. Add the tens.
   1 + 0 + 0 = 1 ten.

   ```
     1
    209
   + 607
   ─────
     16
   ```
   ↑ 1 ten

3. Add the hundreds.
   2 + 6 = 8 hundreds.

   ```
     1
    209
   + 607
   ─────
    816
   ```
   ↑ 8 hundreds

Add.

1.
```
   1
  304
+ 106
─────
  410
```

2.
```
  409
+ 301
─────
```

3.
```
 1,308
+    3
──────
```

4.
```
   907
+ 1,005
───────
```

5.
```
  5,601
+ 1,109
───────
```

6.   5,096 + 68 =

7.   6,004 + 209 =

8.   908 + 84 =

9.   6,808 + 204 =

10.
```
  9,006
    804
+     7
───────
```

11.
```
 17,007
  1,009
+   102
───────
```

12.
```
 14,908
  9,009
+ 3,000
───────
```

13.
```
  9,001
    409
+   800
───────
```

14.
```
  8,601
  4,009
+ 2,000
───────
```

15.   22,005 + 409 + 1,000 =

16.   45,000 + 3,005 + 509 =

Adding Long Columns

When you add columns of four or more numbers, it helps to add the numbers in steps.

Use These Steps

Add   16 + 18 + 82 + 49 + 61

1. Line up the digits in columns. Add groups of digits in the ones column.

```
  2
 16 ———— 6 + 8 = 14
 18
 82 ——— 2 + 9 + 1 = 12
 49              26
+61
  6
```

2. Add groups of digits in the tens column.

```
                      2
2 + 1 + 1 =  4  ———   16
                      18
8 + 4 + 6 = 18  ———   82
              22      49
                    + 61
                     226
```

Add.

1.
```
    6
    4
    3
    9
 +  7
   29
```

2.
```
    7
    8
    5
    5
 +  2
```

3.
```
   41
   19
   63
   27
 + 90
```

4.
```
   88
   19
   13
   41
 + 62
```

5.
```
   430
   762
   148
   299
 + 107
```

6.
```
   827
    33
   143
    69
 +  20
```

7.
```
   1,285
      95
     140
       7
 + 6,581
```

8.
```
   4,281
   5,479
   3,207
   1,800
 + 1,021
```

9.
```
   2,455
   4,532
   3,658
   3,275
 + 8,103
```

10.
```
   3,559
     411
   6,149
   3,622
 +   981
```

11.
```
     675
      25
   4,122
     318
 +   245
```

12.
```
    3,454
   12,357
   44,113
    2,395
 +  7,001
```

Place Value to 1,000,000

The chart on the right shows place value to the millions place.

You read the number 1,476,901 as one million, four hundred seventy-six thousand, nine hundred one.

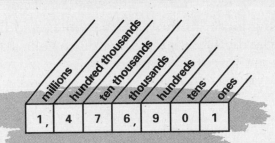

millions	hundred thousands	ten thousands	thousands	hundreds	tens	ones
1,	4	7	6,	9	0	1

Use These Steps

Write the place values of each digit in the number 42,530.

1. Write the digits and their place values.

| 4 ten thousands |
| 2 thousands |
| 5 hundreds |
| 3 tens |
| 0 ones |

2. Write the values of the digits.

| 40,000 |
| 2,000 |
| 500 |
| 30 |
| 0 |

Write the place value for each number. Then write the value of each digit.

1. 3,472,400

3	millions	3,000,000
4	hundred thousands	400,000
7	ten thousands	70,000
2	thousands	2,000
4	hundreds	400
0	tens	00
0	ones	0

2. 6,480,603

6		
4		
8		
0		
6		
0		
3		

Write the value of the underlined digit in each number.

3. 3<u>4</u>5 _____40_____

4. 10<u>3</u> _____

5. <u>4</u>,578 _____

6. 2,<u>9</u>90 _____

7. <u>2</u>4,704 _____

8. 56,<u>9</u>04 _____

9. <u>2</u>34,004 _____

10. 79<u>3</u>,456 _____

11. <u>3</u>,579,844 _____

Adding Larger Numbers

Adding larger numbers is the same as adding small numbers. Be sure that the digits with the same place values are lined up, and that you have not forgotten any digits.

$$4,749,200 + 7,761,035$$

$$\begin{array}{r} 4,749,200 \\ + 7,761,035 \\ \hline 12,510,235 \end{array}$$

Use These Steps

Add   998,206 + 3,044,052

1. Line up the digits in columns.

$$\begin{array}{r} 998,206 \\ + 3,044,052 \\ \hline \end{array}$$

2. Add, beginning with the digits in the ones place.

$$\begin{array}{r} {\scriptstyle 1\ 11} \\ 998,206 \\ + 3,044,052 \\ \hline 4,042,258 \end{array}$$

Add.

1.
$$\begin{array}{r} {\scriptstyle 1\ 1} \\ 20,473 \\ + 99,068 \\ \hline 119,541 \end{array}$$

2.
$$\begin{array}{r} 38,468 \\ + 106,810 \\ \hline \end{array}$$

3.
$$\begin{array}{r} 68,024 \\ + 89,118 \\ \hline \end{array}$$

4.
$$\begin{array}{r} 1,061,247 \\ + \quad 761,785 \\ \hline \end{array}$$

5. $1,460,000 + 39,000 =$

6. $793,047 + 3,799 =$

7. $62,901 + 439 =$

8.
$$\begin{array}{r} 93,486 \\ 129,882 \\ + 1,937,246 \\ \hline \end{array}$$

9.
$$\begin{array}{r} 98,621 \\ 261,084 \\ + 2,689,677 \\ \hline \end{array}$$

10.
$$\begin{array}{r} 237,069 \\ 61,488 \\ + 1,968,984 \\ \hline \end{array}$$

11.
$$\begin{array}{r} 62,949 \\ 981,098 \\ + 6,789,987 \\ \hline \end{array}$$

12. $372,000 + 1,000,497 =$

13. $45,446 + 12,530 + 3,445 =$

14. $3,998 + 133,404 + 12,001 =$

15. $45,978 + 3,166 + 298,566 =$

Problem Solving: Using Rounding and Estimating

When we estimate, we usually round numbers to their greatest place value. The greatest place value is the place value of the first digit on the left, called the *lead digit*.

1,575 rounds to 2,000
925 rounds to 900
39 rounds to 40

Example Last month Kelley drove from Los Angeles to Santa Fe making sales calls. She kept a record of how many miles she drove, how many gallons of gas she used, and how much money she spent.

Look at the chart. About how many miles did Kelley drive the first 2 days of her trip?

Day	Miles	Gallons of Gas	Expenses
1	97	11	$56
2	123	13	$80
3	180	16	$94
4	193	19	$96
5	245	22	$59

Step 1. Round the miles driven each day. To round, look at the digit next to the lead digit.

9<u>7</u>   12<u>3</u>

If the digit to the right of the lead digit is 5 or greater, add 1 to the lead digit and change the other digits to 0. If the digit to the right of the lead digit is less than 5, change all digits except the lead digit to 0.

97 rounds to 100
123 rounds to 100

Step 2. Add the rounded numbers.

$$\begin{array}{r} 100 \\ + 100 \\ \hline 200 \end{array}$$

Kelley drove about 200 miles the first 2 days of her trip.

Solve by rounding to the lead digit.

1. About how many miles did Kelley drive on the last 3 days of her trip?

   Answer _____

2. About how many miles in all did Kelley travel from Los Angeles to Santa Fe?

   Answer _____

3. About how many gallons of gas did she use on the trip?

   Answer _____

4. Estimate how much money Kelley spent on the trip.

   Answer _____

5. Kelley estimated she would spend $500 on her trip. Did she spend more or less than she estimated?

   Answer _____

6. Two months ago, Kelley drove 1,927 miles on a trip. Round this number to the lead digit.

   Answer _____

7. Which month did Kelley drive farther: last month or two months ago?

   Answer _____

8. Next month Kelley plans to drive 2,794 miles from Los Angeles to New York City. Round this number to the lead digit.

   Answer _____

9. About how many total miles will the round trip be from Los Angeles to New York City and back?

   Answer _____

10. Which is the longer trip: the one Kelley took last month or the one she'll take next month?

   Answer _____

Unit 2 *Review*

Add.

1.
$$\begin{array}{r} 6 \\ +\ 5 \\ \hline \end{array}$$

2.
$$\begin{array}{r} 8 \\ +\ 2 \\ \hline \end{array}$$

3.
$$\begin{array}{r} 7 \\ +\ 4 \\ \hline \end{array}$$

4.
$$\begin{array}{r} 7 \\ 2 \\ +\ 3 \\ \hline \end{array}$$

5.
$$\begin{array}{r} 8 \\ 9 \\ +\ 1 \\ \hline \end{array}$$

6.
$$\begin{array}{r} 5 \\ 3 \\ +\ 2 \\ \hline \end{array}$$

7.
$$\begin{array}{r} 89 \\ +\ 10 \\ \hline \end{array}$$

8.
$$\begin{array}{r} 72 \\ +\ 23 \\ \hline \end{array}$$

9.
$$\begin{array}{r} 53 \\ +\ 42 \\ \hline \end{array}$$

10.
$$\begin{array}{r} 69 \\ 20 \\ +\ 10 \\ \hline \end{array}$$

11.
$$\begin{array}{r} 31 \\ 17 \\ +\ 41 \\ \hline \end{array}$$

12.
$$\begin{array}{r} 35 \\ 10 \\ +\ 54 \\ \hline \end{array}$$

13. $40 + 24 =$

14. $76 + 21 =$

15. $30 + 11 + 27 =$

16. $50 + 29 + 10 =$

17.
$$\begin{array}{r} 309 \\ +\ \ 40 \\ \hline \end{array}$$

18.
$$\begin{array}{r} 764 \\ +\ 135 \\ \hline \end{array}$$

19.
$$\begin{array}{r} 41 \\ 7 \\ +\ 401 \\ \hline \end{array}$$

20.
$$\begin{array}{r} 34 \\ 253 \\ +\ 1{,}710 \\ \hline \end{array}$$

21.
$$\begin{array}{r} 45 \\ 843 \\ +\ 6{,}010 \\ \hline \end{array}$$

22. $4{,}037 + 2{,}260 =$

23. $5{,}444 + 434 + 21 =$

24. $100 + 2{,}405 + 50 =$

25.
$$\begin{array}{r} 27 \\ +\ 63 \\ \hline \end{array}$$

26.
$$\begin{array}{r} 56 \\ +\ 39 \\ \hline \end{array}$$

27.
$$\begin{array}{r} 52 \\ +\ 88 \\ \hline \end{array}$$

28.
$$\begin{array}{r} 19 \\ 73 \\ +\ 3 \\ \hline \end{array}$$

29.
$$\begin{array}{r} 25 \\ 75 \\ +\ 5 \\ \hline \end{array}$$

30.
$$\begin{array}{r} 57 \\ 19 \\ +\ 44 \\ \hline \end{array}$$

31. $39 + 68 =$

32. $27 + 27 =$

33. $65 + 75 + 5 =$

34. $47 + 23 + 93 =$

35.
$$268 + 47$$

36.
$$9,974 + 29$$

37.
$$1,381 + 8,739$$

38.
$$693 \\ 378 \\ + \ 29$$

39.
$$948 \\ 96 \\ + 340$$

40.
$$849 + 94 =$$

41.
$$3,938 + 91 =$$

42.
$$1,354 + 788 + 21 =$$

43.
$$9,006 \\ 804 \\ + \quad 7$$

44.
$$17,007 \\ 1,009 \\ + \quad 102$$

45.
$$14,908 \\ 9,009 \\ + \ 3,000$$

46.
$$430 \\ 762 \\ 148 \\ 299 \\ + 107$$

47.
$$827 \\ 33 \\ 143 \\ 69 \\ + \ 20$$

48.
$$56,978 \\ + 49,078$$

49.
$$345,750 \\ + 742,283$$

50.
$$3,740,033 \\ + 4,005,778$$

51.
$$8,798,023 \\ + 3,375,611$$

52.
$$1,569,756 \\ + \ 865,599$$

53.
$$53,890 + 4,877 =$$

54.
$$29,000 + 567,854 + 4,321 =$$

Below is a list of the problems in this review and the pages on which the skills are taught. If you missed any problems, turn to the pages listed and practice the skills. Then correct the problems you missed in the Unit Review.

Problems	Pages	Problems	Pages
1-6	29-32	35-39	43
7-16	34-35	40-42	44
17-24	36-37	43-45	45
25-34	41-43	46-47	46
		48-54	47-48

Unit 3 SUBTRACTING WHOLE NUMBERS

You subtract whole numbers when you take away one amount from another amount. You use subtraction to see how much money you have left after you pay bills, to find how many more days are left in the year, or to learn the difference between sales figures for two months.

In this unit, you will learn how to set up a problem to subtract whole numbers. You will also learn how to borrow, how to subtract with zeros, and how to check answers by using addition.

Getting Ready

You should be familiar with the skills on this page and the next before you begin this unit. To check your answers, turn to page 182.

 When you are working with whole numbers, you need to know the place value of each digit.

The place value chart shows the value of each digit in the number ninety-three thousand, four hundred twenty-seven. Write the value of each digit.

1. 93,427

   9 ten thousands
   _____
   _____
   _____
   _____

2. 42,076

   _____
   _____
   _____
   _____

hundred thousands	ten thousands	thousands	hundreds	tens	ones
	9	3, 4		2	7

Getting Ready

 To set up an addition problem, first line up the digits in columns. Then solve the problem.

Line up the following problems and solve.

3.
467 + 31 =

467
+ 31
498

4.
346 + 29 =

5.
4,960 + 321 =

6.
8,927 + 1,007 =

7.
1,682 + 851 =

8.
605 + 8,126 =

9.
720 + 809 =

10.
2,016 + 8 =

For review, see Unit 2, pages 43-45.

 To round a number, you need to know the place value of each digit.

Round each number to the nearest ten.

11. 29 ___30___ **12.** 155 _____ **13.** 406 _____ **14.** 1,299 _____

Round each number to the nearest hundred.

15. 430 _____ **16.** 792 _____ **17.** 1,007 _____ **18.** 5,383 _____

Round each number to the nearest thousand.

19. 5,830 _____ **20.** 9,436 _____ **21.** 15,099 _____ **22.** 99,650 _____

For review see, Unit 1, pages 20-22.

 In addition, it doesn't matter which number is written first. In subtraction, the larger number must go on top.

Compare the following numbers. Circle the larger number.

23. 30 (300) **24.** 28 18 **25.** 37 73

26. 297 279 **27.** 806 860 **28.** 400 4,000

For review, see Unit 1, page 13.

Subtraction Facts

To subtract larger numbers, you should first know the basic subtraction facts. You will find it helpful to know the following facts by heart.

Subtract the following numbers to complete each row.
Notice that the answers form a pattern.

1.

| $\begin{array}{r}0\\-0\\\hline0\end{array}$ | $\begin{array}{r}1\\-0\\\hline1\end{array}$ | $\begin{array}{r}2\\-0\\\hline2\end{array}$ | $\begin{array}{r}3\\-0\\\hline3\end{array}$ | $\begin{array}{r}4\\-0\\\hline4\end{array}$ | $\begin{array}{r}5\\-0\\\hline5\end{array}$ | $\begin{array}{r}6\\-0\\\hline6\end{array}$ | $\begin{array}{r}7\\-0\\\hline7\end{array}$ | $\begin{array}{r}8\\-0\\\hline8\end{array}$ | $\begin{array}{r}9\\-0\\\hline9\end{array}$ |

2.

| $\begin{array}{r}1\\-1\end{array}$ | $\begin{array}{r}2\\-1\end{array}$ | $\begin{array}{r}3\\-1\end{array}$ | $\begin{array}{r}4\\-1\end{array}$ | $\begin{array}{r}5\\-1\end{array}$ | $\begin{array}{r}6\\-1\end{array}$ | $\begin{array}{r}7\\-1\end{array}$ | $\begin{array}{r}8\\-1\end{array}$ | $\begin{array}{r}9\\-1\end{array}$ | $\begin{array}{r}10\\-1\end{array}$ |

3.

| $\begin{array}{r}2\\-2\end{array}$ | $\begin{array}{r}3\\-2\end{array}$ | $\begin{array}{r}4\\-2\end{array}$ | $\begin{array}{r}5\\-2\end{array}$ | $\begin{array}{r}6\\-2\end{array}$ | $\begin{array}{r}7\\-2\end{array}$ | $\begin{array}{r}8\\-2\end{array}$ | $\begin{array}{r}9\\-2\end{array}$ | $\begin{array}{r}10\\-2\end{array}$ | $\begin{array}{r}11\\-2\end{array}$ |

4.

| $\begin{array}{r}3\\-3\end{array}$ | $\begin{array}{r}4\\-3\end{array}$ | $\begin{array}{r}5\\-3\end{array}$ | $\begin{array}{r}6\\-3\end{array}$ | $\begin{array}{r}7\\-3\end{array}$ | $\begin{array}{r}8\\-3\end{array}$ | $\begin{array}{r}9\\-3\end{array}$ | $\begin{array}{r}10\\-3\end{array}$ | $\begin{array}{r}11\\-3\end{array}$ | $\begin{array}{r}12\\-3\end{array}$ |

5.

| $\begin{array}{r}4\\-4\end{array}$ | $\begin{array}{r}5\\-4\end{array}$ | $\begin{array}{r}6\\-4\end{array}$ | $\begin{array}{r}7\\-4\end{array}$ | $\begin{array}{r}8\\-4\end{array}$ | $\begin{array}{r}9\\-4\end{array}$ | $\begin{array}{r}10\\-4\end{array}$ | $\begin{array}{r}11\\-4\end{array}$ | $\begin{array}{r}12\\-4\end{array}$ | $\begin{array}{r}13\\-4\end{array}$ |

6.

| $\begin{array}{r}5\\-5\end{array}$ | $\begin{array}{r}6\\-5\end{array}$ | $\begin{array}{r}7\\-5\end{array}$ | $\begin{array}{r}8\\-5\end{array}$ | $\begin{array}{r}9\\-5\end{array}$ | $\begin{array}{r}10\\-5\end{array}$ | $\begin{array}{r}11\\-5\end{array}$ | $\begin{array}{r}12\\-5\end{array}$ | $\begin{array}{r}13\\-5\end{array}$ | $\begin{array}{r}14\\-5\end{array}$ |

7.

| $\begin{array}{r}6\\-6\end{array}$ | $\begin{array}{r}7\\-6\end{array}$ | $\begin{array}{r}8\\-6\end{array}$ | $\begin{array}{r}9\\-6\end{array}$ | $\begin{array}{r}10\\-6\end{array}$ | $\begin{array}{r}11\\-6\end{array}$ | $\begin{array}{r}12\\-6\end{array}$ | $\begin{array}{r}13\\-6\end{array}$ | $\begin{array}{r}14\\-6\end{array}$ | $\begin{array}{r}15\\-6\end{array}$ |

8.

| $\begin{array}{r}7\\-7\end{array}$ | $\begin{array}{r}8\\-7\end{array}$ | $\begin{array}{r}9\\-7\end{array}$ | $\begin{array}{r}10\\-7\end{array}$ | $\begin{array}{r}11\\-7\end{array}$ | $\begin{array}{r}12\\-7\end{array}$ | $\begin{array}{r}13\\-7\end{array}$ | $\begin{array}{r}14\\-7\end{array}$ | $\begin{array}{r}15\\-7\end{array}$ | $\begin{array}{r}16\\-7\end{array}$ |

9.

| $\begin{array}{r}8\\-8\end{array}$ | $\begin{array}{r}9\\-8\end{array}$ | $\begin{array}{r}10\\-8\end{array}$ | $\begin{array}{r}11\\-8\end{array}$ | $\begin{array}{r}12\\-8\end{array}$ | $\begin{array}{r}13\\-8\end{array}$ | $\begin{array}{r}14\\-8\end{array}$ | $\begin{array}{r}15\\-8\end{array}$ | $\begin{array}{r}16\\-8\end{array}$ | $\begin{array}{r}17\\-8\end{array}$ |

10.

| $\begin{array}{r}9\\-9\end{array}$ | $\begin{array}{r}10\\-9\end{array}$ | $\begin{array}{r}11\\-9\end{array}$ | $\begin{array}{r}12\\-9\end{array}$ | $\begin{array}{r}13\\-9\end{array}$ | $\begin{array}{r}14\\-9\end{array}$ | $\begin{array}{r}15\\-9\end{array}$ | $\begin{array}{r}16\\-9\end{array}$ | $\begin{array}{r}17\\-9\end{array}$ | $\begin{array}{r}18\\-9\end{array}$ |

Subtraction Facts Practice

You can use the addition facts table to complete subtraction facts, since addition and subtraction are opposite operations.

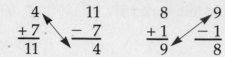

$$\begin{array}{r} 4 \\ +7 \\ \hline 11 \end{array} \qquad \begin{array}{r} 11 \\ -7 \\ \hline 4 \end{array} \qquad \begin{array}{r} 8 \\ +1 \\ \hline 9 \end{array} \qquad \begin{array}{r} 9 \\ -1 \\ \hline 8 \end{array}$$

Use These Steps

Complete the subtraction fact 6 − 4.

1. First, find the smaller number, 4, in the farthest column on the left.

2. Next, move to the right along that row until you find the larger number, 6.

3. Then move to the top of the column to find the answer, 2.

−	0	1	**2**	3	4	5	6	7	8	9
0	0	1	2	3	4	5	6	7	8	9
1	1	2	3	4	5	6	7	8	9	10
2	2	3	4	5	6	7	8	9	10	11
3	3	4	5	6	7	8	9	10	11	12
4	4	5	**6**	7	8	9	10	11	12	13
5	5	6	7	8	9	10	11	12	13	14
6	6	7	8	9	10	11	12	13	14	15
7	7	8	9	10	11	12	13	14	15	16
8	8	9	10	11	12	13	14	15	16	17
9	9	10	11	12	13	14	15	16	17	18

Use the table to complete the following subtraction facts.

1. $12 - 6 = 6$

2. $15 - 8 =$

3. $17 - 9 =$

4. $7 - 3 =$

5. $18 - 9 =$

6. $11 - 6 =$

7. $10 - 5 =$

8. $3 - 0 =$

9. $14 - 8 =$

10. $12 - 9 =$

11. $15 - 6 =$

12. $16 - 7 =$

13. $8 - 6 =$

14. $10 - 2 =$

15. $9 - 4 =$

16. $13 - 5 =$

17. $16 - 0 =$

18. $9 - 9 =$

Subtraction Facts Practice

Subtraction problems can be written vertically or horizontally.

minuend $\longrightarrow$ 9
subtrahend $\longrightarrow$ $-\,6$ is the same as $9 - 6 = 3$
difference $\longrightarrow$ 3

Complete the following subtraction facts. You can use the table on page 56 if you need help remembering the facts.

1. $15 - 7 = \boxed{8}$

2. $8 - 4 = \square$

3. $10 - 6 = \square$

4. $9 - 3 = \square$

5. $7 - \boxed{4} = 3$

6. $12 - \square = 4$

7. $14 - \square = 7$

8. $6 - \square = 6$

9. $\boxed{11} - 2 = 9$

10. $\square - 6 = 5$

11. $\square - 9 = 1$

12. $\square - 8 = 2$

13. $6 - 2 = \square$

14. $9 - 4 = \square$

15. $\square - 3 = 2$

16. $12 - \square = 6$

17. $\square - 8 = 7$

18. $15 - 6 = \square$

19. $13 - \square = 6$

20. $\square - 4 = 3$

21. $5 - 0 = \square$

22. $7 - \square = 5$

23. $18 - \square = 9$

24. $17 - 9 = \square$

25. $10 - \square = 2$

26. $4 - \square = 3$

27. $14 - \square = 14$

28. $\square - 1 = 6$

29. $\square - 2 = 8$

30. $16 - \square = 7$

31. $9 - 9 = \square$

32. $\square - 4 = 1$

Fill in the boxes with any numbers that make the differences. There may be more than one set of numbers that makes a true statement.

33. $\boxed{9} - \boxed{2} = 7$

34. $\square - \square = 9$

35. $\square - \square = 5$

36. $\square - \square = 0$

37. $\square - \square = 4$

38. $\square - \square = 8$

39. $\square - \square = 1$

40. $\square - \square = 6$

41. $\square - \square = 2$

Subtraction as the Opposite of Addition

Subtracting whole numbers is the opposite of adding whole numbers. This means that you can check the answer to a subtraction problem by adding the answer to the number you subtracted. The sum should be the same as the top number.

$$\begin{array}{r} 6 \\ -4 \\ \hline 2 \end{array} \qquad \begin{array}{r} 2 \\ +4 \\ \hline 6 \end{array}$$

Use These Steps

Subtract 17 − 8

1. Line up the digits.

$$\begin{array}{r} 17 \\ -\ 8 \\ \hline \end{array}$$

2. Subtract.

$$\begin{array}{r} 17 \\ -\ 8 \\ \hline 9 \end{array}$$

3. Check by adding the answer, 9, to the bottom number, 8. The sum should be the same as the top number, 17.

Check:

$$\begin{array}{r} 17 \\ -\ 8 \\ \hline 9 \end{array} \qquad \begin{array}{r} 9 \\ +\ 8 \\ \hline 17 \end{array}$$

Subtract. Use addition to check your answers.

1.
$$\begin{array}{r} 12 \\ -\ 3 \\ \hline 9 \end{array} \qquad \begin{array}{r} 9 \\ +\ 3 \\ \hline 12 \end{array}$$

2.
$$\begin{array}{r} 8 \\ -\ 7 \\ \hline \end{array}$$

3.
$$\begin{array}{r} 6 \\ -\ 0 \\ \hline \end{array}$$

4.
$$\begin{array}{r} 10 \\ -\ 2 \\ \hline \end{array}$$

5.
$$\begin{array}{r} 13 \\ -\ 5 \\ \hline \end{array}$$

6.
$$\begin{array}{r} 10 \\ -\ 6 \\ \hline \end{array}$$

7.
$$\begin{array}{r} 9 \\ -\ 0 \\ \hline \end{array}$$

8.
$$\begin{array}{r} 16 \\ -\ 8 \\ \hline \end{array}$$

9.
$$\begin{array}{r} 14 \\ -\ 5 \\ \hline \end{array}$$

10.
$$\begin{array}{r} 9 \\ -\ 6 \\ \hline \end{array}$$

11. $15 - 7 =$

12. $2 - 0 =$

13. $12 - 7 =$

14. $16 - 9 =$

15. $16 - 5 =$

16. $11 - 4 =$

17. $18 - 9 =$

18. $13 - 7 =$

Application

The chart below shows the high and low temperatures on one day in September for twelve cities in the United States.

Example What was the difference between the low and high temperatures for Albany?

$$\begin{array}{r} 63 \\ -\ 43 \\ \hline 20 \end{array}$$

The difference was 20 degrees.

City	High	Low
Albany	63	43
Atlanta	71	54
Boston	62	51
Chicago	60	36
Denver	81	43
Honolulu	89	72
Las Vegas	97	72
Miami	88	81
Omaha	69	42
St. Louis	63	41
Spokane	77	49
Wichita	64	44

Temperature in Degrees Fahrenheit

Solve. Be sure to put the greater number on top when you subtract.

1. Find the difference between the low and high temperatures for Boston.

Answer _____

2. What was the difference between the high and low temperatures for Omaha?

Answer _____

3. How much higher was the high temperature for Las Vegas than the high temperature for Chicago?

Answer _____

4. How much lower was the low temperature for Chicago than the low temperature for Spokane?

Answer _____

5. How much higher was the high temperature for Miami than the low temperature for Wichita?

Answer _____

6. How much lower was the low temperature for St. Louis than the high temperature for Denver?

Answer _____

Subtracting from Two-Digit Numbers

Use the subtraction facts to subtract two-digit numbers. Be sure to line up your answers in the correct columns. You may want to use the table on page 56 to help you.

Use These Steps

Subtract 57 − 36

1. Be sure that the ones and the tens are lined up.

$$
\begin{array}{r}
57 \\
- 36 \\
\hline
\end{array}
$$

2. Subtract the ones. 7 − 6 = 1 one. Put the 1 one in the ones column.

$$
\begin{array}{r}
57 \\
- 36 \\
\hline
1
\end{array}
$$

↖ 1 one

3. Subtract the tens. 5 − 3 = 2 tens. Put the 2 tens in the tens column. Check your answer by adding.

$$
\begin{array}{r}
57 \\
- 36 \\
\hline
21
\end{array}
\qquad
\begin{array}{r}
\text{Check:} \\
21 \\
+ 36 \\
\hline
57
\end{array}
$$

↖ 2 tens

Subtract. Use addition to check your answers.

1.
$$
\begin{array}{r} 78 \\ - 34 \\ \hline 44 \end{array}
\qquad
\begin{array}{r} 44 \\ + 34 \\ \hline 78 \end{array}
$$

2.
$$
\begin{array}{r} 89 \\ - 72 \\ \hline \end{array}
$$

3.
$$
\begin{array}{r} 42 \\ - 21 \\ \hline \end{array}
$$

4.
$$
\begin{array}{r} 96 \\ - 43 \\ \hline \end{array}
$$

5.
$$
\begin{array}{r} 68 \\ - 25 \\ \hline \end{array}
$$

6.
$$
\begin{array}{r} 49 \\ - 37 \\ \hline \end{array}
$$

7.
$$
\begin{array}{r} 32 \\ - 11 \\ \hline \end{array}
$$

8.
$$
\begin{array}{r} 99 \\ - 54 \\ \hline \end{array}
$$

9.
$$
\begin{array}{r} 58 \\ - 30 \\ \hline \end{array}
$$

10.
$$
\begin{array}{r} 22 \\ - 10 \\ \hline \end{array}
$$

11.
$$
\begin{array}{r} 87 \\ - 20 \\ \hline \end{array}
$$

12.
$$
\begin{array}{r} 51 \\ - 30 \\ \hline \end{array}
$$

13.
$$
\begin{array}{r} 86 \\ - 36 \\ \hline 50 \end{array}
$$

14.
$$
\begin{array}{r} 79 \\ - 39 \\ \hline \end{array}
$$

15.
$$
\begin{array}{r} 60 \\ - 50 \\ \hline \end{array}
$$

16.
$$
\begin{array}{r} 28 \\ - 23 \\ \hline \end{array}
$$

17.
$$
\begin{array}{r} 48 \\ - 17 \\ \hline \end{array}
$$

18.
$$
\begin{array}{r} 54 \\ - 22 \\ \hline \end{array}
$$

19.
$$
\begin{array}{r} 63 \\ - 40 \\ \hline \end{array}
$$

20.
$$
\begin{array}{r} 72 \\ - 32 \\ \hline \end{array}
$$

Subtracting from Two-Digit Numbers

To subtract numbers that are not lined up, first put the digits in columns. Line up the digits that have the same place value.

Use These Steps

Subtract 25 − 5

1. Write the digits in columns so that the digits with the same place value are lined up.

```
  25
−  5
```

2. Subtract the ones. 5 − 5 = 0 ones.

```
  25
−  5
   0
```
← 0 ones

3. Subtract the tens. There are no (0) tens in the bottom number. 2 − 0 = 2 tens. Check.

```
  25          Check:
−  5            20
  20          +  5
                25
```
← 2 tens

Subtract. Use addition to check your answers.

1. 36 − 5 =
```
  36        31
−  5      +  5
  31        36
```

2. 77 − 4 =

3. 99 − 6 =

4. 83 − 2 =

5. 18 − 6 =

6. 29 − 7 =

7. 58 − 4 =

8. 99 − 5 =

9. Simon's Pet Store had a shipment of 29 goldfish on Monday. By Saturday, 8 of the goldfish had been bought. How many goldfish were left?

10. Simon's got 46 guppies in the same shipment. By Saturday, 4 of them had been sold. How many guppies were left?

Answer_____

Answer_____

Subtracting from Larger Numbers

To subtract larger numbers, first be sure that the digits with the same place value are lined up. Subtract only the digits with the same place value. Be sure to put your answers in the correct columns.

Use These Steps

Subtract   459
         − 341

1. Be sure that the digits are lined up.

```
  459
− 341
```

2. Subtract each column, starting with the digits in the ones place.

Check:

```
  459        459        459        118
− 341      − 341      − 341      + 341
    8         18        118        459
```

↑ 8 ones   ↑ 1 ten   ↑ 1 hundred

Subtract. Use addition to check your answers.

1.
```
  920       420
− 500     + 500
  420       920
```

2.
```
  876
− 761
```

3.
```
  2,398
− 1,233
```

4.
```
  1,444
− 1,243
```

5.
```
  123
−  23
```

6.
```
  436
−   1
```

7.
```
  7,980
−   920
```

8.
```
  5,874
−     3
```

9. 3,253 − 1,132 =
```
  3,253      2,121
− 1,132    + 1,132
  2,121      3,253
```

10. 4,899 − 236 =

11. 2,789 − 77 =

12. By noon yesterday, the Waverly highway crew had finished paving 1,400 feet of roadway. The entire roadway is 1,456 feet long. How many feet do they have left to pave?

13. The West Branch Library made $465 at its book sale on Saturday and $786 on Sunday. How much more did the library make on Sunday than on Saturday?

Answer _____

Answer _____

Mixed Review

Add or subtract.

1.
$$\begin{array}{r} 2 \\ +1 \\ \hline \end{array}$$

2.
$$\begin{array}{r} 8 \\ -0 \\ \hline \end{array}$$

3.
$$\begin{array}{r} 15 \\ -7 \\ \hline \end{array}$$

4.
$$\begin{array}{r} 8 \\ +6 \\ \hline \end{array}$$

5.
$$\begin{array}{r} 8 \\ +9 \\ \hline \end{array}$$

6.
$$\begin{array}{r} 10 \\ -3 \\ \hline \end{array}$$

7.
$$\begin{array}{r} 7 \\ +4 \\ \hline \end{array}$$

8. $16 - 9 =$

9. $7 + 8 =$

10. $10 - 1 =$

11. $9 + 4 =$

12.
$$\begin{array}{r} 71 \\ +28 \\ \hline \end{array}$$

13.
$$\begin{array}{r} 89 \\ -86 \\ \hline \end{array}$$

14.
$$\begin{array}{r} 54 \\ +40 \\ \hline \end{array}$$

15.
$$\begin{array}{r} 43 \\ -23 \\ \hline \end{array}$$

16. $36 + 13 =$

17. $77 - 54 =$

18. $50 + 10 =$

19. $64 - 30 =$

20.
$$\begin{array}{r} 123 \\ +\ 23 \\ \hline \end{array}$$

21.
$$\begin{array}{r} 434 \\ -\ \ 1 \\ \hline \end{array}$$

22.
$$\begin{array}{r} 7,980 \\ +1,019 \\ \hline \end{array}$$

23.
$$\begin{array}{r} 1,987 \\ -\ \ \ 3 \\ \hline \end{array}$$

24. $6,542 - 2,111 =$

25. $2,699 + 200 =$

26. $5,196 - 71 =$

27. The tailor repaired a torn jacket for $15 and shortened a pair of pants for $15. How much did he charge for his work in all?

28. Sam paid the tailor for the clothes with $40. How much change did Sam get back?

Answer _____

Answer _____

63

Problem Solving: Using a Step-by-Step Plan

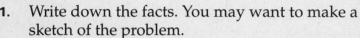

Solving word problems is easier if you follow a step-by-step plan. First, read the problem several times until you understand what the problem is about. Then follow these steps.

1. Write down the facts. You may want to make a sketch of the problem.
2. Think about what you need to do. Decide if you need to add or subtract, or both.
3. Set up a number problem.
4. Solve.
5. Write the answer to the question.

Example This week Marty is building a fence for the back yard of a museum. The yard is in the shape of a rectangle. Two sides of the yard are each 40 feet long. The other sides are each 27 feet long. How many feet of fencing material will Marty need?

Step 1. Write down the facts.

40 feet long on two sides
27 feet long on two sides

Step 2. Decide what to do.

Since you need a total
length, you will need to add the lengths of the four sides of the yard.

Step 3. Set up a number problem.
$$\begin{array}{r} 40 \\ 40 \\ 27 \\ +\ 27 \end{array}$$

Step 4. Solve.
$$\begin{array}{r} 40 \\ 40 \\ 27 \\ +\ 27 \\ \hline 134 \end{array}$$

Step 5. Answer the question.

Marty will need 134 feet of fencing material.

Use the steps on page 64 to solve each problem.

1. By installing storm windows in her house, Carolyn can save $1,850 dollars on her heating bill over the next ten years. Marty is installing these windows for her at a cost of $730. After paying for Marty's work, how much money will Carolyn actually save?

   Step 1.

   Step 2.

   Step 3.

   Step 4.

   Step 5.

2. Della Edwards raises Siamese cats to sell to pet stores. In 1989 she sold 36 cats. In 1990 she sold 52 cats. She sold 72 cats in 1991, and 41 cats in 1992. How many cats all together did Della sell in four years?

   Step 1.

   Step 2.

   Step 3.

   Step 4.

   Step 5.

Subtracting from Two-Digit Numbers with Renaming

When you are subtracting, the digit you are subtracting from can sometimes be too small. When this happens, borrow 1 ten from the next column to the left. Rename 1 ten as 10 ones.

Use These Steps

Subtract   42
          − 19

1. Since you can't subtract 9 from 2, borrow 1 ten. Cross out the 4 and write a 3 above it.

2. Rename the borrowed ten as ten ones. 2 + 10 = 12. Cross out the 2 and write a 12 above it.

3. Subtract the ones. 12 − 9 = 3 ones. Subtract the tens. 3 − 1 = 2 tens. Check your answer.

```
      3                    3 12              3 12        Check:
     4 2                   4 2               4 2           1
    − 1 9                 − 1 9             − 1 9         2 3
                                            2 3         + 1 9
                                                         4 2
```

Subtract. Use addition to check your answers.

1.
```
  3 16
   4 6      1
  − 2 8    1 8
   1 8    + 2 8
          4 6
```

2.
```
   92
 − 73
```

3.
```
   67
 − 49
```

4.
```
   71
 − 33
```

5.
```
   53
 −  8
```

6.
```
   32
 −  7
```

7.
```
   23
 −  6
```

8.
```
   84
 −  9
```

9.
```
   45
 − 37
```

10.
```
   62
 − 59
```

11.
```
   24
 − 15
```

12.
```
   96
 − 88
```

13.
```
   31
 −  6
```

14.
```
   77
 − 49
```

15.
```
   56
 −  8
```

16.
```
   23
 − 17
```

17.
```
   45
 −  6
```

18.
```
   62
 − 55
```

19.
```
   74
 −  9
```

20.
```
   86
 − 18
```

Subtracting from Two-Digit Numbers with Renaming

Line up the numbers carefully. The larger number goes on top. Borrow from the tens column only if you can't subtract the digit in the ones column.

Use These Steps

Subtract 86 − 78

1. Line up the digits in columns.

```
  86
− 78
```

2. Since you can't subtract 8 from 6, borrow 1 ten. Rename.

```
 7 16
  8̸ 6̸
 − 7 8
```

3. Subtract the ones. $16 − 8 = 8$ ones. Subtract the tens. $7 − 7 = 0$ tens. Check.

```
 7 16
  8̸ 6̸
 − 7 8
     8
```

Check:

```
   1
     8
 + 7 8
   8 6
```

Subtract. Use addition to check your answers.

1.
```
 3 14
  4̸ 4̸
 − 2 6
   1 8
```
```
   1
   1 8
 + 2 6
   4 4
```

2.
```
  53
− 34
```

3.
```
  94
− 79
```

4.
```
  82
− 48
```

5. $52 − 43 =$

6. $72 − 59 =$

7. $34 − 26 =$

8. $91 − 87 =$

9. $82 − 9 =$

10. $66 − 7 =$

11. $47 − 8 =$

12. $38 − 9 =$

13. A tune-up at Mike's Repair Shop costs $45. A tune-up kit and spark plugs to do the tune-up yourself cost $28. How much will you save if you do the work yourself?

14. The A & A Auto Shop charges a total of $74 to replace a car muffler. If the muffler alone costs $46, how much can you save if you do the work yourself?

Answer_____

Answer_____

Zeros in Subtraction

To subtract from zero in the ones place, rename just as you have done before.

Subtract. Use addition to check your answers.

1.
```
 2 10      1
  3 0     17
− 13    + 13
  17      30
```

2.
```
  50
− 26
```

3.
```
  70
− 39
```

4.
```
  40
− 14
```

5.
```
  60
− 54
```

6.
```
  80
− 73
```

7.
```
  90
− 88
```

8.
```
  20
− 11
```

9.
```
  30
−  4
```

10.
```
  50
−  7
```

11.
```
  70
−  2
```

12.
```
  90
−  9
```

13.
```
  40
−  3
```

14.
```
  80
−  5
```

15.
```
  20
−  1
```

16.
```
  10
−  6
```

17.
```
  30
− 15
```

18.
```
  70
−  8
```

19.
```
  60
− 39
```

20.
```
  50
−  9
```

68

Zeros in Subtraction

Line up the numbers. Subtract only digits with the same place value.

Subtract. Use addition to check your answers.

1.
$$
\begin{array}{r} {}^{5\ 10} \\ 6\!\!\!/\,0 \\ -\,15 \\ \hline 45 \end{array}
\qquad
\begin{array}{r} {}^{1} \\ 45 \\ +15 \\ \hline 60 \end{array}
$$

2.
$$
\begin{array}{r} 30 \\ -\,7 \\ \hline \end{array}
$$

3.
$$
\begin{array}{r} 40 \\ -\,9 \\ \hline \end{array}
$$

4.
$$
\begin{array}{r} 90 \\ -\,86 \\ \hline \end{array}
$$

5. 50 − 10 =

6. 70 − 11 =

7. 80 − 6 =

8. 20 − 19 =

9. 30 − 23 =

10. 60 − 50 =

11. 50 − 47 =

12. 90 − 40 =

13. A construction crew spent 72 days building one house and 90 days on a second house. How much longer did they spend building the second house than the first?

14. An office supply catalog has printer ribbons on sale for $19. The regular price of the ribbon was $30. How much less is the sale price than the original price?

Answer _____

Answer _____

Mixed Review

Add or subtract.

1.
$$16 - 8$$

2.
$$12 - 5$$

3.
$$6 + 8$$

4.
$$15 + 23$$

5.
$$56 - 25$$

6.
$$132 - 21$$

7. $590 - 430 =$

8. $225 + 10 =$

9. $2,866 - 56 =$

10. $1,304 + 291 =$

11.
$$71 - 36$$

12.
$$55 + 49$$

13.
$$27 - 19$$

14.
$$85 + 6$$

15. $36 + 29 =$

16. $42 - 7 =$

17. $93 - 15 =$

18. $87 - 78 =$

19.
$$30 - 7$$

20.
$$90 - 65$$

21.
$$50 - 8$$

22.
$$40 + 32$$

23. $30 + 16 =$

24. $20 - 11 =$

25. $30 - 10 =$

26. $70 - 67 =$

27. Buster drives a bus for Midway. It takes him 30 hours to go from Los Angeles to New Orleans. On the way, he stops in El Paso. It takes 16 hours to reach El Paso. How long does it take Buster to get from El Paso to New Orleans?

28. Another Midway bus takes 22 hours to travel from Dallas to San Diego. Then it takes 20 hours more to get to Seattle. How many hours does the whole trip take?

Answer _____

Answer _____

Application

Brenda manages the inventory at Better Hardware. The store tries to have a set amount of stock on hand every month. Brenda has a chart of this set amount. At the end of each month, she counts the stock on hand. Then she subtracts this number from the amount on her chart so she will know how much stock to order.

Example The store needs to have 90 boxes of bolts in stock. Brenda counted 42 boxes. How many more boxes of bolts should Brenda order?

$$\begin{array}{r} \overset{8\ 10}{\cancel{9}\cancel{0}} \\ -\ 4\ 2 \\ \hline 4\ 8 \end{array}$$

Brenda should order 48 more boxes.

Solve.

1. Look at Brenda's chart. The chart shows the number of boxes in stock at the end of the month, and the number of boxes the store needs to have in stock. How many boxes of each item should Brenda order? Complete the chart.

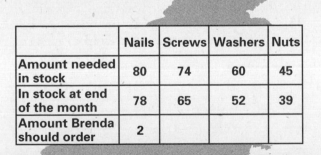

	Nails	Screws	Washers	Nuts
Amount needed in stock	80	74	60	45
In stock at end of the month	78	65	52	39
Amount Brenda should order	2			

2. Last week Brenda counted the cans of paint in stock at the beginning and end of each day. She made a chart to help keep a record. On Monday morning, Brenda counted 87 cans. The store sold 7 cans of paint that day. Each day, she recorded on the chart the number of cans sold. How many cans of paint did Brenda have left at the end of each day? Complete the chart.

	Monday	Tuesday	Wednesday	Thursday	Friday	Saturday
Beginning Count	87	80				
Cans Sold	7	14	12	7	9	28
Ending Count	80					

Subtracting from Larger Numbers with Renaming

To subtract larger numbers, use the same steps you have been using for
two-digit subtraction problems. You may need to rename two or more
times.

Use These Steps

Subtract   367
          − 179

1. To subtract the ones, borrow
   1 ten. Rename.
   17 − 9 = 8 ones.

2. To subtract the tens, borrow
   1 hundred. Rename. Now
   there are 15 tens.
   15 − 7 = 8 tens.

3. Subtract the hundreds.
   2 − 1 = 1 hundred.
   Check your answer.

```
      5 17                    15                      15          Check:
    3 6 7                  2 5 17                  2 5 17          1 1
   3 6 7                   3 6 7                   3 6 7           1 8 8
  − 1 7 9                 − 1 7 9                 − 1 7 9         + 1 7 9
      8                      8 8                   1 8 8           3 6 7
```

Subtract. Use addition to check your answers.

1.
```
    13
  2 3 15        1 1
  3 4 5         177
 − 1 6 8       + 168
  1 7 7         345
```

2.
```
   561
 − 373
```

3.
```
   941
 − 182
```

4.
```
   750
 − 521
```

5.
```
   981
 − 873
```

6.
```
   920
 − 892
```

7.
```
   472
 − 265
```

8.
```
   731
 − 536
```

9.
```
   483
 − 399
```

10.
```
   234
 − 159
```

11.
```
   388
 − 198
```

12.
```
   543
 − 367
```

13.
```
   635
 − 246
```

14.
```
   841
 − 632
```

15.
```
   724
 − 425
```

16.
```
   920
 − 563
```

Subtracting from Larger Numbers with Renaming

When you subtract larger numbers, be sure to line up the digits in the correct columns.

Use These Steps

Subtract   2,890 − 962

1. Line up the digits. To subtract the ones, borrow 1 ten. Rename. 10 − 2 = 8 ones.

$$\begin{array}{r} {\scriptstyle 8\ 10} \\ 2,8\,9\,\cancel{0} \\ -\ \ \ 9\,6\,2 \\ \hline 8 \end{array}$$

2. Subtract the tens. 8 − 6 = 2 tens. No borrowing is needed.

$$\begin{array}{r} {\scriptstyle 8\ 10} \\ 2,8\,9\,\cancel{0} \\ -\ \ \ 9\,6\,2 \\ \hline 2\,8 \end{array}$$

3. To subtract the hundreds, borrow 1 thousand. Rename 1 thousand as 10 hundreds. 18 − 9 = 9 hundreds. Subtract the thousands. 1 − 0 = 1 thousand. Check your answer.

$$\begin{array}{r} {\scriptstyle 1\ 18\ 8\ 10} \\ 2,8\,9\,0 \\ -\ \ \ 9\,6\,2 \\ \hline 1,9\,2\,8 \end{array}$$

Check:
$$\begin{array}{r} {\scriptstyle 1\ \ \ 1} \\ 1,9\,2\,8 \\ +\ \ \ 9\,6\,2 \\ \hline 2,8\,9\,0 \end{array}$$

Subtract. Use addition to check your answers.

1.
3,640 − 1,983 =

$$\begin{array}{r} {\scriptstyle 15\ 13} \\ {\scriptstyle 2\ 5\ 3\ 10} \\ 3,6\,4\,0 \\ -\ 1,9\,8\,3 \\ \hline 1,6\,5\,7 \end{array} \qquad \begin{array}{r} {\scriptstyle 1\ 11} \\ 1,6\,5\,7 \\ +\ 1,9\,8\,3 \\ \hline 3,6\,4\,0 \end{array}$$

2.
4,794 − 1,887 =

3.
6,550 − 3,458 =

4.
11,832 − 4,659 =

5.
25,611 − 14,703 =

6.
37,730 − 1,982 =

7.
124,653 − 48,927 =

8.
362,141 − 183,529 =

9.
943,217 − 56,199 =

73

Mixed Review

Subtract.

1.
$$258 - 169$$

2.
$$961 - 382$$

3.
$$1,545 - 39$$

4.
$$652 - 399$$

5. $276 - 93 =$

6. $772 - 89 =$

7. $2,435 - 95 =$

8.
$$12,490 - 1,652$$

9.
$$53,925 - 41,799$$

10.
$$98,324 - 990$$

11. $14,320 - 11,965 =$

12. $25,030 - 19,019 =$

13. $52,340 - 967 =$

14.
$$125,330 - 26,592$$

15.
$$980,352 - 30,199$$

16.
$$247,822 - 172,653$$

17. The diameter (distance through the center) of the smallest planet, Pluto, is 1,420 miles. The diameter of the largest planet, Jupiter, is 88,640 miles. How much larger is the diameter of Jupiter than the diameter of Pluto?

18. The diameter of Earth is 7,926 miles. The sun has a diameter of 863,027 miles. How much larger is the diameter of the sun than the diameter of Earth?

Answer_____

Answer_____

Zeros in Subtraction

Zeros may be in two places in larger numbers. When you subtract from two zeros, you will need to borrow two or more times.

Subtract   700
         − 375

1. There are no ones and no tens in the top number. To subtract, borrow from the hundreds column. Rename 1 hundred as 10 tens.

```
  6 10
  7 0 0
− 3 7 5
```

2. There are now 10 tens. Rename 1 ten as 10 ones.

```
      9
  6 10 10
  7 0 0
− 3 7 5
```

3. There are now 10 ones, 9 tens, and 6 hundreds. Subtract.
   10 − 5 = 5 ones.
   9 − 7 = 2 tens.
   6 − 3 = 3 hundreds.
   Check your answer.

```
      9
  6 10 10
  7 0 0
− 3 7 5
  3 2 5
```

Check:
```
  1 1
  3 2 5
+ 3 7 5
  7 0 0
```

Subtract. Use addition to check your answers.

1.
```
      9
  4 10 10        1 1
  5 0 0        2 3 7
− 2 6 3      + 2 6 3
  2 3 7        5 0 0
```

2.
```
  300
−  98
```

3.
```
  400
−  56
```

4.
```
  900
− 398
```

5.
```
  3,100
− 1,642
```

6.
```
  5,500
− 2,307
```

7.
```
  2,600
−   593
```

8.
```
  8,700
−   477
```

9.
```
  18,700
− 17,856
```

10.
```
  26,900
−  9,459
```

11.
```
  57,300
−  3,750
```

12.
```
  95,500
− 10,022
```

13.
```
  6,200
− 2,341
```

14.
```
  27,100
−  5,248
```

15.
```
  83,300
− 17,306
```

16.
```
  41,600
−    782
```

Zeros in Subtraction

To subtract from three or more zeros, you will need to borrow three or more times.

Use These Steps

Subtract 3,000 − 2,506

1. Line up the digits.

```
  3,000
− 2,506
```

2. Rename three times.

```
      9 9
  2 10 10 10
  3,0 0 0
− 2,5 0 6
```

3. Subtract.

10 − 6 = 4 ones.
9 − 0 = 9 tens.
9 − 5 = 4 hundreds.
2 − 2 = 0 thousands.
Check your answer.

```
      9 9                 Check:
  2 10 10 10              1 1 1
  3,0 0 0                   4 9 4
− 2,5 0 6               + 2,5 0 6
    4 9 4                 3,0 0 0
```

Subtract. Use addition to check your answers.

1.
```
  9 9
4 10 10 10      1 1 1
5,0 0 0     3,505
− 1,4 9 5   + 1,495
3,5 0 5     5,000
```

2.
```
  7,000
− 6,703
```

3.
```
  1,000
−   985
```

4.
```
  3,000
−   770
```

5.
```
  26,000
−  2,891
```

6.
```
  42,000
− 15,407
```

7.
```
  196,000
−  99,396
```

8.
```
  437,000
− 256,930
```

9. 53,000 − 47,926 =

10. 148,000 − 129,672 =

11. 539,000 − 2,659 =

12. 290,000 − 32,619 =
```
      9 9 9
  8 10 10 10 10      1 1 1 1
  2 9 0,0 0 0      257,381
−     3 2,6 1 9    + 32,619
  2 5 7,3 8 1      290,000
```

13. 300,000 − 56,032 =

14. 800,000 − 136,275 =

Borrowing Across Zeros

Some subtraction problems may have one or more zeros in the middle part of the top number. When this happens, you will need to borrow across the zeros.

Use These Steps

Subtract 501 − 299

1. Line up the digits. To subtract ones, borrow 1 hundred across the zero from the hundreds column. Rename 1 hundred as 10 tens.

$$\begin{array}{r} {}^{4\ 10}\\ \cancel{5}\cancel{0}1 \\ -299 \\ \hline \end{array}$$

2. Borrow 1 ten and rename as 10 ones. There are now 4 hundreds, 9 tens, and 11 ones.

$$\begin{array}{r} {}^{9}\\ {}^{4\ \cancel{10}\ 11}\\ \cancel{5}\cancel{0}\cancel{1} \\ -299 \\ \hline \end{array}$$

3. Subtract.
   $11 − 9 = 2$ ones.
   $9 − 9 = 0$ tens.
   $4 − 2 = 2$ hundreds. Check your answer.

$$\begin{array}{r} {}^{9}\\ {}^{4\ \cancel{10}\ 11}\\ \cancel{5}\cancel{0}\cancel{1} \\ -299 \\ \hline 202 \end{array}$$

Check:
$$\begin{array}{r} {}^{1\ 1}\\ 202 \\ +299 \\ \hline 501 \end{array}$$

Subtract. Use addition to check your answers.

1.
$$\begin{array}{r} {}^{9}\\ {}^{6\ \cancel{10}\ 16}\\ 7\cancel{0}\cancel{6} \\ -257 \\ \hline 449 \end{array} \qquad \begin{array}{r} {}^{11}\\ 449 \\ +257 \\ \hline 706 \end{array}$$

2.
$$\begin{array}{r} 301 \\ -199 \\ \hline \end{array}$$

3.
$$\begin{array}{r} 508 \\ -369 \\ \hline \end{array}$$

4.
$$\begin{array}{r} 903 \\ -424 \\ \hline \end{array}$$

5.
$$\begin{array}{r} 207 \\ -78 \\ \hline \end{array}$$

6.
$$\begin{array}{r} 403 \\ -56 \\ \hline \end{array}$$

7.
$$\begin{array}{r} 503 \\ -88 \\ \hline \end{array}$$

8.
$$\begin{array}{r} 707 \\ -99 \\ \hline \end{array}$$

9.
$$\begin{array}{r} 1{,}603 \\ -348 \\ \hline \end{array}$$

10.
$$\begin{array}{r} 4{,}302 \\ -773 \\ \hline \end{array}$$

11.
$$\begin{array}{r} 9{,}206 \\ -3{,}837 \\ \hline \end{array}$$

12.
$$\begin{array}{r} 7{,}701 \\ -2{,}995 \\ \hline \end{array}$$

13. $406 − 249 =$

14. $301 − 93 =$

15. $1{,}702 − 635 =$

Borrowing Across Zeros

To subtract across one or more zeros, you may need to borrow across
the zeros from the hundreds or thousands place.

Use These Steps

Subtract   35,003 − 3,236

1. Line up the digits.

$$
\begin{array}{r}
35{,}003 \\
-\ \ 3{,}236 \\
\end{array}
$$

2. To subtract the ones, borrow
across the zeros from the
thousands column. Rename.
There are now 4 thousands,
9 hundreds, 9 tens, and
13 ones.

$$
\begin{array}{r}
^{9\ 9} \\
^{4\,10\,10\,13} \\
3\,5{,}0\,0\,3 \\
-\ \ \ 3{,}2\,3\,6 \\
\end{array}
$$

3. Subtract. Check your
answer.

$$
\begin{array}{r}
^{9\ 9} \\
^{4\,10\,10\,13} \\
3\,5{,}0\,0\,3 \\
-\ \ \ 3{,}2\,3\,6 \\
\hline
3\,1{,}7\,6\,7 \\
\end{array}
$$

Check:
$$
\begin{array}{r}
^{1\ 1\ 1} \\
3\,1{,}7\,6\,7 \\
+\ \ 3{,}2\,3\,6 \\
\hline
3\,5{,}0\,0\,3 \\
\end{array}
$$

Subtract. Use addition to check your answers.

1.
$$
\begin{array}{r}
^{9\ 9} \\
^{5\,10\,10\,13} \\
6{,}0\,0\,3 \\
-\ 3{,}4\,8\,7 \\
\hline
2{,}5\,1\,6 \\
\end{array}
\qquad
\begin{array}{r}
^{1\ 1\ 1} \\
2{,}516 \\
+\ 3{,}487 \\
\hline
6{,}003 \\
\end{array}
$$

2.
$$
\begin{array}{r}
4{,}001 \\
-\ 1{,}892 \\
\end{array}
$$

3.
$$
\begin{array}{r}
1{,}007 \\
-\ \ \ 998 \\
\end{array}
$$

4.
$$
\begin{array}{r}
2{,}006 \\
-\ \ \ 347 \\
\end{array}
$$

5. $7{,}002 - 685 =$

6. $19{,}006 - 8{,}149 =$

7. $25{,}009 - 7{,}658 =$

8. $10{,}032 - 765 =$

9. $90{,}026 - 1{,}493 =$

10. $130{,}082 - 15{,}996 =$

11. $3{,}002 - 926 =$

12. $20{,}029 - 1{,}577 =$

13. $100{,}251 - 74{,}844 =$

Problem Solving: Using Rounding and Estimating

When you work with larger numbers, it is sometimes easier to use rounded numbers rather than exact numbers. In rounding a number to the nearest thousand, remember that if the digit in the hundreds place ends in 5, round to the next higher number in the thousands place.

Example This chart lists ten of the most famous mountains in the world and their height above sea level. About how many feet taller is Mount McKinley than Mont Blanc?

Mountain	Height in Feet	Mountain	Height in Feet
Aconcagua	22,831	Kilimanjaro	19,340
Mauna Loa	13,677	Mont Blanc	15,771
Mount Everest	29,028	Mount Fuji	12,388
Mount Kenya	17,058	Mount Logan	19,524
Mount McKinley	20,320	Mount Rainier	14,410

▶ **Step 1.** Round each number to the nearest thousand.

Mount McKinley   20,320   rounds to 20,000
Mont Blanc   15,771   rounds to 16,000

▶ **Step 2.** Compare the rounded numbers.

20,000 > 16,000, so Mount McKinley is taller than Mont Blanc.

▶ **Step 3.** Subtract the smaller number from the larger number.

$$\begin{array}{r} \overset{110}{2\cancel{0},000} \\ -16,000 \\ \hline 4,000 \end{array}$$

Mount McKinley is about 4,000 feet taller than Mont Blanc.

Solve.

1. Round the height of Kilimanjaro to the nearest thousand.

2. Round the height of Aconcagua to the nearest thousand.

Answer_____

Answer_____

3. Round the height of Mount Rainier to the nearest thousand.

Answer_____

4. Round the height of Mauna Loa to the nearest thousand.

Answer_____

5. Round the height of Mount Fuji to the nearest thousand.

Answer_____

6. Compare the rounded heights of Kilimanjaro and Mauna Loa. Which mountain is taller?

Answer_____

7. Compare the rounded heights of Mount Fuji and Mount McKinley. Which mountain is taller?

Answer_____

8. About how many feet taller is Mauna Loa than Mount Fuji?

Answer_____

9. About how many feet taller is Aconcagua than Mount Rainier?

Answer_____

10. About how many feet shorter than Mount Everest is Mount Logan?

Answer_____

11. About how many feet shorter than Mount McKinley is Mount Kenya?

Answer_____

12. About how many feet shorter than Kilimanjaro is Mont Blanc?

Answer_____

Unit 3 *Review*

Subtract. Use addition to check your answers.

1.
$$17 - 8$$

2.
$$13 - 7$$

3.
$$12 - 4$$

4.
$$27 - 13$$

5.
$$94 - 83$$

6.
$$85 - 15$$

7. $16 - 9 =$

8. $11 - 9 =$

9. $36 - 4 =$

10. $72 - 10 =$

11.
$$367 - 243$$

12.
$$935 - 25$$

13.
$$657 - 343$$

14.
$$1,507 - 1,402$$

15. $193 - 141 =$

16. $280 - 140 =$

17. $2,327 - 1,304 =$

18.
$$53 - 17$$

19.
$$26 - 9$$

20.
$$47 - 38$$

21.
$$93 - 86$$

22. $65 - 56 =$

23. $44 - 9 =$

24. $52 - 42 =$

25. $72 - 29 =$

26.
$$20 - 15$$

27.
$$30 - 29$$

28.
$$90 - 56$$

29.
$$50 - 3$$

30. $60 - 6 =$

31. $80 - 5 =$

32. $40 - 26 =$

33. $70 - 62 =$

Subtract. Use addition to check your answers.

34.
$$\begin{array}{r} 641 \\ -572 \\ \hline \end{array}$$

35.
$$\begin{array}{r} 916 \\ -709 \\ \hline \end{array}$$

36.
$$\begin{array}{r} 2,350 \\ -\ 291 \\ \hline \end{array}$$

37.
$$\begin{array}{r} 1,552 \\ -\ 497 \\ \hline \end{array}$$

38. $5,623 - 1,927 =$

39. $17,420 - 15,523 =$

40. $25,062 - 9,059 =$

41.
$$\begin{array}{r} 400 \\ -293 \\ \hline \end{array}$$

42.
$$\begin{array}{r} 700 \\ -654 \\ \hline \end{array}$$

43.
$$\begin{array}{r} 800 \\ -427 \\ \hline \end{array}$$

44.
$$\begin{array}{r} 3,506 \\ -1,968 \\ \hline \end{array}$$

45. $15,006 - 13,558 =$

46. $72,008 - 9,662 =$

47. $90,800 - 1,857 =$

48. $29,000 - 17,627 =$

49. $700,000 - 493,274 =$

50. $680,000 - 14,901 =$

Below is a list of the problems in this review and the pages on which the skills are taught. If you missed any problems, turn to the pages listed and practice the skills. Then correct the problems you missed in the Unit Review.

Problems	Pages	Problems	Pages
1–3, 7–8	55–58	26–33	68–69
4–6, 9–10	60–61	34–40	72–73
11–17	62	41–50	75–78
18–25	66–67		

Unit 4 MULTIPLYING WHOLE NUMBERS

Multiplication is the same as repeated addition. For example, if you have a case of cherry soda that has 4 six-packs in it, you could add sixes to find out how many cans of soda you have. 6 + 6 + 6 + 6 = 24 cans. It is much easier, though, to multiply 4 by 6 to find the answer.

To be successful at multiplying numbers, you must memorize the multiplication facts. These facts are the basis of every multiplication problem. In this unit, you will learn the multiplication facts and how to multiply by one-digit, two-digit, and three-digit numbers. You will also learn about multiplying with zeros.

Getting Ready

You should be familiar with the skills on this page and the next before you begin this unit. To check your answers, turn to page 187.

 When you are working with whole numbers, place value is important in setting up problems, renaming, and lining up answers.

Write the value of the underlined digit in each number.

1. 3<u>2</u> _____ 2 ones _____

2. <u>5</u>47 _____

3. 1,0<u>6</u>1 _____

4. <u>1</u>,495 _____

5. <u>6</u>,886 _____

6. 5,0<u>00</u> _____

For review, see Unit 1, pages 18-19.

Getting Ready

 To set up an addition problem, first line up the digits.
Then solve the problem.

Line up the digits in each problem and solve.

7.
$$342 + 11 =$$
$$\begin{array}{r} 342 \\ +\ 11 \\ \hline 353 \end{array}$$

8.
$$1,365 + 32 =$$

9.
$$15,341 + 1,231 =$$

For review, see Unit 2, pages 36-37.

 Renaming in addition will help you learn to rename in multiplication.

Add.

10.
$$297 + 48 =$$
$$\begin{array}{r} {\scriptstyle 1\ 1} \\ 297 \\ +\ \ 48 \\ \hline 345 \end{array}$$

11.
$$1,619 + 391 =$$

12.
$$83,457 + 19,543 =$$

For review, see Unit 2, pages 43-44.

Zero plus any number is that number.

Add.

13.
$$\begin{array}{r} 200 \\ +\ 591 \\ \hline 791 \end{array}$$

14.
$$\begin{array}{r} 1,709 \\ +\ \ \ \ 3 \\ \hline \end{array}$$

15.
$$\begin{array}{r} 506 \\ +\ \ 37 \\ \hline \end{array}$$

16.
$$\begin{array}{r} 7,006 \\ +\ 8,906 \\ \hline \end{array}$$

17.
$$\begin{array}{r} 20,009 \\ +\ 36,304 \\ \hline \end{array}$$

18.
$$306 + 42 =$$

19.
$$1,030 + 2,091 =$$

20.
$$600 + 5,300 =$$

21.
$$30,004 + 502 + 2,007 =$$

22.
$$10,600 + 3,400 + 20 =$$

For review, see Unit 2, page 45.

Multiplication Facts

To multiply larger numbers, you should first know the basic multiplication facts. You will find it helpful to know the following facts by heart.

Multiply the following numbers to complete each row. Notice that the answers form a pattern. Notice also that zero times any number equals zero.

1.
$$\begin{array}{c} 0 \\ \times 1 \\ \hline 0 \end{array} \quad \begin{array}{c} 1 \\ \times 1 \\ \hline 1 \end{array} \quad \begin{array}{c} 2 \\ \times 1 \\ \hline 2 \end{array} \quad \begin{array}{c} 3 \\ \times 1 \\ \hline 3 \end{array} \quad \begin{array}{c} 4 \\ \times 1 \\ \hline 4 \end{array} \quad \begin{array}{c} 5 \\ \times 1 \\ \hline 5 \end{array} \quad \begin{array}{c} 6 \\ \times 1 \\ \hline 6 \end{array} \quad \begin{array}{c} 7 \\ \times 1 \\ \hline 7 \end{array} \quad \begin{array}{c} 8 \\ \times 1 \\ \hline 8 \end{array} \quad \begin{array}{c} 9 \\ \times 1 \\ \hline 9 \end{array}$$

2.
$$\begin{array}{c} 0 \\ \times 2 \end{array} \quad \begin{array}{c} 1 \\ \times 2 \end{array} \quad \begin{array}{c} 2 \\ \times 2 \end{array} \quad \begin{array}{c} 3 \\ \times 2 \end{array} \quad \begin{array}{c} 4 \\ \times 2 \end{array} \quad \begin{array}{c} 5 \\ \times 2 \end{array} \quad \begin{array}{c} 6 \\ \times 2 \end{array} \quad \begin{array}{c} 7 \\ \times 2 \end{array} \quad \begin{array}{c} 8 \\ \times 2 \end{array} \quad \begin{array}{c} 9 \\ \times 2 \end{array}$$

3.
$$\begin{array}{c} 0 \\ \times 3 \end{array} \quad \begin{array}{c} 1 \\ \times 3 \end{array} \quad \begin{array}{c} 2 \\ \times 3 \end{array} \quad \begin{array}{c} 3 \\ \times 3 \end{array} \quad \begin{array}{c} 4 \\ \times 3 \end{array} \quad \begin{array}{c} 5 \\ \times 3 \end{array} \quad \begin{array}{c} 6 \\ \times 3 \end{array} \quad \begin{array}{c} 7 \\ \times 3 \end{array} \quad \begin{array}{c} 8 \\ \times 3 \end{array} \quad \begin{array}{c} 9 \\ \times 3 \end{array}$$

4.
$$\begin{array}{c} 0 \\ \times 4 \end{array} \quad \begin{array}{c} 1 \\ \times 4 \end{array} \quad \begin{array}{c} 2 \\ \times 4 \end{array} \quad \begin{array}{c} 3 \\ \times 4 \end{array} \quad \begin{array}{c} 4 \\ \times 4 \end{array} \quad \begin{array}{c} 5 \\ \times 4 \end{array} \quad \begin{array}{c} 6 \\ \times 4 \end{array} \quad \begin{array}{c} 7 \\ \times 4 \end{array} \quad \begin{array}{c} 8 \\ \times 4 \end{array} \quad \begin{array}{c} 9 \\ \times 4 \end{array}$$

5.
$$\begin{array}{c} 0 \\ \times 5 \end{array} \quad \begin{array}{c} 1 \\ \times 5 \end{array} \quad \begin{array}{c} 2 \\ \times 5 \end{array} \quad \begin{array}{c} 3 \\ \times 5 \end{array} \quad \begin{array}{c} 4 \\ \times 5 \end{array} \quad \begin{array}{c} 5 \\ \times 5 \end{array} \quad \begin{array}{c} 6 \\ \times 5 \end{array} \quad \begin{array}{c} 7 \\ \times 5 \end{array} \quad \begin{array}{c} 8 \\ \times 5 \end{array} \quad \begin{array}{c} 9 \\ \times 5 \end{array}$$

6.
$$\begin{array}{c} 0 \\ \times 6 \end{array} \quad \begin{array}{c} 1 \\ \times 6 \end{array} \quad \begin{array}{c} 2 \\ \times 6 \end{array} \quad \begin{array}{c} 3 \\ \times 6 \end{array} \quad \begin{array}{c} 4 \\ \times 6 \end{array} \quad \begin{array}{c} 5 \\ \times 6 \end{array} \quad \begin{array}{c} 6 \\ \times 6 \end{array} \quad \begin{array}{c} 7 \\ \times 6 \end{array} \quad \begin{array}{c} 8 \\ \times 6 \end{array} \quad \begin{array}{c} 9 \\ \times 6 \end{array}$$

7.
$$\begin{array}{c} 0 \\ \times 7 \end{array} \quad \begin{array}{c} 1 \\ \times 7 \end{array} \quad \begin{array}{c} 2 \\ \times 7 \end{array} \quad \begin{array}{c} 3 \\ \times 7 \end{array} \quad \begin{array}{c} 4 \\ \times 7 \end{array} \quad \begin{array}{c} 5 \\ \times 7 \end{array} \quad \begin{array}{c} 6 \\ \times 7 \end{array} \quad \begin{array}{c} 7 \\ \times 7 \end{array} \quad \begin{array}{c} 8 \\ \times 7 \end{array} \quad \begin{array}{c} 9 \\ \times 7 \end{array}$$

8.
$$\begin{array}{c} 0 \\ \times 8 \end{array} \quad \begin{array}{c} 1 \\ \times 8 \end{array} \quad \begin{array}{c} 2 \\ \times 8 \end{array} \quad \begin{array}{c} 3 \\ \times 8 \end{array} \quad \begin{array}{c} 4 \\ \times 8 \end{array} \quad \begin{array}{c} 5 \\ \times 8 \end{array} \quad \begin{array}{c} 6 \\ \times 8 \end{array} \quad \begin{array}{c} 7 \\ \times 8 \end{array} \quad \begin{array}{c} 8 \\ \times 8 \end{array} \quad \begin{array}{c} 9 \\ \times 8 \end{array}$$

9.
$$\begin{array}{c} 0 \\ \times 9 \end{array} \quad \begin{array}{c} 1 \\ \times 9 \end{array} \quad \begin{array}{c} 2 \\ \times 9 \end{array} \quad \begin{array}{c} 3 \\ \times 9 \end{array} \quad \begin{array}{c} 4 \\ \times 9 \end{array} \quad \begin{array}{c} 5 \\ \times 9 \end{array} \quad \begin{array}{c} 6 \\ \times 9 \end{array} \quad \begin{array}{c} 7 \\ \times 9 \end{array} \quad \begin{array}{c} 8 \\ \times 9 \end{array} \quad \begin{array}{c} 9 \\ \times 9 \end{array}$$

Multiplication Facts Practice

Use the multiplication facts from page 85 to complete the table.

Example Find an empty box in the table. Look up the column to the top row of numbers. Then move left from the box to the number at the beginning of the row. Multiply these two numbers. Write the answer in the empty box.

×	0	1	2	3	4	5	6	7	8	9
0	0									
1		1								
2			4							
3				9						
4					16					
5						25				
6							36			
7								49		
8									64	
9										81

To use the table to complete the multiplication facts, find one number at the top of a column and the other number at the beginning of a row. The answer is the number in the box where the row and the column meet.

Complete the following multiplication facts.

1. $6 \times 7 = 42$

2. $3 \times 9 =$

3. $5 \times 7 =$

4. $2 \times 0 =$

5. $9 \times 9 =$

6. $8 \times 4 =$

7. $5 \times 6 =$

8. $3 \times 4 =$

9. $7 \times 8 =$

10. $2 \times 6 =$

11. $6 \times 6 =$

12. $3 \times 2 =$

13. $4 \times 4 =$

14. $0 \times 8 =$

15. $1 \times 5 =$

16. $9 \times 8 =$

17. $4 \times 1 =$

18. $7 \times 3 =$

19. $6 \times 9 =$

20. $8 \times 5 =$

21. $4 \times 2 =$

22. $3 \times 3 =$

23. $0 \times 1 =$

24. $2 \times 5 =$

Multiplication Facts Practice

Multiplication problems can be written vertically or horizontally.

$$\begin{array}{r} \text{multiplicand} \longrightarrow \quad 9 \\ \text{multiplier} \longrightarrow \underline{\times\, 6} \\ \text{product} \longrightarrow \quad 54 \end{array} \qquad \text{is the same as } 6 \times 9 = 54$$

Complete the following multiplication facts. You can use the table on page 86 if you need help remembering the facts.

1. $5 \times 5 = \boxed{25}$

2. $2 \times 8 = \square$

3. $7 \times 3 = \square$

4. $9 \times 4 = \square$

5. $4 \times \boxed{8} = 32$

6. $6 \times \square = 0$

7. $8 \times \square = 8$

8. $2 \times \square = 10$

9. $\square \times 6 = 24$

10. $\square \times 3 = 9$

11. $\square \times 7 = 42$

12. $\square \times 2 = 18$

13. $1 \times \square = 0$

14. $5 \times 9 = \square$

15. $\square \times 6 = 18$

16. $9 \times \square = 36$

17. $8 \times \square = 40$

18. $\square \times 4 = 12$

19. $7 \times 8 = \square$

20. $5 \times 6 = \square$

Fill in the boxes with any numbers that make the products. There may be more than one set of numbers that makes a true statement. Use the table on page 86 if you need help.

21. $\boxed{5} \times \boxed{4} = 20$

22. $\square \times \square = 16$

23. $\square \times \square = 27$

24. $\square \times \square = 32$

25. $\square \times \square = 42$

26. $\square \times \square = 12$

27. $\square \times \square = 9$

28. $\square \times \square = 0$

29. $\square \times \square = 8$

30. $\square \times \square = 54$

31. $\square \times \square = 45$

32. $\square \times \square = 64$

33. $\square \times \square = 15$

34. $\square \times \square = 21$

35. $\square \times \square = 36$

36. $\square \times \square = 72$

37. $\square \times \square = 24$

38. $\square \times \square = 25$

39. $\square \times \square = 10$

40. $\square \times \square = 18$

Application

You can use multiplication to help you figure out total cost when you are buying more than one of the same thing.

Barron's Office Supply   *21*

Write Idea pens $2 per box   Staplers $4 each   Notebooks $2 each   Calendars $3 each

For each problem below, use the prices from the catalog to work out each answer. Circle the letter next to the correct choice.

1. Carlos is ordering supplies for his company. He wants to buy 6 boxes of pens. How much will 6 boxes of pens cost?

   a. $9
   b. $12
   c. $18

2. Carlos doesn't want to spend more than $20 for pens. If he buys 6 boxes, he will spend

   a. less than $20.
   b. more than $20.
   c. exactly $20.

3. There are 9 pens in each box. If Carlos orders 6 boxes, how many pens will he get?

   a. 27
   b. 54
   c. 15

4. There are 5 offices in Carlos' company. He needs to order 1 stapler for each office. Which choice shows how to find the total cost of the staplers?

   a. 5 + $4
   b. 5 − $4
   c. 5 × $4

5. Carlos needs to order 8 notebooks. How much will 8 notebooks cost?

   a. $10
   b. $16
   c. $20

6. Carlos also wants to order 5 calendars. How much will it cost for the 5 calendars and the 8 notebooks all together?
   (Hint: Use the answer for question 5 to solve this problem.)

   a. less than $40
   b. more than $40
   c. exactly $40

Multiplying by One-Digit Numbers

When you multiply by a one-digit number, use the multiplication facts. Begin by multiplying the ones digits. Be sure to line up your answers in the correct column.

Use These Steps

Multiply   12
            $\times\,4$

1. Be sure that the digits are lined up.

$$\begin{array}{r} 12 \\ \times\ 4 \\ \hline \end{array}$$

2. Multiply the ones. $4 \times 2 = 8$ ones. Put the 8 in the ones column.

$$\begin{array}{r} 12 \\ \times\ 4 \\ \hline 8 \end{array}$$

8 ones

3. Multiply the tens. $4 \times 1 = 4$ tens. Put the 4 in the tens column.

$$\begin{array}{r} 12 \\ \times\ 4 \\ \hline 48 \end{array}$$

4 tens

Multiply.

1.
$$\begin{array}{r} 23 \\ \times\ 3 \\ \hline 69 \end{array}$$

2.
$$\begin{array}{r} 11 \\ \times\ 2 \\ \hline \end{array}$$

3.
$$\begin{array}{r} 13 \\ \times\ 3 \\ \hline \end{array}$$

4.
$$\begin{array}{r} 24 \\ \times\ 2 \\ \hline \end{array}$$

5.
$$\begin{array}{r} 21 \\ \times\ 3 \\ \hline \end{array}$$

6.
$$\begin{array}{r} 11 \\ \times\ 3 \\ \hline \end{array}$$

7.
$$\begin{array}{r} 32 \\ \times\ 1 \\ \hline \end{array}$$

8.
$$\begin{array}{r} 41 \\ \times\ 2 \\ \hline \end{array}$$

9.
$$\begin{array}{r} 21 \\ \times\ 4 \\ \hline \end{array}$$

10.
$$\begin{array}{r} 42 \\ \times\ 2 \\ \hline \end{array}$$

11.
$$\begin{array}{r} 33 \\ \times\ 2 \\ \hline \end{array}$$

12.
$$\begin{array}{r} 22 \\ \times\ 4 \\ \hline \end{array}$$

13.
$$\begin{array}{r} 153 \\ \times\ 1 \\ \hline \end{array}$$

14.
$$\begin{array}{r} 243 \\ \times\ 2 \\ \hline \end{array}$$

15.
$$\begin{array}{r} 233 \\ \times\ 3 \\ \hline \end{array}$$

16.
$$\begin{array}{r} 432 \\ \times\ 2 \\ \hline \end{array}$$

17.
$$\begin{array}{r} 312 \\ \times\ 3 \\ \hline \end{array}$$

18.
$$\begin{array}{r} 211 \\ \times\ 4 \\ \hline \end{array}$$

19.
$$\begin{array}{r} 123 \\ \times\ 3 \\ \hline \end{array}$$

20.
$$\begin{array}{r} 231 \\ \times\ 2 \\ \hline \end{array}$$

21.
$$\begin{array}{r} 562 \\ \times\ 1 \\ \hline \end{array}$$

22.
$$\begin{array}{r} 403 \\ \times\ 2 \\ \hline \end{array}$$

23.
$$\begin{array}{r} 330 \\ \times\ 3 \\ \hline \end{array}$$

24.
$$\begin{array}{r} 120 \\ \times\ 4 \\ \hline \end{array}$$

25. $36 \times 1 =$
$$\begin{array}{r} 36 \\ \times\ 1 \\ \hline 36 \end{array}$$

26. $23 \times 3 =$

27. $102 \times 4 =$

28. $344 \times 2 =$

Multiplying by One-Digit Numbers

When you multiply, write the answer from right to left, starting with the ones column.

Use These Steps

Multiply   312
          ×   4

1. Be sure that the digits are lined up. Multiply the ones. 4 × 2 = 8 ones. Put the 8 in the ones column.

2. Multiply the tens. 4 × 1 = 4 tens. Put the 4 in the tens column.

3. Multiply the hundreds. 4 × 3 = 12 hundreds. The answer is more than 10. Put the 2 in the hundreds column. Put the 1 in the thousands column.

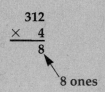
```
   312
 ×   4
     8
```
8 ones

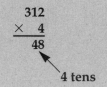
```
   312
 ×   4
    48
```
4 tens

```
   312
 ×   4
 1,248
```
2 hundreds
1 thousand

Multiply.

1.
```
   53
 × 2
  106
```

2.
```
   41
 × 3
```

3.
```
   32
 × 4
```

4.
```
  211
 ×  5
```

5.
```
  412
 ×  4
```

6.
```
  422
 ×  3
```

7.
```
  311
 ×  7
```

8.
```
  522
 ×  4
```

9.
```
 7,112
 ×   3
```

10.
```
 6,113
 ×   2
```

11.   62 × 4 =

12.   83 × 3 =

13.   71 × 7 =

14.   812 × 4 =

15. A display rack holds 52 packages of tulip bulbs. If Ryan fills 3 racks completely, how many packages of bulbs will he need?

16. Alejandro bought 21 sheets of plywood to build a garage. Each sheet cost $5. How much did he spend for plywood?

Answer_____

Answer_____

Multiplying with Zeros

When you multiply zeros, you will have a zero in your answer.
Remember that zero times any number is zero.

Use These Steps

Multiply   903
          × 2

1. Be sure that the digits are lined up. Multiply the ones. 2 × 3 = 6 ones. Put the 6 in the ones column.

2. Multiply the tens. 2 × 0 = 0 tens. Put the 0 in the tens column.

3. Multiply the hundreds. 2 × 9 = 18 hundreds. The answer is more than 10. Put the 8 in the hundreds column. Put the 1 in the thousands column.

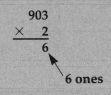

6 ones

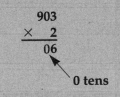

0 tens

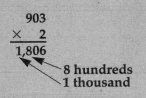

8 hundreds
1 thousand

Multiply.

1.
```
  503
× 3
─────
1,509
```

2.
```
  60
× 4
```

3.
```
  201
× 9
```

4.
```
  40
× 3
```

5.
```
  704
× 2
```

6.
```
  3,002
×    4
```

7.
```
  5,023
×    2
```

8.
```
  7,001
×    8
```

9.
```
  6,020
×    3
```

10.
```
  4,002
×    4
```

11. 2,001 × 7 =

12. 6,013 × 3 =

13. 5,102 × 4 =

14. 6,010 × 8 =

15. Dot's paycheck is $603 every 2 weeks. How much does she make in 4 weeks?

16. To move into her new house, Dot has to pay 3 months' rent in advance. Rent is $302. How much will she have to pay?

Answer_____

Answer_____

Mixed Review

Add, subtract, or multiply.

1.	2.	3.	4.	5.	6.	7.
3 + 9	7 × 6	4 × 8	9 − 6	18 − 9	8 + 9	5 × 6

8.	9.	10.	11.	12.	13.	14.
45 − 4	66 + 3	42 × 2	12 + 7	31 × 3	54 − 4	90 + 9

15. $86 - 6 =$

16. $15 + 4 =$

17. $12 \times 4 =$

18. $63 - 2 =$

19. $20 \times 3 =$

20. $40 \times 2 =$

21. $96 + 3 =$

22. $30 \times 3 =$

23.	24.	25.	26.	27.	28.
210 × 4	433 × 2	534 + 3	1,986 − 6	2,102 × 3	6,407 + 2

29.	30.	31.	32.	33.	34.
30 × 5	51 × 7	93 + 7	3,105 − 6	2,001 × 9	1,400 + 8

35. $53 \times 3 =$

36. $82 + 9 =$

37. $177 - 8 =$

38. $400 \times 7 =$

39. $6,200 \times 4 =$

40. $9,860 + 50 =$

41. $8,700 - 125 =$

42. $7,000 \times 9 =$

Problem Solving: Using a Circle Graph

When you are using information from a graph, decide which facts you need to solve the problem.

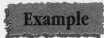 A circle graph gives you information in pie-shaped pieces. The sections of this circle graph show the items collected by the Oak Ridge Recycling Center each week.

Use the information from the graph to find how many pounds of glass the center collects every 2 weeks.

▶ **Step 1.** Decide which facts you need from the graph.

600 pounds of glass each week

▶ **Step 2.** Decide what you need to do to solve the problem.

Since the problem asks you to find the number of pounds collected every 2 weeks, multiply 600 pounds of glass by 2.

▶ **Step 3.** Set up the problem and solve.

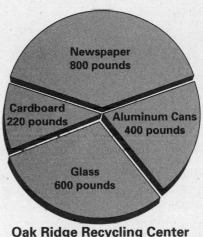

**Oak Ridge Recycling Center
Weekly Collection**

$$\begin{array}{r} 600 \\ \times\ \ \ 2 \\ \hline 1{,}200 \end{array}$$

The recycling center collects 1,200 pounds of glass every 2 weeks.

Use the information from the graph to answer the questions.

1. How many pounds of cardboard does the recycling center collect every week?

2. How many pounds of newspaper does the recycling center collect every week?

Answer _____

Answer _____

Use the information from the graph on page 93 to answer each question.

3. How many pounds of aluminum cans does the center collect every week?

    Answer_____

4. How many pounds of aluminum cans does the center collect every 2 weeks?

    Answer_____

5. How many pounds of aluminum cans does the center collect every month? (Hint: Use 4 weeks for 1 month.)

    Answer_____

6. How many pounds of newspaper does the center collect every 3 weeks?

    Answer_____

7. How many pounds of newspaper does the center collect every 2 months? (Hint: Use 8 weeks for 2 months.)

    Answer_____

8. How many pounds of cardboard does the center collect every month?

    Answer_____

9. How many pounds of aluminum cans and newspaper does the center collect every week?

    Answer_____

10. How many pounds of aluminum cans and newspaper does the center collect every month?

    Answer_____

11. How many pounds of cardboard and newspaper does the center collect every week?

    Answer_____

12. How many pounds of cardboard and newspaper does the center collect every month?

    Answer_____

Multiplying by Two-Digit Numbers

When you multiply by a two-digit number, multiply each digit in the top number by each digit in the bottom number. You will get two partial products. Add the partial products to get the answer.

Use These Steps

Multiply 31
         $\times$ 42

1. Be sure that the digits are lined up. Multiply by 2 ones. $2 \times 1 = 2$ ones. Put the 2 in the ones column. $2 \times 3 = 6$ tens. Put the 6 in the tens column.

$$\begin{array}{r} 31 \\ \times 42 \\ \hline 62 \end{array}$$ ← partial product

2. Multiply by 4 tens. $4 \times 1 = 4$ tens. Put the 4 in the tens column under the 6. $4 \times 3 = 12$ hundreds. Put the 12 to the left of the 4 tens.

$$\begin{array}{r} 31 \\ \times 42 \\ \hline 62 \\ 124 \end{array}$$ ← partial product

3. Add the partial products to get the answer.

$$\begin{array}{r} 31 \\ \times 42 \\ \hline 62 \\ +124 \\ \hline 1,302 \end{array}$$

Multiply.

1.
$$\begin{array}{r} 31 \\ \times 22 \\ \hline 62 \\ +62 \\ \hline 682 \end{array}$$

2.
$$\begin{array}{r} 12 \\ \times 34 \\ \hline \end{array}$$

3.
$$\begin{array}{r} 23 \\ \times 13 \\ \hline \end{array}$$

4.
$$\begin{array}{r} 11 \\ \times 56 \\ \hline \end{array}$$

5.
$$\begin{array}{r} 42 \\ \times 12 \\ \hline \end{array}$$

6.
$$\begin{array}{r} 23 \\ \times 21 \\ \hline \end{array}$$

7.
$$\begin{array}{r} 14 \\ \times 12 \\ \hline \end{array}$$

8.
$$\begin{array}{r} 42 \\ \times 22 \\ \hline \end{array}$$

9.
$$\begin{array}{r} 10 \\ \times 89 \\ \hline \end{array}$$

10.
$$\begin{array}{r} 12 \\ \times 43 \\ \hline \end{array}$$

11.
$$\begin{array}{r} 30 \\ \times 33 \\ \hline \end{array}$$

12.
$$\begin{array}{r} 40 \\ \times 21 \\ \hline \end{array}$$

13.
$$\begin{array}{r} 10 \\ \times 75 \\ \hline \end{array}$$

14.
$$\begin{array}{r} 20 \\ \times 44 \\ \hline \end{array}$$

15.
$$\begin{array}{r} 60 \\ \times 11 \\ \hline \end{array}$$

Multiplying by Two-Digit Numbers

When you multiply larger numbers by a two-digit number, you still get two partial products. Add the partial products to get the answer.

Use These Steps

Multiply 520×23

1. Line up the digits.

```
  520
×  23
```

2. Multiply by 3 ones.
   Multiply by 2 tens.

```
   520
×   23
 1 560
10 40
```

3. Add the partial products.

```
    520
×    23
  1 560
+ 10 40
 11,960
```

Multiply.

1.
```
    52
×  21
    52
+ 1 04
 1,092
```

2.
```
   73
× 13
```

3.
```
   40
× 35
```

4.
```
  211
× 15
```

5.
```
  800
× 27
```

6. $602 \times 43 =$

7. $320 \times 34 =$

8. $900 \times 56 =$

9. $602 \times 33 =$

10.
```
  5,021
×    34
```

11.
```
  6,234
×    22
```

12.
```
 43,001
×    31
```

13.
```
 80,421
×    12
```

14. $3,012 \times 44 =$

15. $70,022 \times 32 =$

16. $51,000 \times 97 =$

17. $90,301 \times 22 =$

Multiplying by Three-Digit Numbers

When you multiply by a three-digit number, multiply each digit in the top number by each digit in the bottom number. You will get three partial products. Add all three partial products to get the answer.

Use These Steps

Multiply
```
   120
 × 321
```

1. Be sure that the digits are lined up.

```
   120
 × 321
```

2. Multiply by 1 one.
   $1 \times 120 = 120$.
   Multiply by 2 tens.
   $2 \times 120 = 240$.
   Multiply by 3 hundreds.
   $3 \times 120 = 360$.

```
   120
 × 321
   120
  2 40
 36 0
```

3. Add the partial products to get the answer.

```
    120
  × 321
    120
   2 40
 + 36 0
  38,520
```

Multiply.

1.
```
     312
  × 312
     624
    3 12
 + 93 6
  97,344
```

2.
```
   430
 × 112
```

3.
```
   202
 × 133
```

4.
```
   301
 × 221
```

5.
```
   401
 × 212
```

6.
```
   240
 × 121
```

7.
```
   331
 × 213
```

8.
```
   100
 × 434
```

9.
```
   602
 × 111
```

10.
```
   400
 × 211
```

11.
```
   302
 × 323
```

12.
```
   200
 × 413
```

Multiplying by Three-Digit Numbers

When you multiply each digit in the top number by each digit in the bottom number, be sure to write the partial products in the correct columns.

Use These Steps

Multiply 321 × 124

1. Line up the digits.

```
  321
× 124
```

2. Multiply by 4 ones.
   Multiply by 2 tens.
   Multiply by 1 hundred.

```
  321
× 124
 1 284
 6 42
32 1
```

3. Add the partial products.

```
   321
 × 124
  1 284
  6 42
 + 32 1
 39,804
```

Multiply.

1.
```
    530
  × 231
    530
  15 90
+ 106 0
122,430
```

2.
```
   600
 × 325
```

3.
```
  4,122
×   124
```

4.
```
 91,000
×    753
```

5. 201 × 564 =

6. 4,100 × 628 =

7. 31,011 × 739 =

8. 80,110 × 692 =

9. Alicia owns a typing service. Alicia's employees typed 112 pages each day for 111 days. How many total pages did they type?

10. If Alicia charges $2 per page, how much did her company earn for typing the 112 pages?

Answer_____

Answer_____

Application

When you are taking inventory, using multiplication can make your job easier. For example, most grocery store items come to the warehouse in cases. When you take inventory, you count the number of cases. Then you multiply by the number of items in the case to get a total.

Example | Albert is the Freshway Grocery warehouse supervisor. He is taking inventory of paper goods. He counted 2,031 cases of paper towels. There are 12 rolls of towels to a case. How many rolls of paper towels are there in the warehouse?

Set up the problem. Then multiply.

$$
\begin{array}{r}
2,031 \\
\times \quad 12 \\
\hline
4\,062 \\
+ \ 20\,31 \\
\hline
24,372
\end{array}
$$

There are 24,372 rolls of paper towels in the Freshway warehouse.

Solve.

1. Albert counted cases of tissues. There are 25 boxes of tissues in a case. He counted 3,001 cases. How many boxes of tissues are there in the warehouse?

2. Albert counted 4,010 cases of paper plates. There are 45 packages of paper plates to the case. How many packages of paper plates are there in the warehouse?

Answer_____

Answer_____

3. In the store, Pete counted rolls of paper towels. He counted 10 shelves of paper towels. There were 36 rolls on each shelf. How many rolls of paper towels are there?

4. Pete counted 402 boxes of tissues on each of 3 shelves in the store. How many boxes of tissues are there in the store?

Answer_____

Answer_____

Mixed Review

Add, subtract, or multiply.

1. $6 \times 70 =$

2. $5 + 8 =$

3. $12 \times 4 =$

4. $10 - 9 =$

5. $20 \times 33 =$

6. $56 - 15 =$

7. $382 + 7 =$

8. $122 \times 4 =$

9. $321 \times 4 =$

10. $923 \times 23 =$

11. $457 + 9 =$

12. $660 - 50 =$

13. $509 + 625 =$

14. $3,120 \times 41 =$

15. $9,002 + 998 =$

16. $7,051 - 151 =$

17. $801 \times 49 =$

18. $900 \times 32 =$

19. $6,000 + 7,000 =$

20. $1,000 - 500 =$

21. $5,102 \times 4 =$

22. $297 + 3 =$

23. $7,802 - 802 =$

24. $4,000 \times 17 =$

25. $1,022 \times 301 =$

26. $603 + 977 =$

27. $490 - 376 =$

28. $3,011 \times 509 =$

Multiplying by 10, 100, and 1,000

When you multiply by 10, 100, or 1,000, you don't have to write a row of partial products with zeros. There is an easier way to work these problems.

Use These Steps

Multiply 3,471
$\times$ 10

1. Multiply by 0 ones. Write the zero in the ones column.

2. Multiply by 1. Write the answer to the left of the zero. The answer is the same as the top number plus one zero.

$$\begin{array}{r} 3,471 \\ \times \quad 10 \\ \hline 0 \end{array}$$

$$\begin{array}{r} 3,471 \\ \times \quad 10 \\ \hline 34,710 \end{array}$$

Multiply.

1.
$$\begin{array}{r} 96 \\ \times 10 \\ \hline 960 \end{array}$$

2.
$$\begin{array}{r} 520 \\ \times \ 10 \\ \hline \end{array}$$

3.
$$\begin{array}{r} 1,085 \\ \times \quad 10 \\ \hline \end{array}$$

4.
$$\begin{array}{r} 7,831 \\ \times \quad 10 \\ \hline \end{array}$$

5.
$$\begin{array}{r} 76,300 \\ \times \quad 10 \\ \hline \end{array}$$

6.
$$\begin{array}{r} 461 \\ \times 100 \\ \hline 46,100 \end{array}$$

7.
$$\begin{array}{r} 982 \\ \times 100 \\ \hline \end{array}$$

8.
$$\begin{array}{r} 3,305 \\ \times \quad 100 \\ \hline \end{array}$$

9.
$$\begin{array}{r} 46,720 \\ \times \quad 100 \\ \hline \end{array}$$

10.
$$\begin{array}{r} 39,900 \\ \times \quad 100 \\ \hline \end{array}$$

11.
$$\begin{array}{r} 3,382 \\ \times 1,000 \\ \hline 3,382,000 \end{array}$$

12.
$$\begin{array}{r} 1,590 \\ \times 1,000 \\ \hline \end{array}$$

13.
$$\begin{array}{r} 2,706 \\ \times 1,000 \\ \hline \end{array}$$

14.
$$\begin{array}{r} 25,400 \\ \times 1,000 \\ \hline \end{array}$$

15.
$$\begin{array}{r} 17,000 \\ \times 1,000 \\ \hline \end{array}$$

16. $546 \times 10 =$

17. $2,389 \times 10 =$

18. $477 \times 100 =$

19. $12,903 \times 100 =$

20. $29 \times 100 =$

21. $36 \times 1,000$

22. $1,109 \times 1,000 =$

23. $20,000 \times 1,000 =$

Multiplying by 10, 100, and 1,000

When you multiply by 10, 100, or 1,000, you can figure out the answers without working them out on paper. Remember to use a comma.

Use These Steps

Multiply 297×100

1. Write the number you started with, 297.

   297

2. Count the number of zeros in 100. There are 2. Put 2 zeros after 297.

   $297 \times 100 = 29{,}700$

Multiply.

1. $27 \times 10 = \mathbf{270}$

2. $195 \times 10 =$

3. $3{,}402 \times 10 =$

4. $31 \times 100 = \mathbf{3{,}100}$

5. $286 \times 100 =$

6. $15{,}029 \times 100 =$

7. $490 \times 1{,}000 = \mathbf{490{,}000}$

8. $1{,}830 \times 1{,}000 =$

9. $27{,}600 \times 1{,}000 =$

10. $2{,}101 \times 1{,}000 =$

11. $133 \times 100 =$

12. $6{,}997 \times 10 =$

13. $41 \times 10 =$

14. $201 \times 100 =$

15. $33{,}032 \times 1{,}000 =$

16. $20 \times 100 =$

17. $3{,}100 \times 100 =$

18. $21{,}000 \times 1{,}000 =$

19. $89 \times 10 =$

20. $420 \times 10 =$

21. $5{,}100 \times 10 =$

22. $36 \times 1{,}000 =$

23. $500 \times 1{,}000 =$

24. $99 \times 100 =$

Problem Solving: Using Pictographs

A *pictograph* shows information by using symbols or pictures. Each picture stands for a certain number. That number is found in the *key*.

This pictograph shows some of the leading potato–growing countries in the world. The pictures stand for the number of bags of potatoes produced in one year.

Example How many million bags of potatoes does the United States produce in one year?

▶ **Step 1.** Count each ⬤. There are two.

▶ **Step 2.** One ⬤ equals 200 million bags of potatoes. To find the number of bags for two ⬤, multiply 200 million by 2.

200 million × 2 = 400 million

Leading Potato–Growing Countries

Poland	⬤ ⬤ ⬤ ⬤
Germany	⬤ ⬤ ⬤
United States	⬤ ⬤
France	⬤

Key: One ⬤ equals 200 million bags of potatoes.

The United States produces 400 million bags of potatoes in one year.

Solve.

1. How many million bags of potatoes does Germany produce in one year?

2. How many million bags of potatoes does Poland produce in one year?

Answer_____

Answer_____

3. How many million bags of potatoes does France produce in one year?

4. How many million bags of potatoes does the United States produce in two years?
(Hint: Multiply the number of bags by 2.)

Answer_____

Answer_____

This pictograph shows the leading rice—growing countries in the world.
The pictures stand for the number of tons of rice grown in one year.

Leading Rice–Growing Countries

China	🌾 🌾 🌾 🌾 🌾 🌾 🌾 🌾 🌾 🌾
India	🌾 🌾 🌾 🌾 🌾 🌾
Indonesia	🌾 🌾 🌾
Bangladesh	🌾 🌾
Thailand	🌾

Key: One 🌾 equals 20 million tons of rice.

Solve.

1. How many million tons of rice does India grow in one year?

Answer_____

2. How many million tons of rice does Bangladesh grow in one year?

Answer_____

3. How many million tons of rice does Indonesia grow in one year?

Answer_____

4. There are 2,000 pounds in one ton. How many million pounds of rice does Thailand grow in one year? (Hint: Multiply the number of tons by 2,000.)

Answer_____

5. How many million tons of rice does Indonesia grow in two years?

Answer_____

6. How many million tons of rice does India grow in five years?

Answer_____

Multiplying by One-Digit Numbers with Renaming

When you multiply two digits, the product is sometimes 10 or more. As in addition, when an answer is 10 or more, rename by carrying to the next column.

Use These Steps

Multiply
```
  35
×  5
```

1. Be sure the digits are lined up.

2. Multiply the 5 by 5 ones. 5 × 5 = 25 ones. Rename 25 as 2 tens and 5 ones. Put the 5 in the ones column. Carry 2 tens to the top of the next column.

3. Multiply the 3 by 5 ones. 5 × 3 = 15 tens. Then add the carried 2 tens. 15 + 2 = 17 tens. Write 17.

```
   35          2           2
 ×  5         35          35
             ×  5        ×  5
                5         175
```

Multiply.

1.
```
   2
  47
×  3
 141
```

2.
```
  32
×  8
```

3.
```
  93
×  7
```

4.
```
  45
×  4
```

5.
```
  78
×  9
```

6.
```
  54
×  6
```

7.
```
  62
×  5
```

8.
```
  94
×  3
```

9.
```
  57
×  7
```

10.
```
  82
×  9
```

11.
```
  250
×   4
```

12.
```
  175
×   6
```

13.
```
  340
×   5
```

14.
```
  625
×   4
```

15.
```
  875
×   9
```

16.
```
  916
×   7
```

17.
```
  432
×   8
```

18.
```
  520
×   5
```

19.
```
  899
×   3
```

20.
```
  770
×   2
```

Multiplying by One-Digit Numbers with Renaming

When the product of two digits is 10 or more, rename by carrying to the next column. Multiply first, and then add carried numbers. You may need to rename several times.

Use These Steps

Multiply 4,769 × 3

1. Line up the digits.

$$\begin{array}{r} 4,769 \\ \times \quad 3 \\ \hline \end{array}$$

2. Multiply by 3 ones.

$$\begin{array}{r} {}^{2} \\ 4,769 \\ \times \quad 3 \\ \hline 7 \end{array} \qquad \begin{array}{r} {}^{22} \\ 4,769 \\ \times \quad 3 \\ \hline 07 \end{array} \qquad \begin{array}{r} {}^{222} \\ 4,769 \\ \times \quad 3 \\ \hline 307 \end{array} \qquad \begin{array}{r} {}^{222} \\ 4,769 \\ \times \quad 3 \\ \hline 14,307 \end{array}$$

Multiply.

1.
$$\begin{array}{r} {}^{3\ 15} \\ 5,416 \\ \times \quad 9 \\ \hline 48,744 \end{array}$$

2.
$$\begin{array}{r} 7,328 \\ \times \quad 6 \\ \hline \end{array}$$

3.
$$\begin{array}{r} 4,465 \\ \times \quad 4 \\ \hline \end{array}$$

4.
$$\begin{array}{r} 9,270 \\ \times \quad 3 \\ \hline \end{array}$$

5.
$$\begin{array}{r} 26,347 \\ \times \quad 2 \\ \hline \end{array}$$

6.
$$\begin{array}{r} 52,180 \\ \times \quad 5 \\ \hline \end{array}$$

7.
$$\begin{array}{r} 39,400 \\ \times \quad 7 \\ \hline \end{array}$$

8.
$$\begin{array}{r} 92,000 \\ \times \quad 9 \\ \hline \end{array}$$

9. $3,362 \times 4 =$

10. $11,900 \times 8 =$

11. $76,543 \times 2 =$

12. $6,989 \times 6 =$

13. Kay makes $24,500 each year as an office manager. She has worked for 3 years at this salary. How much money has she earned all together in the last 3 years?

14. Kay got a raise of $1,200 this year. How much will she earn after 2 years at her new salary?
(Hint: You need to add before you multiply.)

Answer＿＿＿＿＿＿＿＿＿＿＿

Answer＿＿＿＿＿＿＿＿＿＿＿

Multiplying with Zeros

When you multiply, there will sometimes be a zero in the top number. Remember that zero times any number is always zero. Don't forget to add carried numbers.

Use These Steps

Multiply   403
         × 7

1. Multiply the 3 by 7 ones. 3 × 7 = 21. Carry 2 tens.

$$\begin{array}{r} 2 \\ 403 \\ \times\ \ 7 \\ \hline 1 \end{array}$$

2. Multiply the 0 by 7 ones. 0 × 7 = 0. Add the carried 2.

$$\begin{array}{r} 2 \\ 403 \\ \times\ \ 7 \\ \hline 21 \end{array}$$

3. Multiply the 4 by 7 ones. 4 × 7 = 28. Write 28.

$$\begin{array}{r} 2 \\ 403 \\ \times\ \ 7 \\ \hline 2,821 \end{array}$$

Multiply.

1.
$$\begin{array}{r} 5 \\ 509 \\ \times\ \ 6 \\ \hline 3,054 \end{array}$$

2.
$$\begin{array}{r} 307 \\ \times\ \ 5 \\ \hline \end{array}$$

3.
$$\begin{array}{r} 906 \\ \times\ \ 8 \\ \hline \end{array}$$

4.
$$\begin{array}{r} 205 \\ \times\ \ 7 \\ \hline \end{array}$$

5.
$$\begin{array}{r} 404 \\ \times\ \ 4 \\ \hline \end{array}$$

6.
$$\begin{array}{r} 702 \\ \times\ \ 9 \\ \hline \end{array}$$

7.
$$\begin{array}{r} 907 \\ \times\ \ 3 \\ \hline \end{array}$$

8.
$$\begin{array}{r} 609 \\ \times\ \ 5 \\ \hline \end{array}$$

9.
$$\begin{array}{r} 506 \\ \times\ \ 6 \\ \hline \end{array}$$

10.
$$\begin{array}{r} 302 \\ \times\ \ 8 \\ \hline \end{array}$$

11. $703 \times 4 =$

12. $208 \times 9 =$

13. $805 \times 8 =$

14. $605 \times 5 =$

15. $808 \times 8 =$

16. $903 \times 6 =$

17. $707 \times 7 =$

18. $309 \times 9 =$

19. $504 \times 2 =$

20. $601 \times 3 =$

21. $809 \times 4 =$

22. $109 \times 8 =$

Multiplying with Zeros

Multiply first, and then add carried numbers.

Multiply.

1.
$$
\begin{array}{r}
{}^{4}\ \ {}^{4} \\
4,707 \\
\times\quad 6 \\
\hline
28,242 \\
\end{array}
$$

2.
$$
\begin{array}{r}
9,073 \\
\times\quad 3 \\
\hline
\end{array}
$$

3.
$$
\begin{array}{r}
8,089 \\
\times\quad 5 \\
\hline
\end{array}
$$

4.
$$
\begin{array}{r}
3,605 \\
\times\quad 7 \\
\hline
\end{array}
$$

5.
$$
\begin{array}{r}
10,702 \\
\times\quad 8 \\
\hline
\end{array}
$$

6.
$$
\begin{array}{r}
66,095 \\
\times\quad 4 \\
\hline
\end{array}
$$

7.
$$
\begin{array}{r}
80,096 \\
\times\quad 2 \\
\hline
\end{array}
$$

8.
$$
\begin{array}{r}
90,909 \\
\times\quad 9 \\
\hline
\end{array}
$$

9. $42,008 \times 5 =$

10. $30,506 \times 7 =$

11. $20,005 \times 9 =$

12. Juanita collects the rent for the Sunnyvale Apartments. There are 6 apartments on each floor. She collects $405 per month for each apartment. How much rent does she collect from each floor every month?

13. If there are 10 floors in the building, how much rent in all does Juanita collect each month?

Answer_____

Answer_____

Mixed Review

Add, subtract, or multiply.

1.	2.	3.	4.	5.	6.
7	17	85	131	260	582
× 6	+ 3	− 13	× 3	− 1	+ 8

7.	8.	9.	10.	11.
603	478	930	9,016	70,005
× 2	− 6	+ 6	× 4	× 9

12.	13.	14.	15.	16.	17.
25	62	59	88	93	46
× 4	× 8	+ 6	+ 2	− 7	− 9

18.	19.	20.	21.	22.	23.
31	53	63	56	21	91
× 24	+ 87	− 19	× 11	× 59	− 89

24.	25.	26.	27.	28.
412	521	752	3,220	5,867
+ 98	× 16	− 59	× 27	− 77

29.	30.	31.	32.	33.
782	812	660	4,123	1,575
− 394	× 422	− 570	× 313	+ 225

34.	35.	36.	37.	38.
220	1,012	1,400	5,032	7,301
× 10	× 302	− 296	× 100	× 203

Multiplying by Two-Digit Numbers with Renaming

When you multiply by a two-digit number, first multiply by the ones digit. Then multiply by the tens digit. When a product is 10 or more, rename by carrying to the next column.

Use These Steps

Multiply
$$\begin{array}{r} 35 \\ \times\, 29 \end{array}$$

1. Be sure that the digits are lined up. Multiply by 9 ones. $9 \times 5 = 45$ ones. Carry the 4. $9 \times 3 = 27$ tens. Add the carried 4.

$$\begin{array}{r} 4 \\ 35 \\ \times\, 29 \\ \hline 315 \end{array}$$

2. Multiply by 2 tens. $2 \times 5 = 10$ tens. Carry the 1. $2 \times 3 = 6$ hundreds. Add the carried 1.

$$\begin{array}{r} 1 \\ 35 \\ \times\, 29 \\ \hline 315 \\ 70 \end{array}$$

3. Add the partial products.

$$\begin{array}{r} 35 \\ \times\, 29 \\ \hline 315 \\ +\, 70 \\ \hline 1{,}015 \end{array}$$

Multiply.

1.
$$\begin{array}{r} 46 \\ \times\, 35 \\ \hline 230 \\ +\, 1\,38 \\ \hline 1{,}610 \end{array}$$

2.
$$\begin{array}{r} 59 \\ \times\, 24 \end{array}$$

3.
$$\begin{array}{r} 75 \\ \times\, 53 \end{array}$$

4.
$$\begin{array}{r} 62 \\ \times\, 49 \end{array}$$

5.
$$\begin{array}{r} 86 \\ \times\, 75 \end{array}$$

6.
$$\begin{array}{r} 234 \\ \times\, 57 \end{array}$$

7.
$$\begin{array}{r} 603 \\ \times\, 78 \end{array}$$

8.
$$\begin{array}{r} 574 \\ \times\, 39 \end{array}$$

9.
$$\begin{array}{r} 409 \\ \times\, 68 \end{array}$$

10.
$$\begin{array}{r} 775 \\ \times\, 23 \end{array}$$

11.
$$\begin{array}{r} 802 \\ \times\, 99 \end{array}$$

12.
$$\begin{array}{r} 625 \\ \times\, 44 \end{array}$$

13.
$$\begin{array}{r} 306 \\ \times\, 67 \end{array}$$

14.
$$\begin{array}{r} 504 \\ \times\, 29 \end{array}$$

15.
$$\begin{array}{r} 207 \\ \times\, 33 \end{array}$$

Multiplying by Two-Digit Numbers with Renaming

When the product of two digits is 10 or more, rename by carrying to the next column. You may need to carry several times.

Use These Steps

Multiply   2,030 × 45

1. Line up the digits.

$$\begin{array}{r} 2,030 \\ \times \quad 45 \\ \hline \end{array}$$

2. Multiply by 5 ones.
   Multiply by 4 tens.

$$\begin{array}{r} 2,030 \\ \times \quad 45 \\ \hline 10\ 150 \\ 81\ 20 \end{array}$$

3. Add the partial products.

$$\begin{array}{r} 2,030 \\ \times \quad 45 \\ \hline 10\ 150 \\ +\ 81\ 20 \\ \hline 91,350 \end{array}$$

Multiply.

1.

$5,316 \times 25 =$

$$\begin{array}{r} 5,316 \\ \times \quad 25 \\ \hline 26\ 580 \\ +\ 106\ 32 \\ \hline 132,900 \end{array}$$

2.

$4,069 \times 18 =$

3.

$9,208 \times 45 =$

4.

$15,037 \times 72 =$

5.

$24,005 \times 37 =$

6.

$80,067 \times 93 =$

7. At the equator, the distance around Earth is about 24,902 miles. If a train could travel this distance 45 times, how many miles would it cover?

8. The distance from Earth to the moon and back is 477,720 miles. If the space shuttle goes to the moon and back 5 times, how many miles does it travel?

Answer_____

Answer_____

Multiplying by Three-Digit Numbers with Renaming

When you multiply by a three-digit number, you get three partial products. You may need to rename by carrying several times. Be sure to add the carried numbers.

Use These Steps

Multiply 516
      × 312

1. Be sure that the digits are lined up.

```
  516
× 312
```

2. Multiply by 2 ones.
Multiply by 1 ten.
Multiply by 3 hundreds.

```
  516
× 312
 1 032
 5 16
154 8
```

3. Add the partial products.

```
    516
  × 312
   1 032
   5 16
+ 154 8
 160,992
```

Multiply.

1.
```
    270
  × 483
    810
  21 60
+ 108 0
130,410
```

2.
```
  486
× 132
```

3.
```
  895
× 546
```

4.
```
  922
× 317
```

5.
```
  771
× 439
```

6.
```
 1,397
×  262
```

7.
```
 5,926
×  453
```

8.
```
 13,311
×   899
```

9.
```
 25,658
×   581
```

10.
```
 93,427
×   316
```

11. 450 × 185 =

12. 918 × 576 =

13. 2,820 × 193 =

14. 17,462 × 761 =

Multiplying by Three-Digit Numbers with Renaming

When the product of two digits is 10 or more, rename by carrying to the next column. You may need to rename several times. Remember to add the carried numbers when multiplying zeros.

Use These Steps

Multiply   409
          × 365

1. Be sure that the digits are lined up.

```
    409
  × 365
```

2. Multiply by 5 ones.
Multiply by 6 tens.
Multiply by 3 hundreds.

```
    409
  × 365
  2 045
  24 54
 122 7
```

3. Add the partial products.

```
    409
  × 365
  2 045
  24 54
+ 122 7
 149,285
```

Multiply.

1.
```
    506
  × 432
  1 012
  15 18
+ 202 4
 218,592
```

2.
```
    208
  × 593
```

3.
```
    709
  × 946
```

4.
```
    405
  × 127
```

5.
```
    302
  × 279
```

6.
```
  1,082
  × 743
```

7.
```
  5,070
  × 629
```

8.
```
  8,603
  × 558
```

9.
```
  2,009
  × 417
```

10.
```
  7,730
  × 256
```

11.
```
  10,340
  × 145
```

12.
```
  25,007
  × 622
```

13.
```
  50,603
  × 254
```

14.
```
  70,005
  × 437
```

15.
```
  62,400
  × 618
```

Multiplying with Zeros

When there are one or more zeros in the bottom number, you can use this shortcut. Put a zero in the partial product. Put the next partial product to the left of the zero.

Use These Steps

Multiply 423 × 207

1. Line up the digits.

```
  423
× 207
```

2. Multiply by 7 ones. Multiply by 0 tens, and put a zero in the tens column. Multiply by 2 hundreds, and put this partial product to the left of the zero.

```
         423
       × 207
        2 961
partial product → 84 60 ← partial product
```

3. Add the partial products.

```
  423
× 207
 2 961
+84 60
87,561
```

Multiply.

1.
```
   569
 × 309
 5 121
+170 70
175,821
```

2.
```
   640
 × 605
```

3.
```
   872
 × 504
```

4.
```
   330
 × 708
```

5.
```
   400
 × 307
```

6.
```
    3,040
 ×    900
2,736,000
```

7.
```
   7,300
 ×   400
```

8.
```
   5,688
 ×   300
```

9.
```
   1,402
 ×   700
```

10.
```
   9,000
 ×   600
```

11. 13,025 × 500 =

12. 50,236 × 906 =

13. 72,000 × 403 =

14. 10,006 × 502 =

Multiplying with Zeros

When the number you are multiplying by has a zero, be sure to include zero in the partial product.

Use These Steps

Multiply 19,361
$\times$ 409

1. Multiply by 9 ones.

2. Multiply by 0 tens. Put a zero in the partial product in the tens column. Multiply by 4 hundreds. Put the partial product to the left of the zero.

3. Add the partial products.

```
      19,361
  ×      409
     174 249
```

```
      19,361
  ×      409
     174 249
partial product → 7 744 40 ← partial product
```

```
      19,361
  ×      409
     174 249
 +  7 744 40
   7,918,649
```

Multiply.

1.
```
       629
    × 302
     1 258
 + 188 70
  189,958
```

2.
```
       583
    × 500
```

3.
```
       641
    × 106
```

4.
```
       870
    × 401
```

5.
```
     1,409
    ×  200
```

6.
```
     5,664
    ×  704
```

7.
```
     8,306
    ×  800
```

8.
```
     9,200
    ×  907
```

9.
```
    43,099
    ×  102
```

10.
```
    54,320
    ×  300
```

11.
```
    89,003
    ×  705
```

12.
```
    17,000
    ×  400
```

Problem Solving: Using Rounding and Estimating

Multiplying rounded numbers is one way to estimate monthly and yearly income and expenses.

365 days	= 1 year
52 weeks	= 1 year
12 months	= 1 year
30 days	= 1 month
4 weeks	= 1 month

Example Mike makes $291 each week. About how much does he make in 1 year?

▶ **Step 1.** In the table, find how many weeks are in 1 year.

52 weeks = 1 year

▶ **Step 2.** Round Mike's weekly salary and the number of weeks in a year to the lead digit.

$291 rounds up to $300
52 rounds down to 50

▶ **Step 3.** Multiply the rounded numbers.

$$\begin{array}{r} \$300 \\ \times\ \ 50 \\ \hline \$15,000 \end{array}$$

Mike makes about $15,000 in 1 year.

Solve by rounding to the lead digit and then multiplying.

1. Estella makes $385 each week. About how much does she make in 1 year?

2. Lisa spends $415 per month on rent. About how much does she spend on rent in 1 year?

Answer＿＿＿＿＿＿＿＿＿＿＿

Answer＿＿＿＿＿＿＿＿＿＿＿

3. Eric's car payment is $107 each month. About how much does he spend on car payments in 1 year?

4. Harris spends $68 per month for bus fare. About how much does he spend in 1 year?

Answer＿＿＿＿＿＿＿＿＿＿＿

Answer＿＿＿＿＿＿＿＿＿＿＿

Solve.

5. Irving's car insurance costs $47 per month. About how much does he spend on car insurance in 1 year?

Answer_____

6. Mickey's students pay $12 each week for cooking lessons at the adult ed center. About how much does he earn per student for the lessons in 1 year?

Answer_____

7. Ed spends about $11 for gas each week. About how much does he spend on gas in 1 month?

Answer_____

8. Loni earns about $50 each week selling cosmetics door-to-door. About how much does she earn selling cosmetics in 1 year?

Answer_____

9. Art goes to a community college at night. He pays $110 each month for tuition and books. About how much does he pay for tuition and books in 1 year?

Answer_____

10. Sonia is saving $20 a week to upgrade the computer in her home office. The upgrade will cost $600. If she saves for 6 months, will she have enough money?
(Hint: Use 24 weeks for 6 months.)

Answer_____

Unit 4 *Review*

Multiply.

1.
$$\begin{array}{r} 9 \\ \times 9 \\ \hline \end{array}$$

2.
$$\begin{array}{r} 5 \\ \times 7 \\ \hline \end{array}$$

3.
$$\begin{array}{r} 9 \\ \times 8 \\ \hline \end{array}$$

4.
$$\begin{array}{r} 6 \\ \times 4 \\ \hline \end{array}$$

5.
$$\begin{array}{r} 8 \\ \times 3 \\ \hline \end{array}$$

6.
$$\begin{array}{r} 3 \\ \times 7 \\ \hline \end{array}$$

7.
$$\begin{array}{r} 5 \\ \times 8 \\ \hline \end{array}$$

8.
$$\begin{array}{r} 9 \\ \times 0 \\ \hline \end{array}$$

9.
$$\begin{array}{r} 23 \\ \times 2 \\ \hline \end{array}$$

10.
$$\begin{array}{r} 40 \\ \times 2 \\ \hline \end{array}$$

11.
$$\begin{array}{r} 82 \\ \times 4 \\ \hline \end{array}$$

12.
$$\begin{array}{r} 12 \\ \times 4 \\ \hline \end{array}$$

13. $63 \times 3 =$

14. $221 \times 3 =$

15. $411 \times 7 =$

16. $71 \times 6 =$

17.
$$\begin{array}{r} 30 \\ \times 6 \\ \hline \end{array}$$

18.
$$\begin{array}{r} 703 \\ \times 3 \\ \hline \end{array}$$

19.
$$\begin{array}{r} 402 \\ \times 5 \\ \hline \end{array}$$

20.
$$\begin{array}{r} 7,001 \\ \times 9 \\ \hline \end{array}$$

21.
$$\begin{array}{r} 6,200 \\ \times 4 \\ \hline \end{array}$$

22.
$$\begin{array}{r} 3,014 \\ \times 2 \\ \hline \end{array}$$

23.
$$\begin{array}{r} 42 \\ \times 12 \\ \hline \end{array}$$

24.
$$\begin{array}{r} 20 \\ \times 34 \\ \hline \end{array}$$

25.
$$\begin{array}{r} 241 \\ \times 21 \\ \hline \end{array}$$

26.
$$\begin{array}{r} 302 \\ \times 14 \\ \hline \end{array}$$

27.
$$\begin{array}{r} 500 \\ \times 39 \\ \hline \end{array}$$

28.
$$\begin{array}{r} 9,021 \\ \times 43 \\ \hline \end{array}$$

29. $8,312 \times 33 =$

30. $1,010 \times 96 =$

31. $23,312 \times 32 =$

32. $80,001 \times 56 =$

Multiply.

33.
$$\begin{array}{r} 340 \\ \times\ 122 \\ \hline \end{array}$$

34.
$$\begin{array}{r} 100 \\ \times\ 567 \\ \hline \end{array}$$

35.
$$\begin{array}{r} 612 \\ \times\ 343 \\ \hline \end{array}$$

36.
$$\begin{array}{r} 7,021 \\ \times\ \ \ 422 \\ \hline \end{array}$$

37.
$$\begin{array}{r} 61,000 \\ \times\ \ \ \ 759 \\ \hline \end{array}$$

38.
$$\begin{array}{r} 47 \\ \times\ 10 \\ \hline \end{array}$$

39.
$$\begin{array}{r} 189 \\ \times\ \ 10 \\ \hline \end{array}$$

40.
$$\begin{array}{r} 157 \\ \times\ 100 \\ \hline \end{array}$$

41.
$$\begin{array}{r} 2,890 \\ \times\ \ \ 100 \\ \hline \end{array}$$

42.
$$\begin{array}{r} 2,586 \\ \times\ 1,000 \\ \hline \end{array}$$

43.
$$\begin{array}{r} 10,000 \\ \times\ \ 1,000 \\ \hline \end{array}$$

44. $36 \times 100 =$

45. $295 \times 1,000 =$

46. $25 \times 10 =$

47. $3,406 \times 100 =$

48.
$$\begin{array}{r} 89 \\ \times\ 3 \\ \hline \end{array}$$

49.
$$\begin{array}{r} 227 \\ \times\ \ 9 \\ \hline \end{array}$$

50.
$$\begin{array}{r} 6,420 \\ \times\ \ \ \ 7 \\ \hline \end{array}$$

51.
$$\begin{array}{r} 11,650 \\ \times\ \ \ \ \ 4 \\ \hline \end{array}$$

52.
$$\begin{array}{r} 3,407 \\ \times\ \ \ \ 2 \\ \hline \end{array}$$

53.
$$\begin{array}{r} 15,009 \\ \times\ \ \ \ \ 6 \\ \hline \end{array}$$

54. $40,077 \times 8 =$

55. $6,020 \times 7 =$

56. $23,067 \times 6 =$

57. $99,090 \times 9 =$

58.
$$\begin{array}{r} 75 \\ \times\ 25 \\ \hline \end{array}$$

59.
$$\begin{array}{r} 46 \\ \times\ 39 \\ \hline \end{array}$$

60.
$$\begin{array}{r} 476 \\ \times\ \ 52 \\ \hline \end{array}$$

61.
$$\begin{array}{r} 607 \\ \times\ \ 44 \\ \hline \end{array}$$

62.
$$\begin{array}{r} 4,702 \\ \times\ \ \ \ 73 \\ \hline \end{array}$$

63.
$$\begin{array}{r} 8,066 \\ \times\ \ \ \ 45 \\ \hline \end{array}$$

Multiply.

64.
$6{,}835 \times 47 =$

65.
$9{,}054 \times 93 =$

66.
$20{,}067 \times 82 =$

67.
$35{,}023 \times 51 =$

68.
$$\begin{array}{r} 900 \\ \times\ 623 \\ \hline \end{array}$$

69.
$$\begin{array}{r} 5{,}476 \\ \times\ 213 \\ \hline \end{array}$$

70.
$$\begin{array}{r} 18{,}460 \\ \times\ 725 \\ \hline \end{array}$$

71.
$$\begin{array}{r} 854 \\ \times\ 472 \\ \hline \end{array}$$

72.
$$\begin{array}{r} 1{,}497 \\ \times\ 501 \\ \hline \end{array}$$

73.
$521 \times 203 =$

74.
$110 \times 907 =$

75.
$3{,}021 \times 201 =$

76.
$784 \times 101 =$

77.
$$\begin{array}{r} 400 \\ \times\ 203 \\ \hline \end{array}$$

78.
$$\begin{array}{r} 1{,}804 \\ \times\ 409 \\ \hline \end{array}$$

79.
$$\begin{array}{r} 78{,}009 \\ \times\ 104 \\ \hline \end{array}$$

80.
$$\begin{array}{r} 39{,}000 \\ \times\ 506 \\ \hline \end{array}$$

Below is a list of the problems in this review and the pages on which the skills are taught. If you missed any problems, turn to the pages listed and practice the skills. Then correct the problems you missed in the Unit Review.

Unit 5 DIVIDING WHOLE NUMBERS

Dividing whole numbers is the opposite of multiplying them. Instead of finding a total, you split a total into equal groups. When 4 people split the cost of lunch, they divide the total cost equally by 4 to find the amount each person will pay.

In this unit, you will learn the division facts, and how to divide by one-digit, two-digit, and three-digit numbers. You will also learn about dividing with zeros.

Getting Ready

You should be familiar with the skills on this page and the next before you begin this unit. To check your answers, turn to page 194.

 You will need to round to the tens and hundreds places when you divide larger numbers.

Round each number to the nearest ten.

1. 14 _____10_____ **2.** 27 _____ **3.** 45 _____ **4.** 73 _____

Round each number to the nearest hundred.

5. 186 _____200_____ **6.** 550 _____ **7.** 641 _____ **8.** 397 _____

For review, see Unit 1, pages 20-21.

Getting Ready

 To set up a subtraction problem, first line up the digits. Then solve the problem.

Line up the digits in each problem and solve.

9.
$74 - 72 =$

$$\begin{array}{r} 74 \\ -\ 72 \\ \hline 2 \end{array}$$

10.
$468 - 354 =$

11.
$16 - 16 =$

12.
$599 - 490 =$

For review, see Unit 3, pages 60-62.

 When subtracting from zero, borrow from the next column. You may need to borrow two or more times.

Solve.

13.
$$\begin{array}{r} {\scriptstyle 3\,10} \\ 24\!\!\!/0 \\ -\ 137 \\ \hline 103 \end{array}$$

14.
$$\begin{array}{r} 5{,}000 \\ -\ 1{,}657 \\ \hline \end{array}$$

15.
$$\begin{array}{r} 13{,}002 \\ -\ 7{,}937 \\ \hline \end{array}$$

16.
$$\begin{array}{r} 9{,}026 \\ -\ 8{,}900 \\ \hline \end{array}$$

For review, see Unit 3, pages 72-78.

 Knowing the multiplication facts will help you with division and with checking your answers.

Complete the following multiplication facts and multiplication problems.

17.
$6 \times \boxed{5} = 30$

18.
$9 \times \boxed{} = 72$

19.
$3 \times \boxed{} = 21$

20.
$5 \times \boxed{} = 40$

21.
$32 \times 6 =$

$$\begin{array}{r} 32 \\ \times\ 6 \\ \hline 192 \end{array}$$

22.
$47 \times 69 =$

23.
$1{,}130 \times 25 =$

24.
$136 \times 259 =$

25.
$\boxed{} \times 7 = 56$

26.
$\boxed{} \times 4 = 12$

27.
$\boxed{} \times 9 = 81$

28.
$\boxed{} \times 6 = 48$

29.
$653 \times 45 =$

30.
$98 \times 37 =$

31.
$4{,}571 \times 126 =$

32.
$502 \times 312 =$

For review, see Unit 4, pages 85-98.

Division Facts

To divide larger numbers, you should first know the basic division facts.
You will find it helpful to know the following facts by heart.

Divide the following numbers to complete each row. Notice that the answers form a pattern.

1. $1\overline{)0}$ $1\overline{)1}$ $1\overline{)2}$ $1\overline{)3}$ $1\overline{)4}$ $1\overline{)5}$ $1\overline{)6}$ $1\overline{)7}$ $1\overline{)8}$ $1\overline{)9}$

2. $2\overline{)0}$ $2\overline{)2}$ $2\overline{)4}$ $2\overline{)6}$ $2\overline{)8}$ $2\overline{)10}$ $2\overline{)12}$ $2\overline{)14}$ $2\overline{)16}$ $2\overline{)18}$

3. $3\overline{)0}$ $3\overline{)3}$ $3\overline{)6}$ $3\overline{)9}$ $3\overline{)12}$ $3\overline{)15}$ $3\overline{)18}$ $3\overline{)21}$ $3\overline{)24}$ $3\overline{)27}$

4. $4\overline{)0}$ $4\overline{)4}$ $4\overline{)8}$ $4\overline{)12}$ $4\overline{)16}$ $4\overline{)20}$ $4\overline{)24}$ $4\overline{)28}$ $4\overline{)32}$ $4\overline{)36}$

5. $5\overline{)0}$ $5\overline{)5}$ $5\overline{)10}$ $5\overline{)15}$ $5\overline{)20}$ $5\overline{)25}$ $5\overline{)30}$ $5\overline{)35}$ $5\overline{)40}$ $5\overline{)45}$

6. $6\overline{)0}$ $6\overline{)6}$ $6\overline{)12}$ $6\overline{)18}$ $6\overline{)24}$ $6\overline{)30}$ $6\overline{)36}$ $6\overline{)42}$ $6\overline{)48}$ $6\overline{)54}$

7. $7\overline{)0}$ $7\overline{)7}$ $7\overline{)14}$ $7\overline{)21}$ $7\overline{)28}$ $7\overline{)35}$ $7\overline{)42}$ $7\overline{)49}$ $7\overline{)56}$ $7\overline{)63}$

8. $8\overline{)0}$ $8\overline{)8}$ $8\overline{)16}$ $8\overline{)24}$ $8\overline{)32}$ $8\overline{)40}$ $8\overline{)48}$ $8\overline{)56}$ $8\overline{)64}$ $8\overline{)72}$

9. $9\overline{)0}$ $9\overline{)9}$ $9\overline{)18}$ $9\overline{)27}$ $9\overline{)36}$ $9\overline{)45}$ $9\overline{)54}$ $9\overline{)63}$ $9\overline{)72}$ $9\overline{)81}$

Division Facts Practice

You can use the multiplication facts table to complete division facts since multiplication and division are opposite operations.

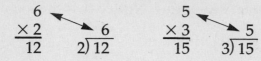

Use These Steps

Complete the division fact   20 ÷ 5

1. First, find the smaller number, 5, in the farthest row on the left.

2. Next, move to the right along that same row until you find the larger number, 20.

3. Then move to the top of the column to find the answer, 4.

÷	0	1	2	3	4	5	6	7	8	9
1	0	1	2	3	4	5	6	7	8	9
2	0	2	4	6	8	10	12	14	16	18
3	0	3	6	9	12	15	18	21	24	27
4	0	4	8	12	16	20	24	28	32	36
5	0	5	10	15	20	25	30	35	40	45
6	0	6	12	18	24	30	36	42	48	54
7	0	7	14	21	28	35	42	49	56	63
8	0	8	16	24	32	40	48	56	64	72
9	0	9	18	27	36	45	54	63	72	81

Use the table to complete the following division facts.

1. $2\overline{)8}$ (4)   2. $7\overline{)14}$ 3. $6\overline{)24}$ 4. $3\overline{)9}$ 5. $6\overline{)30}$ 6. $6\overline{)36}$

7. $8\overline{)16}$ 8. $7\overline{)49}$ 9. $8\overline{)56}$ 10. $9\overline{)45}$ 11. $7\overline{)63}$ 12. $9\overline{)81}$

13. $6\overline{)48}$ 14. $7\overline{)42}$ 15. $3\overline{)24}$ 16. $5\overline{)35}$ 17. $4\overline{)12}$ 18. $4\overline{)32}$

Division Facts Practice

Division problems can be written two ways.

$$\text{quotient} \longrightarrow \overset{4}{3\overline{)12}} \quad \text{is the same as} \quad 12 \div 3 = 4$$

quotient ⟶ 4
divisor ⟶ 3)12
dividend ⟶

Complete the following division facts. You can use the table on page 124 if you need help remembering the facts.

1. $16 \div 8 = \boxed{2}$

2. $12 \div 4 = \boxed{}$

3. $0 \div 3 = \boxed{}$

4. $18 \div 9 = \boxed{}$

5. $20 \div \boxed{5} = 4$

6. $24 \div \boxed{} = 4$

7. $30 \div \boxed{} = 5$

8. $27 \div \boxed{} = 3$

9. $\boxed{} \div 7 = 5$

10. $\boxed{} \div 6 = 7$

11. $\boxed{} \div 9 = 5$

12. $\boxed{} \div 8 = 0$

13. $72 \div 8 = \boxed{}$

14. $81 \div \boxed{} = 9$

15. $64 \div 8 = \boxed{}$

16. $10 \div \boxed{} = 2$

17. $\boxed{} \div 2 = 7$

18. $20 \div \boxed{} = 5$

19. $\boxed{} \div 7 = 3$

20. $25 \div 5 = \boxed{}$

21. $27 \div \boxed{} = 3$

22. $30 \div 5 = \boxed{}$

23. $32 \div \boxed{} = 8$

24. $\boxed{} \div 6 = 6$

25. $\boxed{} \div 8 = 5$

26. $42 \div 6 = \boxed{}$

27. $45 \div \boxed{} = 9$

28. $54 \div \boxed{} = 9$

29. $56 \div \boxed{} = 7$

30. $\boxed{} \div 8 = 8$

31. $14 \div 7 = \boxed{}$

32. $63 \div 9 = \boxed{}$

Fill in the boxes with numbers that complete the division facts. There may be more than one set of numbers that makes a true statement.

33. $\boxed{6} \div \boxed{2} = 3$

34. $\boxed{} \div \boxed{} = 2$

35. $\boxed{} \div \boxed{} = 4$

36. $\boxed{} \div \boxed{} = 0$

37. $\boxed{} \div \boxed{} = 8$

38. $\boxed{} \div \boxed{} = 7$

39. $\boxed{} \div \boxed{} = 5$

40. $\boxed{} \div \boxed{} = 9$

41. $\boxed{} \div \boxed{} = 6$

Division as the Opposite of Multiplication

Dividing is the opposite of multiplying. This means that you can check the answer to a division problem by multiplying the answer by the number you divided by. The answer should be the same as the number you divided into.

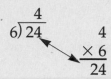

Use These Steps

Divide 32 ÷ 8

1. Set up the problem.

$$8\overline{)32}$$

2. Divide.

$$8\overline{)32}^{\ 4}$$

3. Check by multiplying the answer, 4, by the number you divided by, 8. The answer should be the same as the number you divided into, 32.

$$8\overline{)32}^{\ 4} \qquad \begin{array}{r} 4 \\ \times\ 8 \\ \hline 32 \end{array}$$

Divide. Use multiplication to check your answers.

1.
$$4\overline{)20}^{\ 5} \qquad \begin{array}{r} 5 \\ \times\ 4 \\ \hline 20 \end{array}$$

2. $6\overline{)36}$

3. $5\overline{)45}$

4. $3\overline{)27}$

5. $7\overline{)35}$

6. $4\overline{)28}$

7. $2\overline{)18}$

8. $1\overline{)8}$

9. $0 \div 5 =$

10. $42 \div 6 =$

11. $56 \div 8 =$

12. $32 \div 4 =$

13. $40 \div 8 =$

14. $49 \div 7 =$

15. $64 \div 8 =$

16. $72 \div 8 =$

Dividing by One-Digit Numbers

When you divide by a one-digit number, use the division facts. Be sure to put each answer in the correct column.

Use These Steps

Divide $3\overline{)249}$

1. Divide. Since you can't divide 2 by 3 evenly, divide 24 by 3. $24 \div 3 = 8$. Write the 8 above the 4.

$$\begin{array}{r} 8 \\ 3\overline{)249} \end{array}$$

$24 \div 3 = 8$

2. Divide again. $9 \div 3 = 3$. Write the 3 above the 9.

$$\begin{array}{r} 83 \\ 3\overline{)249} \end{array}$$

3. Check by multiplying the answer, 83, by the number you divided by, 3.

$$\begin{array}{r} 83 \\ 3\overline{)249} \end{array}$$

$$\begin{array}{r} 83 \\ \times\ 3 \\ \hline 249 \end{array}$$

Divide. Use multiplication to check your answers.

1.
$$\begin{array}{r} 4 \\ 4\overline{)16} \end{array}$$
$$\begin{array}{r} 4 \\ \times\ 4 \\ \hline 16 \end{array}$$

2. $5\overline{)45}$

3. $7\overline{)63}$

4. $9\overline{)54}$

5. $5\overline{)105}$

6. $4\overline{)128}$

7. $2\overline{)144}$

8. $8\overline{)488}$

9. $6\overline{)126}$

10. $9\overline{)189}$

11. $3\overline{)213}$

12. $5\overline{)255}$

13. $186 \div 2 =$

14. $168 \div 4 =$

15. $189 \div 3 =$

16. $568 \div 8 =$

17. $637 \div 7 =$

18. $426 \div 6 =$

19. $305 \div 5 =$

20. $128 \div 2 =$

Dividing by One-Digit Numbers Using Long Division

Long division has several steps: divide, multiply, subtract, and bring down.

Use These Steps

Divide 8) 256

1. Divide. Since you can't divide 2 by 8 evenly, divide 25 by 8. 25 ÷ 8 is not a basic fact. Use the closest fact. 24 ÷ 8 = 3, so 25 ÷ 8 = 3, plus an amount left over. Write 3 above the 5.

$$\begin{array}{r} 3 \\ 8\overline{)256} \end{array}$$

2. Multiply. 3 × 8 = 24. Subtract 24 from 25 to find the amount left over. The amount left must be less than 8. 25 − 24 = 1. Bring down the next digit, 6.

$$\begin{array}{r} 3 \\ 8\overline{)256} \\ -24\downarrow \\ \hline 16 \end{array}$$

3. Divide. 16 ÷ 8 = 2. Write 2 above the 6. Multiply. Subtract. Check the answer.

$$\begin{array}{r} 32 \\ 8\overline{)256} \\ -24 \\ \hline 16 \\ -16 \\ \hline 0 \end{array} \qquad \begin{array}{r} 32 \\ \times\ 8 \\ \hline 256 \end{array}$$

Divide.

1.
$$\begin{array}{r} 42 \\ 7\overline{)294} \\ -28 \\ \hline 14 \\ -14 \\ \hline 0 \end{array} \qquad \begin{array}{r} 42 \\ \times\ 7 \\ \hline 294 \end{array}$$

2. 6) 384

3. 5) 275

4. 4) 184

5. 9) 738

6. 3) 282

7. 2) 172

8. 8) 432

9. 2) 172

10. 5) 475

11. 3) 168

12. 6) 288

13. 7) 224

14. 6) 318

15. 4) 268

16. 8) 416

Dividing by One-Digit Numbers with Remainders

When you divide, you will sometimes have an amount left over. This amount is called a *remainder*. Use the letter *R* to stand for remainder. The remainder is part of the answer.

Use These Steps

Divide $9\overline{)28}$

1. Divide. 28 ÷ 9 is not a basic fact. Use the closest basic fact. 27 ÷ 9 = 3, so 28 ÷ 9 = 3, plus an amount left over. Write the 3 above the 8.

$$\begin{array}{r} 3 \\ 9\overline{)28} \end{array}$$

2. Multiply. 3 × 9 = 27. Subtract 27 from 28 to find the amount left over. The amount left over must be less than the number you divided by. 28 − 27 = 1. The remainder is 1. Write R1 in the answer.

$$\begin{array}{r} 3\ \text{R1} \\ 9\overline{)28} \\ -27 \\ \hline 1 \end{array}$$

3. Check by multiplying the answer by the number you divided by. Then add the remainder. The answer should be the same as the number you divided into.

$$\begin{array}{r} 3\ \text{R1} \\ 9\overline{)28} \\ -27 \\ \hline 1 \end{array} \qquad \begin{array}{r} 3 \\ \times\ 9 \\ \hline 27 \\ +\ 1 \\ \hline 28 \end{array}$$

Divide. Use multiplication to check your answers.

1.
$$\begin{array}{r} 5\ \text{R2} \\ 5\overline{)27} \\ -25 \\ \hline 2 \end{array} \qquad \begin{array}{r} 5 \\ \times\ 5 \\ \hline 25 \\ +\ 2 \\ \hline 27 \end{array}$$

2. $3\overline{)10}$

3. $9\overline{)30}$

4. $7\overline{)59}$

5. $6\overline{)20}$

6. $8\overline{)44}$

7. $2\overline{)11}$

8. $4\overline{)34}$

9. 36 ÷ 7 =

10. 43 ÷ 6 =

11. 88 ÷ 9 =

12. 15 ÷ 2 =

13. 59 ÷ 8 =

14. 33 ÷ 4 =

15. 29 ÷ 5 =

16. 17 ÷ 3 =

Dividing by One-Digit Numbers with Remainders

When you divide into a larger number, you need to repeat the division steps two or more times. With each division step, you may have an amount left over.

Use These Steps

Divide $5\overline{)187}$

1. Divide. Since you can't divide 1 by 5 evenly, divide 18 by 5. $18 \div 5 = 3$, plus an amount left over. Write the 3 above the 8. Multiply. $3 \times 5 = 15$. Write the 15 under the 18 and subtract. The amount left is 3.

$$\begin{array}{r} 3 \\ 5\overline{)187} \\ -15 \\ \hline 3 \end{array}$$

2. Divide again by bringing down the next digit, 7. The 7 brought down beside the 3 makes 37. $37 \div 5 = 7$, plus an amount left over. Multiply. $7 \times 5 = 35$. Write the 35 under the 37 and subtract. $37 - 35 = 2$. The remainder is 2.

$$\begin{array}{r} 37 \text{ R2} \\ 5\overline{)187} \\ -15\downarrow \\ \hline 37 \\ -35 \\ \hline 2 \end{array}$$

3. Check your answer by multiplying. Add the remainder.

$$\begin{array}{r} 37 \\ \times\ 5 \\ \hline 185 \\ +\ 2 \\ \hline 187 \end{array}$$

Divide. Use multiplication to check your answers.

1.
$$\begin{array}{r} 29 \text{ R5} \\ 7\overline{)208} \\ -14 \\ \hline 68 \\ -63 \\ \hline 5 \end{array} \qquad \begin{array}{r} 29 \\ \times\ 7 \\ \hline 203 \\ +\ 5 \\ \hline 208 \end{array}$$

2. $5\overline{)192}$

3. $6\overline{)272}$

4. $9\overline{)424}$

5. $380 \div 6 =$

6. $395 \div 4 =$

7. $657 \div 8 =$

8. $508 \div 7 =$

9. $541 \div 7 =$

10. $178 \div 3 =$

11. $139 \div 2 =$

12. $566 \div 6 =$

Dividing by One-Digit Numbers with Remainders

Sometimes you will be able to divide into the first digit of a number.

Use These Steps

Divide $2\overline{)433}$

1. Divide. 4 ÷ 2 = 2. Write the 2 above the 4. Multiply. Subtract. Bring down 3.

$$
\begin{array}{r}
2 \\
2\overline{)433} \\
-4 \downarrow \\
\hline
03
\end{array}
$$

2. Divide. 3 ÷ 2 = 1, plus an amount left over. Write 1 in the answer. Multiply. Subtract. Bring down 3.

$$
\begin{array}{r}
21 \\
2\overline{)433} \\
-4 \\
\hline
03 \\
-2 \downarrow \\
\hline
13
\end{array}
$$

3. Divide again. 13 ÷ 2 = 6, plus an amount left over. Multiply. Subtract. The remainder is 1.

$$
\begin{array}{r}
216 \text{ R1} \\
2\overline{)433} \\
-4 \\
\hline
03 \\
-2 \\
\hline
13 \\
-12 \\
\hline
1
\end{array}
\qquad
\begin{array}{r}
216 \\
\times\ 2 \\
\hline
432 \\
+\ 1 \\
\hline
433
\end{array}
$$

Divide.

1.
$$
\begin{array}{r}
214 \text{ R1} \\
4\overline{)857} \\
-8 \\
\hline
05 \\
-4 \\
\hline
17 \\
-16 \\
\hline
1
\end{array}
\qquad
\begin{array}{r}
214 \\
\times\ 4 \\
\hline
856 \\
+\ 1 \\
\hline
857
\end{array}
$$

2. $3\overline{)674}$

3. $2\overline{)479}$

4. $4\overline{)875}$

5. $9{,}486 \div 4 =$

6. $7{,}991 \div 3 =$

7. $6{,}789 \div 6 =$

8. $8{,}979 \div 8 =$

9. $6{,}687 \div 5 =$

10. $9{,}432 \div 7 =$

11. $3{,}527 \div 2 =$

12. $7{,}769 \div 6 =$

Application

You can use division to help you split large amounts into smaller, equal groups.

Example A computer repair company received 18 requests for service calls. If the work is divided equally among 6 technicians, how many calls will each technician make? To find equal amounts, divide.

$$18 \div 6 = 3$$

Each technician will make 3 service calls.

Solve.

1. Bob, Tim, Rita, and Ellie share office space in a downtown office building. They split their monthly expenses equally. Last month their electric bill was $144. How much did each of them pay?

    Answer _____

2. Last month their water bill was $24. How much did each of them pay?

    Answer _____

3. The rent on their office space is $580 per month. How much rent does each of them pay every month?

    Answer _____

4. The 4 office mates are thinking about asking another person to share the space with them. If 5 people share the rent, how much will each person pay per month?

    Answer _____

Mixed Review

Add, subtract, multiply, or divide.

1. $7\overline{)56}$

2. $\begin{array}{r} 5 \\ \times\,6 \\ \hline \end{array}$

3. $8\overline{)72}$

4. $\begin{array}{r} 15 \\ -\,7 \\ \hline \end{array}$

5. $6\overline{)42}$

6. $\begin{array}{r} 9 \\ +\,8 \\ \hline \end{array}$

7. $24 \div 6 =$

8. $12 - 4 =$

9. $5\overline{)205}$

10. $\begin{array}{r} 32 \\ \times\,4 \\ \hline \end{array}$

11. $4\overline{)288}$

12. $\begin{array}{r} 60 \\ +\,9 \\ \hline \end{array}$

13. $203 \times 3 =$

14. $819 \div 9 =$

15. $355 - 5 =$

16. $147 \div 7 =$

17. $5\overline{)14}$

18. $3\overline{)23}$

19. $\begin{array}{r} 57 \\ +\,9 \\ \hline \end{array}$

20. $4\overline{)30}$

21. $\begin{array}{r} 50 \\ \times\,5 \\ \hline \end{array}$

22. $29 \div 8 =$

23. $52 \times 7 =$

24. $33 \div 4 =$

25. $20 - 3 =$

26. $\begin{array}{r} 330 \\ \times\,6 \\ \hline \end{array}$

27. $2\overline{)196}$

28. $5\overline{)188}$

29. $\begin{array}{r} 670 \\ -\,8 \\ \hline \end{array}$

30. $520 \div 8 =$

31. $174 \times 3 =$

32. $549 + 7 =$

33. $353 \div 4 =$

Dividing Larger Numbers

To divide larger numbers, follow the steps you learned on pages 129-131. You will need to divide two or more times.

Use These Steps

Divide $9\overline{)3,890}$

1. Divide. $38 \div 9 = 4$, plus an amount left over. Multiply. $4 \times 9 = 36$. Subtract. $38 - 36 = 2$. Bring down the next digit, 9.

```
      4
9)3,890
  -36↓
    29
```

2. Divide. $29 \div 9 = 3$, plus an amount left over. Multiply. $3 \times 9 = 27$. Subtract. $29 - 27 = 2$. Bring down the 0.

```
     43
9)3,890
  -36
    29
   -27↓
     20
```

3. Divide. $20 \div 9 = 2$, plus an amount left over. Multiply. $2 \times 9 = 18$. Subtract. $20 - 18 = 2$. Write R2 in the answer. Check your answer.

```
    432 R2           432
9)3,890            ×   9
  -36              3,888
    29            +    2
   -27             3,890
     20
    -18
      2
```

Divide. Use multiplication to check your answers.

1.
```
    438 R5
8)3,509        438
 -32         ×   8
   30        3 504
  -24        +   5
   69        3,509
  -64
    5
```

2. $6\overline{)1,614}$

3. $5\overline{)2,137}$

4. $3\overline{)1,934}$

5. $2,935 \div 4 =$

6. $5,828 \div 8 =$

7. $1,458 \div 6 =$

8. $1,843 \div 5 =$

9. $1,779 \div 2 =$

10. $3,286 \div 7 =$

11. $2,533 \div 4 =$

12. $3,818 \div 9 =$

Dividing Larger Numbers

Remember, there are four parts to each division step: divide, multiply, subtract, and bring down the next digit.

Use These Steps

Divide   1,868 ÷ 6

1. Set up the problem. Divide. 18 ÷ 6 = 3. Multiply. Subtract. 18 − 18 = 0. Put the 0 under the 8. Bring down the 6.

```
      3
6)1,868
 −18↓
    06
```

2. Divide. 6 ÷ 6 = 1. Multiply. Subtract. Bring down the 8.

```
     31
6)1,868
 −18
    06
   − 6↓
     08
```

3. Divide. 8 ÷ 6 = 1, plus an amount left over. Multiply. Subtract. Write the remainder in the answer. Check your answer.

```
   311 R2
6)1,868        311
 −18         ×   6
    06       1,866
   − 6       +   2
     08      1,868
    − 6
      2
```

Divide. Use multiplication to check your answers.

1.
```
     361 R8
9)3,257       361
 −27        ×   9
   55       3,249
  −54       +   8
   17       3,257
  − 9
    8
```

2. 8)6,888

3. 7)42,859

4. 6)57,486

5. 18,942 ÷ 3 =

6. 26,476 ÷ 5 =

7. 67,589 ÷ 4 =

8. 42,953 ÷ 6 =

9. 18,431 ÷ 2 =

10. 82,136 ÷ 9 =

Dividing into Zeros

When you divide a number with one or more zeros in the dividend, use the same steps as with other division problems: divide, multiply, and subtract. Bring down the next digit, even if it is a zero.

Use These Steps

Divide $5\overline{)1{,}105}$

1. Divide. $11 \div 5 = 2$, plus an amount left over. Multiply, subtract, and bring down the 0.

$$
\begin{array}{r}
2 \\
5\overline{)1{,}105} \\
-10\downarrow \\
\hline
10
\end{array}
$$

2. Divide. $10 \div 5 = 2$. Multiply and subtract. Be sure to write the 0. Bring down the 5.

$$
\begin{array}{r}
22 \\
5\overline{)1{,}105} \\
-10 \\
\hline
10 \\
-10\downarrow \\
\hline
05
\end{array}
$$

3. Divide. $5 \div 5 = 1$. Multiply and subtract. There is no remainder. Check your answer.

$$
\begin{array}{r}
221 \\
5\overline{)1{,}105} \\
-10 \\
\hline
10 \\
-10 \\
\hline
05 \\
-5 \\
\hline
0
\end{array}
\qquad
\begin{array}{r}
221 \\
\times5 \\
\hline
1{,}105
\end{array}
$$

Divide. Use multiplication to check your answers.

1.
$$
\begin{array}{r}
15 \\
7\overline{)105} \\
-7 \\
\hline
35 \\
-35 \\
\hline
0
\end{array}
\qquad
\begin{array}{r}
15 \\
\times7 \\
\hline
105
\end{array}
$$

2. $8\overline{)209}$

3. $6\overline{)504}$

4. $5\overline{)406}$

5. $6{,}008 \div 8 =$

$$
\begin{array}{r}
751 \\
8\overline{)6{,}008} \\
-56 \\
\hline
40 \\
-40 \\
\hline
08 \\
-8 \\
\hline
0
\end{array}
\qquad
\begin{array}{r}
751 \\
\times8 \\
\hline
6{,}008
\end{array}
$$

6. $2{,}008 \div 7 =$

7. $5{,}003 \div 6 =$

8. $13{,}007 \div 8 =$

9. $16{,}076 \div 3 =$

10. $10{,}006 \div 6 =$

Dividing into Zeros

The number you are dividing into may have 1 or more zeros. Use the same steps as in other division problems: divide, multiply, subtract, and bring down. Bring down the next digit, even if it is a zero. When dividing into zero, write 0 in the answer.

Use These Steps

Divide $9 \overline{)8,100}$

1. Divide. $81 \div 9 = 9$. Multiply and subtract. Bring down the 0.

```
       9
9 )8,100
 - 81↓
     00
```

2. Divide. $0 \div 9 = 0$. Multiply and subtract. Write 0 in the answer. Bring down the next 0.

```
      90
9 )8,100
 - 81 |
    00 |
   - 0↓
     00
```

3. Divide. $0 \div 9 = 0$. Multiply and subtract. Write 0 in the answer. Check your answer.

```
     900
9 )8,100            900
 - 81             ×   9
    00            8,100
   - 0
    00
   - 0
     0
```

Divide.

1.
```
      400
4 )1,600      400
 - 16       ×   4
    00      1,600
   - 0
    00
   - 0
     0
```

2. $5 \overline{)3,000}$

3. $6 \overline{)2,400}$

4. $2 \overline{)4,000}$

5. $64,000 \div 8 =$

6. $42,000 \div 7 =$

7. $18,000 \div 3 =$

8. $36,000 \div 9 =$

9. $48,000 \div 6 =$

10. $81,000 \div 9 =$

11. $42,000 \div 6 =$

12. $56,000 \div 7 =$

Problem Solving: Using Rounding and Estimating

When you are dividing one large payment into several small payments, you can use rounding and estimating.

Example Audrey has a bookkeeping business. She needs a computer and printer stand that costs $298. Instead of paying for it all at once, she wants to take 6 months to pay. About how much will Audrey have to pay each month?

▶ **Step 1.** Round the cost of the stand to the nearest hundred.
$298 rounds to $300.

▶ **Step 2.** Divide to estimate the monthly payments.

$$\begin{array}{r} \$\ 50 \\ 6\overline{)\$300} \\ -\underline{30} \\ 00 \end{array}$$

Audrey will pay about $50 each month for 6 months.

Solve by rounding to the nearest hundred. Then divide.

1. Ace Flooring bought an answering machine for $209. If they pay for it in 5 monthly payments, about how much will they pay each month?

2. A photography studio spent $378 for chairs for the reception area. They will pay for the chairs in 8 monthly payments. About how much will they pay each month?

Answer _____

Answer _____

3. Bud is planning to buy a word processor for $599. He wants to make 5 monthly payments. About how much will he pay each month?

4. If Bud decides to make 8 monthly payments for the word processor, about how much will he pay each month?

Answer _____

Answer _____

5. Joe wants to buy a used taxi that costs $4,819. If he splits the cost into 2 payments, about how much will each payment be?

Answer_____

6. If Joe pays for the taxi in 6 months, about how much will he pay each month?

Answer_____

7. Joe has decided that he can afford to pay for the taxi in 4 monthly payments. About how much will he pay each month?

Answer_____

8. Brian is buying a truck for his carpet cleaning business for $8,215. If he splits the cost into 8 payments, about how much will each payment be?

Answer_____

9. Ellen has to buy car insurance. The insurance costs $619 for one year. If Ellen decides to split the cost into 2 payments, about how much will each payment be?

Answer_____

10. If Ellen decides to pay for her insurance by the month, about how much will she pay each month? (Hint: There are 12 months in a year.)

Answer_____

11. Two departments at a shipping company want to share the cost of hiring a temporary clerk during their busy season. The clerk's salary is $445 a month. If they split the cost, about how much will each department pay a month?

Answer_____

12. A building manager requires a cleaning deposit of $175 on all new apartment leases. If a renter pays the deposit in 4 payments, about how much will each payment be?

Answer_____

Dividing by Two-Digit Numbers

When you divide by a two-digit number, you may need to estimate.

Use These Steps

Divide $25\overline{)95}$

1. Divide 95 by 25 by estimating how many times 2 goes into 9. $9 \div 2$ is about 4. Write the 4 above the 5. Multiply. $4 \times 25 = 100$. 100 is larger than 95, so 4 is too large.

$$25\overline{)95}^{\,4}$$

2. Try a smaller number, 3. $25 \times 3 = 75$. 75 is smaller than 95. Subtract. $95 - 75 = 20$. The answer is 3, plus a remainder of 20.

$$
\begin{array}{r}
3\ R20 \\
25\overline{)95} \\
-\ 75 \\
\hline
20
\end{array}
$$

3. Check your answer.

$$
\begin{array}{r}
25 \\
\times\ \ 3 \\
\hline
75 \\
+\ 20 \\
\hline
95
\end{array}
$$

Divide. Use multiplication to check your answers.

1.
$$
\begin{array}{r}
3\ R2 \\
27\overline{)83} \\
-\ 81 \\
\hline
2
\end{array}
\qquad
\begin{array}{r}
27 \\
\times\ \ 3 \\
\hline
81 \\
+\ \ 2 \\
\hline
83
\end{array}
$$

2. $12\overline{)50}$

3. $31\overline{)93}$

4. $45\overline{)90}$

5. $24\overline{)360}$

6. $33\overline{)530}$

7. $56\overline{)677}$

8. $62\overline{)809}$

9. $566 \div 19 =$

10. $996 \div 83 =$

11. $702 \div 48 =$

12. $800 \div 61 =$

Dividing by Two-Digit Numbers

When you divide by a two-digit number, first estimate, then multiply. If the answer is too large, try dividing by a smaller number.

Use These Steps

Divide $34\overline{)2,096}$

1. Divide. Since you can't divide 20 by 34 evenly, divide 209 by 34. Estimate how many times 3 goes into 20. $20 \div 3$ is about 6. Try 6. Put the 6 above the 9. Multiply. $6 \times 34 = 204$. Subtract. Bring down the next digit.

$$\begin{array}{r} 6 \\ 34\overline{)2,096} \\ -2\ 04\downarrow \\ \hline 56 \end{array}$$

2. Divide. $5 \div 3$ is about 1. Multiply. Subtract. The answer is 61, plus a remainder of 22.

$$\begin{array}{r} 61\ \text{R22} \\ 34\overline{)2,096} \\ -2\ 04 \\ \hline 56 \\ -34 \\ \hline 22 \end{array}$$

3. Check your answer.

$$\begin{array}{r} 61 \\ \times 34 \\ \hline 244 \\ +1\ 83 \\ \hline 2,074 \\ +\quad 22 \\ \hline 2,096 \end{array}$$

Divide. Use multiplication to check your answers.

1.
$$\begin{array}{r} 3\ \text{R24} \\ 32\overline{)120} \\ -\ 96 \\ \hline 24 \end{array} \qquad \begin{array}{r} 32 \\ \times\ 3 \\ \hline 96 \\ +24 \\ \hline 120 \end{array}$$

2. $22\overline{)162}$

3. $46\overline{)351}$

4. $54\overline{)327}$

5. $96\overline{)4,320}$

6. $56\overline{)1,650}$

7. $36\overline{)1,900}$

8. $93\overline{)8,026}$

9. $6,550 \div 75 =$

10. $3,000 \div 42 =$

11. $7,452 \div 96 =$

Dividing by Two-Digit Numbers

When you divide by two-digit numbers, line up the digits in the correct columns for the subtraction step. If you round the number you are dividing by, you will get an estimate.

Use These Steps

Divide $59 \overline{)13{,}865}$

1. Divide. 59 rounds to 60. Use 6 to estimate each answer. Multiply. Subtract, and bring down.

$$\begin{array}{r} 2 \\ 59\overline{)13{,}865} \\ -11\ 8\downarrow \\ \hline 2\ 06 \end{array}$$

$$\begin{array}{r} 23 \\ 59\overline{)13{,}865} \\ -11\ 8 \\ \hline 2\ 06 \\ -1\ 77\downarrow \\ \hline 295 \end{array}$$

$$\begin{array}{r} 235 \\ 59\overline{)13{,}865} \\ -11\ 8 \\ \hline 2\ 06 \\ -1\ 77 \\ \hline 295 \\ -295 \\ \hline 0 \end{array}$$

2. Check your answer.

$$\begin{array}{r} 235 \\ \times\ 59 \\ \hline 2\ 115 \\ +11\ 75 \\ \hline 13{,}865 \end{array}$$

Divide. Use multiplication to check your answers.

1.
$$\begin{array}{r} 169\ \text{R}18 \\ 32\overline{)5{,}426} \\ -3\ 2 \\ \hline 2\ 22 \\ -1\ 92 \\ \hline 306 \\ -288 \\ \hline 18 \end{array}$$

$$\begin{array}{r} 169 \\ \times\ 32 \\ \hline 338 \\ +5\ 07 \\ \hline 5\ 408 \\ +\ \ 18 \\ \hline 5{,}426 \end{array}$$

2. $51 \overline{)4{,}896}$

3. $65 \overline{)3{,}371}$

4. $29 \overline{)3{,}326}$

5. $47 \overline{)52{,}687}$

6. $38 \overline{)28{,}559}$

7. $26 \overline{)14{,}726}$

8. $63 \overline{)73{,}017}$

9. $26{,}000 \div 32 =$

10. $65{,}200 \div 58 =$

11. $99{,}424 \div 52 =$

Dividing with Zeros

In a division problem, the number you divide by sometimes ends in zero. Be sure to include the zero when you multiply and subtract.

Use These Steps

Divide $80)\overline{44,083}$

1. Divide, multiply, subtract, and bring down.

$$
\begin{array}{r}
5 \\
80)\overline{44,083} \\
-40\ 0\downarrow \\
\hline
4\ 08
\end{array}
\qquad
\begin{array}{r}
55 \\
80)\overline{44,083} \\
-40\ 0 \\
\hline
4\ 08 \\
-4\ 00\downarrow \\
\hline
83
\end{array}
\qquad
\begin{array}{r}
551\ \text{R3} \\
80)\overline{44,083} \\
-40\ 0 \\
\hline
4\ 08 \\
-4\ 00 \\
\hline
83 \\
-80 \\
\hline
3
\end{array}
$$

2. Check your answer.

$$
\begin{array}{r}
551 \\
\times\ \ 80 \\
\hline
44,080 \\
+\ \ \ \ \ 3 \\
\hline
44,083
\end{array}
$$

Divide. Use multiplication to check your answers.

1.
$$
\begin{array}{r}
35 \\
10)\overline{350} \\
-30 \\
\hline
50 \\
-50 \\
\hline
0
\end{array}
\qquad
\begin{array}{r}
35 \\
\times\ 10 \\
\hline
350
\end{array}
$$

2. $30)\overline{930}$

3. $50)\overline{4,225}$

4. $20)\overline{1,182}$

5. $60)\overline{3,900}$

6. $30)\overline{54,630}$

7. $10)\overline{29,340}$

8. $80)\overline{79,040}$

9. $25,007 \div 40 =$

10. $95,550 \div 50 =$

11. $86,310 \div 10 =$

12. $17,040 \div 20 =$

13. $41,940 \div 90 =$

14. $91,876 \div 70 =$

Mixed Review

Add, subtract, multiply, or divide.

1.
$$\begin{array}{r} 15 \\ + 67 \\ \hline \end{array}$$

2.
$$\begin{array}{r} 48 \\ - 39 \\ \hline \end{array}$$

3.
$$\begin{array}{r} 56 \\ + 42 \\ \hline \end{array}$$

4. $31\overline{)217}$

5.
$$\begin{array}{r} 61 \\ \times 43 \\ \hline \end{array}$$

6. $25\overline{)300}$

7.
$$\begin{array}{r} 50 \\ - 37 \\ \hline \end{array}$$

8. $59\overline{)178}$

9.
$$\begin{array}{r} 24 \\ + 76 \\ \hline \end{array}$$

10. $86\overline{)774}$

11.
$$\begin{array}{r} 99 \\ \times 30 \\ \hline \end{array}$$

12. $980 \div 20 =$

13. $70 \times 70 =$

14. $80 - 10 =$

15. $60 + 70 =$

16.
$$\begin{array}{r} 362 \\ \times \ \ 45 \\ \hline \end{array}$$

17. $50\overline{)9,132}$

18.
$$\begin{array}{r} 403 \\ - \ \ 99 \\ \hline \end{array}$$

19. $95\overline{)2,470}$

20. $15\overline{)8,439}$

21.
$$\begin{array}{r} 478 \\ \times \ \ 96 \\ \hline \end{array}$$

22.
$$\begin{array}{r} 500 \\ - 452 \\ \hline \end{array}$$

23. $40\overline{)3,440}$

Add, subtract, multiply, or divide.

24.
$$2,679 + 43 =$$

25.
$$2,359 \div 31 =$$

26.
$$4,320 \times 90 =$$

27.
$$41 \overline{)29,563}$$

28.
$$\begin{array}{r} 5,432 \\ \times 126 \\ \hline \end{array}$$

29.
$$\begin{array}{r} 4,792 \\ -1,849 \\ \hline \end{array}$$

30.
$$\begin{array}{r} 6,540 \\ +9,873 \\ \hline \end{array}$$

31.
$$10 \overline{)83,270}$$

32.
$$46 \overline{)5,402}$$

33.
$$\begin{array}{r} 8,729 \\ \times 557 \\ \hline \end{array}$$

34.
$$\begin{array}{r} 9,000 \\ -7,430 \\ \hline \end{array}$$

35.
$$5,486 + 297 + 54 =$$

36.
$$27,800 - 18,922 =$$

37.
$$99,800 \div 42 =$$

38.
$$2,000 \times 409 =$$

39.
$$80 \overline{)50,320}$$

40.
$$35 \overline{)26,430}$$

41.
$$\begin{array}{r} 25,040 \\ \times 37 \\ \hline \end{array}$$

42.
$$\begin{array}{r} 70,000 \\ -3,428 \\ \hline \end{array}$$

Application

When you want to find the best buy at the grocery store, you compare prices. To do this, you need to know the unit cost of items. For example, if soup is on sale at 3 cans for 99 cents, the unit cost is 99 ÷ 3, or 33 cents per can.

Example Morton's Market is advertising Mealtime soup on sale at 2 cans for 52 cents. If 3 cans of Valley Fresh soup sell for 99 cents, which soup costs more: Mealtime or Valley Fresh?

Divide to find the unit cost. Then compare.

Valley Fresh
$$\begin{array}{r} 33 \text{ cents} \\ 3\overline{)99} \end{array}$$

Mealtime
$$\begin{array}{r} 26 \text{ cents} \\ 2\overline{)52} \end{array}$$

33 cents > 26 cents
Valley Fresh soup costs more than Mealtime soup.

Solve.

1. Bunty paper towels cost 49 cents per roll. Diva paper towels are on sale at 2 for 94 cents. Which brand costs more: Bunty or Diva?

   Answer _____

2. Meaty Chow dog food is on sale at 4 cans for 80 cents. Barker's dog food costs 85 cents for 5 cans. Which dog food costs more: Meaty Chow or Barker's?

   Answer _____

3. An 8-ounce package of Curly's noodles costs 63 cents. A 10-ounce package of Italia noodles costs 90 cents. Which costs more: Curly's or Italia?

   Answer _____

4. You can buy onions for 20 cents a pound, or you can buy a 3-pound bag for 57 cents. How much money will you save if you buy the 3-pound bag?

   Answer _____

Dividing by Three-Digit Numbers

When you divide by a three-digit number, first estimate. Then multiply to see if your estimate is correct.

Use These Steps

Divide 341$\overline{)9,930}$

1. Divide 993 by 341 by estimating how many times 3 goes into 9. 9 ÷ 3 = 3. Multiply. 341 × 3 = 1,023. Try a smaller number. 341 × 2 = 682. Subtract. Bring down.

2. Divide 31 by 3 to estimate. 31 ÷ 3 = 10. The number 10 will not fit in the answer. Try 9. 341 × 9 = 3,069. Subtract. Check your answer.

$$\begin{array}{r} 2 \\ 341\overline{)9,930} \\ -6\,82\downarrow \\ \hline 3\,110 \end{array}$$

$$\begin{array}{r} 29\ \text{R}41 \\ 341\overline{)9,930} \\ -6\,82 \\ \hline 3\,110 \\ -3\,069 \\ \hline 41 \end{array} \qquad \begin{array}{r} 341 \\ \times\ 29 \\ \hline 3\,069 \\ +6\,82 \\ \hline 9,889 \\ +\quad 41 \\ \hline 9,930 \end{array}$$

Divide. Use multiplication to check your answers.

1.
$$\begin{array}{r} 13 \\ 529\overline{)6,877} \\ -5\,29 \\ \hline 1\,587 \\ -1\,587 \\ \hline 0 \end{array} \qquad \begin{array}{r} 529 \\ \times\ 13 \\ \hline 1\,587 \\ +5\,29 \\ \hline 6,877 \end{array}$$

2.
$$692\overline{)8,304}$$

3.
$$478\overline{)6,697}$$

4.
$$861\overline{)9,614}$$

5.
$$525\overline{)9,450}$$

6.
$$117\overline{)6,669}$$

7.
$$9,297 \div 101 =$$

8.
$$5,916 \div 348 =$$

9.
$$6,488 \div 926 =$$

Dividing by Three-Digit Numbers

When you subtract and bring down, be sure to keep the digits lined up in the correct columns.

Use These Steps

Divide $601\overline{)369,615}$

1. Divide, multiply, subtract, and bring down.

```
        6              61             615
601)369,615    601)369,615    601)369,615
   − 360 6↓       − 360 6         − 360 6
      9 01          9 01            9 01
                  − 6 01↓         − 6 01
                    3 005          3 005
                                 − 3 005
                                       0
```

2. Check your answer.

```
     601
   × 615
   3 005
   6 01
 + 360 6
 369,615
```

Divide. Use multiplication to check your answers.

1.
```
          318
915) 290,970        318
   − 274 5        × 915
     16 47        1 590
   −  9 15        3 18
     7 320      + 286 2
   − 7 320      290,970
         0
```

2. $653\overline{)594,913}$

3. $491\overline{)33,388}$

4. $97,498 \div 402 =$

5. $118,692 \div 756 =$

6. $94,552 \div 109 =$

7. $324\overline{)264,859}$

8. $502\overline{)59,514}$

9. $369\overline{)176,751}$

Dividing with Zeros in the Answer

When you subtract and bring down, you sometimes get a number that is smaller than the number you are dividing into. When this happens, write a zero in the answer and bring down the next digit.

Use These Steps

Divide $5\overline{)3,010}$

1. Divide. Multiply. Subtract. Bring down.

$$
\begin{array}{r}
6 \\
5\overline{)3,010} \\
-30\downarrow \\
\hline
01
\end{array}
$$

2. Five is larger than 1, so you can't divide. Put a zero in the answer, and bring down the next number.

$$
\begin{array}{r}
60 \\
5\overline{)3,010} \\
-30\downarrow \\
\hline
010
\end{array}
$$

3. Divide. Multiply. Subtract. Check your answer.

$$
\begin{array}{r}
602 \\
5\overline{)3,010} \\
-30 \\
\hline
010 \\
-10 \\
\hline
0
\end{array}
\qquad
\begin{array}{r}
602 \\
\times\quad 5 \\
\hline
3,010
\end{array}
$$

Divide. Use multiplication to check your answers.

1.
$$
\begin{array}{r}
203 \\
75\overline{)15,225} \\
-150 \\
\hline
225 \\
-225 \\
\hline
0
\end{array}
\qquad
\begin{array}{r}
203 \\
\times\quad 75 \\
\hline
1\ 015 \\
+14\ 21 \\
\hline
15,225
\end{array}
$$

2. $7\overline{)7,014}$

3. $3\overline{)1,518}$

4. $28,210 \div 35 =$

5. $27,336 \div 68 =$

6. $77,125 \div 96 =$

7. $418\overline{)211,511}$

8. $523\overline{)53,869}$

9. $290\overline{)261,581}$

Dividing with Zeros in the Answer

When you divide, use zero as you would use any other digit.

Use These Steps

Divide $49\overline{)98,980}$

1. Divide, multiply, subtract, and bring down. Repeat these steps as many times as necessary to solve the problem.

```
      2              2 0            2 02           2,020
49) 98,980     49) 98,980     49) 98,980     49) 98,980
  − 98 ↓         − 98 ↓         − 98            − 98
    0 9            0 98           0 98            0 98
                                − 98 ↓          − 98
                                   00              00
```

2. Check your answer.

```
     2,020
  ×     49
    18 180
  + 80 80
    98,980
```

Divide. Use multiplication to check your answers.

1.
```
        306  R2
28) 8,570              306
  − 8 40             ×   28
    170              2 448
  − 168            + 61 2
      2              8 568
                   +     2
                     8,570
```

2. $9\overline{)54,023}$

3. $3\overline{)15,272}$

4. $76\overline{)61,409}$

5. $91\overline{)456,820}$

6. $882\overline{)793,814}$

7. $375,769 \div 501 =$

8. $243,405 \div 405 =$

9. $70,200 \div 702 =$

Application

Elaine is a route manager for the city newspaper. She counts the number of newspapers each newsstand needs, delivers the bundles of papers, and collects the unsold papers and money from each stand.

Example On Monday, Elaine delivered 10,125 papers to 135 newsstands. Each newsstand gets the same number of newspapers. How many newspapers did Elaine deliver to each stand?

$$
\begin{array}{r}
75 \\
135\overline{)10{,}125} \\
-\;9\,45 \\
\hline
675 \\
-\;675 \\
\hline
0
\end{array}
$$

Elaine delivered 75 newspapers to each stand.

Solve.

1. On Tuesday, Elaine delivered 15,600 papers. Each stand received 100 papers. How many stands did she deliver papers to on Tuesday?

2. Elaine delivered the same number of papers on Wednesday, Thursday, and Friday. If she delivered 58,995 papers in all, how many did she deliver each day?

Answer _____

Answer _____

3. On Sunday, Elaine delivered 20,150 papers. There are 25 papers to a bundle. How many bundles of papers did Elaine deliver?

4. Eduardo's newsstand took in a total of $300 for the Sunday paper. If Eduardo sold 150 papers, how much did he charge for each paper?

Answer _____

Answer _____

Unit 5 *Review*

Divide. Use multiplication to check your answers.

1. $6\overline{)18}$ **2.** $8\overline{)24}$ **3.** $9\overline{)72}$ **4.** $5\overline{)45}$ **5.** $7\overline{)42}$

6. $10 \div 2 =$ **7.** $15 \div 3 =$ **8.** $25 \div 5 =$ **9.** $32 \div 8 =$ **10.** $0 \div 9 =$

11. $2\overline{)24}$ **12.** $3\overline{)396}$ **13.** $5\overline{)555}$ **14.** $9\overline{)369}$ **15.** $6\overline{)426}$

16. $693 \div 3 =$ **17.** $482 \div 2 =$ **18.** $728 \div 8 =$

19. $5\overline{)145}$ **20.** $6\overline{)324}$ **21.** $8\overline{)1,864}$ **22.** $7\overline{)377}$

23. $4\overline{)159}$ **24.** $9\overline{)3,229}$ **25.** $2\overline{)11,159}$

26. $4\overline{)500}$ **27.** $7\overline{)3,024}$ **28.** $75,705 \div 5$ **29.** $10,023 \div 3$

Divide. Use multiplication to check your answers.

30.
$14\overline{)28}$

31.
$22\overline{)66}$

32.
$32\overline{)96}$

33.
$42\overline{)84}$

34.
$54\overline{)486}$

35.
$87\overline{)2,267}$

36.
$65\overline{)5,050}$

37.
$91\overline{)19,201}$

38.
$3,029 \div 42 =$

39.
$26,098 \div 59 =$

40.
$80,582 \div 86 =$

41.
$60\overline{)3,950}$

42.
$10\overline{)2,165}$

43.
$30\overline{)9,360}$

44.
$50\overline{)16,450}$

45.
$32,067 \div 90 =$

46.
$82,674 \div 70 =$

47.
$95,020 \div 20 =$

Divide. Use multiplication to check your answers.

48.

$326\overline{)815}$

49.

$270\overline{)339}$

50.

$792\overline{)862}$

51.

$530\overline{)862}$

52.

$521\overline{)3,824}$

53.

$862\overline{)1,588}$

54.

$711\overline{)25,622}$

55.

$451\overline{)23,001}$

56.

$3\overline{)32,983}$

57.

$412\overline{)8,360}$

58.

$330\overline{)16,500}$

59.

$54,120 \div 902 =$

60.

$95,000 \div 500 =$

61.

$50,000 \div 200 =$

Below is a list of the problems in this review and the pages on which the skills are taught. If you missed any problems, turn to the pages listed and practice the skills. Then correct the problems you missed in the Unit Review.

Problems	Pages	Problems	Pages
1-10	123-125	30-40	140-142
11-18	127	41-47	143
19-25	128-135	48-55	147-148
26-29	136-137	56-61	149-150

You have studied four operations with whole numbers — addition, subtraction, multiplication, and division. You have applied these skills to real-life problems, and you have learned techniques for solving word problems.

In this unit, you will study how to choose the correct operation needed to solve problems. You will also learn how to solve problems that require you to use more than one operation to find the answers.

Getting Ready

You should be familiar with the skills on this page and the next before you begin this unit. To check your answers, turn to page 202.

 To add whole numbers, be sure the digits are lined up. Start by adding the digits in the ones column. You may need to rename by carrying to the next column.

Add.

1.	2.	3.	4.	5.
15	25	162	103	386
+ 32	+ 47	+ 89	+ 47	+ 499
47				

6.	7.	8.	9.	10.
1,487	5,429	2,032	15,300	70,000
+ 613	+ 1,876	+ 8,961	+ 25,800	+ 42,037

Getting Ready

To subtract whole numbers, be sure the digits are lined up. Start by subtracting the digits in the ones column. You may need to rename by borrowing from the next column.

Subtract.

11.	12.	13.	14.	15.
96 − 43 ‾‾ 53	84 − 74	73 − 26	247 − 89	347 − 268

16.	17.	18.	19.	20.
3,420 − 932	5,809 − 2,532	9,030 − 4,672	10,500 − 4,670	40,000 − 29,641

For review, see Unit 3.

To multiply whole numbers, line up the digits. Start by multiplying by the ones digit. You may need to rename by carrying to the next column.

Multiply.

21.	22.	23.	24.	25.
32 × 4 ‾‾ 128	20 × 30	41 × 36	89 × 3	90 × 36

26.	27.	28.	29.	30.
138 × 30	507 × 53	1,406 × 198	420 × 307	2,065 × 100

For review, see Unit 4.

To divide, set up the problem. Start by dividing into the digits on the left. You may need to bring down one or more digits.

Divide.

31.
$$\begin{array}{r} 51 \\ 5\overline{)255} \\ -25 \\ \hline 05 \\ -5 \\ \hline 0 \end{array}$$

32. $7\overline{)432}$

33. $9\overline{)936}$

34. $62\overline{)4,340}$

35. $41\overline{)3,772}$

For review, see Unit 5.

Choose an Operation: Being a Consumer

Cholesterol is a fatty substance found in many foods. Many doctors say that to prevent heart disease, people should lower their cholesterol levels. One way to do this is to eat foods that are low in cholesterol.

Example A nurse is trying to help his elderly patients lower their cholesterol level. What will be the difference in milligrams of cholesterol if a patient drinks 1 cup of skim milk instead of 1 cup of whole milk for breakfast?

▶ **Step 1.** To find the difference, subtract.

▶ **Step 2.** Use the chart to find the amounts of cholesterol.

1 cup of skim milk = 5 milligrams
1 cup of whole milk = 34 milligrams

▶ **Step 3.** Subtract.

$$34 - 5 = 29$$

Cholesterol Content in Milligrams (mgs) of Some Common Foods

	serving	cholesterol
skim milk	1 cup	5 mgs
cottage cheese	$\frac{1}{2}$ cup	7
ice cream	$\frac{1}{2}$ cup	28
cheddar cheese	1 ounce	28
whole milk	1 cup	34
butter	1 tablespoon	35
chicken	3 ounces	67
beef	3 ounces	75
egg	1	250

The patient will take in 29 fewer milligrams of cholesterol if she drinks skim milk.

Solve.

1. A patient had 1 cup of skim milk and 1 egg for breakfast. How many total milligrams of cholesterol were in his breakfast?

Answer_____

2. If the nurse tells his patient to have 2 servings of beef for dinner tomorrow, how many milligrams of cholesterol will she take in?

Answer_____

3. Which expression would you use to find how many milligrams of cholesterol there are in 2 servings of chicken?

   a. 2×6 Solve for the answer.
   b. 67×2
   c. $67 + 2$
   d. $67 - 2$

Answer_____

4. Circle the expression you would use to find how many more milligrams of cholesterol there are in 3 ounces of beef than in 3 ounces of chicken.

   a. $67 + 3$ Solve for the answer.
   b. $67 \div 3$
   c. $75 - 67$
   d. 75×67

Answer_____

Choose an Operation: Using Measurement

To change from one unit of measurement to another, remember that when you change a small unit to a large unit, you divide. When you change a large unit to a small unit, you multiply.

12 inches	=	1 foot
3 feet	=	1 yard
1,760 yards	=	1 mile
5,280 feet	=	1 mile

Example Maude used 48 inches of cord to rope off an area in the park where she had planted new grass. How many feet of cord did she use?

▶ **Step 1.** You are changing inches to feet. To change a small unit to a large unit, divide.

▶ **Step 2.** Use the chart to find out how many inches there are in one foot. 12 inches = 1 foot

▶ **Step 3.** Divide. 48 ÷ 12 = 4 feet

Solve.

1. Hank used a 6-foot long electrical cord to rewire a refrigerator. How many inches long is the cord?

2. It is 2 miles from the doctor's office where Michiko works to the lab where she sends patients for x-rays. How many yards are in 2 miles?

Answer_____

Answer_____

3. Alberto bought some boards to repair a porch. Each board is 9 feet long. Circle the expression you would use to find how long each board is in inches.

   a. 9 × 3   Solve for the answer.
   b. 9 ÷ 3
   c. 9 × 12
   d. 9 ÷ 12

4. Circle the expression you would use to find how long each of Alberto's boards is in yards.

   a. 9 × 3   Solve for the answer.
   b. 9 ÷ 3
   c. 12 ÷ 3
   d. 12 × 3

Answer_____

Answer_____

Choose an Operation: Using a Bar Graph

The total monthly rainfall for a ten–year period in Petersburg is shown in the bar graph. The numbers in the column on the left show inches of rain. Each bar shows the amount of rainfall for that month.

Example What was the total rainfall for April and May in Petersburg?

▶ **Step 1.** To find the total, add.

▶ **Step 2.** Use the graph to find the rainfall amounts. They are shown by the height of each bar.

April = 10 inches / May = 30 inches

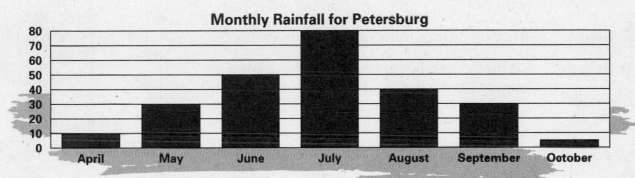

Monthly Rainfall for Petersburg

▶ **Step 3.** Add.

10 + 30 = 40 inches

In April and May, 40 inches of rain fell in Petersburg.

Solve.

1. How much more rain fell in July than in June?

   Answer_____

2. The rainfall for August was exactly half the rainfall for which month?

   Answer_____

3. Circle the expression you would use to find how much more rain fell in April than in October.

   a. 10 + 10   Solve for the answer.
   b. 10 ÷ 5
   c. 10 − 0
   d. 10 − 5

   Answer_____

4. Circle the expression you would use to find how much total rain fell in July and August.

   a. 80 + 40   Solve for the answer.
   b. 40 × 80
   c. 80 − 40
   d. 80 ÷ 40

   Answer_____

Two-Step Problems: Using a Map

You may need to use two operations to solve some problems.
Look at the city map. Each block is a square that is 500 feet long on each
side. Each intersection is marked with a letter. The shaded part is the
park. The diagonal lines show paths across the park. Each path is 1,120
feet long.

Example The high school football coach had the team run
the following route. They started at point A and
ran to the park, point B. They took the path
through the park to point H. They returned to
the school, passing through intersections G, F,
D, and back to A. How many total feet did the
team run?

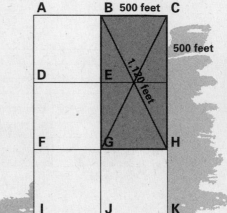

Step 1. Trace the team's route on the city map.

Step 2. Count the number of times they ran a 500-foot
length. There are 5. Multiply by 500 feet to find
a total.

500 feet × 5 = 2,500

Step 3. Add the length of the diagonal path across
the park.

2,500 + 1,120 = 3,620

They ran a total of 3,620 feet.

Solve.

1. Carolyn lives at intersection J. Every
   morning she takes her son to child care.
   She walks to the park, point G, across
   the park to point C, and back home
   again the same way. How many feet
   does Carolyn walk in one round trip?

2. Yesterday Lynette had a job interview
   at a hotel at point B. She lives at
   intersection K. She walked to point B
   by going from point K to point H and
   across the park on the diagonal path.
   How many feet did she walk to get to
   the interview?

Answer_____

Answer_____

3. Lynette walked home from point B by walking through intersections E, G, J, and then back home to K. How many feet did she walk in all, from point B back home?

4. Brad drives a delivery truck for the Pizza Parlor, which is at intersection G. One evening he needed to make stops at points E, C, A, and D. He went from the Pizza Parlor across the park to point C. Then he went to point A, and then to points D and E, and back to point G. How many total feet did Brad drive?

Answer_____

Answer_____

5. The distance around the outside edges of something is called the perimeter. Name the 4 corners of the perimeter of City Park.

6. How many feet is the perimeter of City Park?

Answer_____

Answer_____

7. On Secretaries Day, Bob delivered flowers around the city. He started from the florist's at point I. He walked through intersections J, K, H, G, and F before returning to point I. Is the perimeter of City Park greater than the distance Bob walked?

8. What is the length of the shortest path going only once through every point on the map?
(Hint: Go from point I to A, from A to B, from B to J, from J to K, and from K to C.)

Answer_____

Answer_____

Two-Step Problems: Comparing Prices

Pete sells tickets at the concert hall. The prices for summer concert tickets are shown below.

Example Pete is selling tickets for one concert to the Chen family. There are 2 adults and 3 children in the Chen family. How much money should Pete collect from the Chens?

▶ **Step 1.** To find the total cost for the adults and the total cost for the children, multiply.

$10 × 2 = $20
$5 × 3 = $15

▶ **Step 2.** To find the total for the adults and the children, add.

$20 + $15 = $35

Pete should collect $35.

Solve.

1. Mr. and Mrs. Chen want to buy season tickets. How much will the 2 adults save if they buy 2 season tickets instead of paying the adult prices for 12 concerts?

2. The Chen children have four grandparents, who are senior citizens. The grandparents attend 6 concerts each season. How much do the grandparents spend all together for the 6 concerts?

Answer_____   Answer_____

3. At its last performance, the concert hall sold a total of 2,527 tickets. Of these, 1,595 were adult tickets, 100 were season tickets, 530 were children's tickets, and the rest were senior citizens' tickets. How many senior citizens' tickets did they sell?

Answer_____

4. The concert hall has 3,000 seats. Of these, 100 seats are reserved for season ticket holders and 150 seats are reserved for families of the performers. How many seats are not reserved?

Answer_____

5. If the concert hall sold 1,926 adult tickets and 732 children's tickets, how much money did it make all together?

Answer_____

6. If the concert hall sold 342 tickets to senior citizens on Saturday and 418 on Sunday, how much money did it make on senior citizens' tickets?

Answer_____

7. The concert hall sold 1,263 children's tickets for an afternoon performance. How much more money would they have made if they had sold the same number of adult tickets?

Answer_____

8. On Friday night, the concert hall was sold out. They sold 1,900 adult tickets and 925 children's tickets. The rest were senior citizens' tickets. How many senior citizens' tickets did they sell?

Answer_____

Two-Step Problems: Finding An Average

Finding an average amount gives you a number that represents a group of numbers. Some examples are average rainfall, average miles per gallon, and average income.

To find an average, use two steps. First add the numbers in the group. Then divide the sum by the total number of items in the group.

Example The Berger's family income for 1987 to 1991 is listed in the chart. What was their average income for the 4 years?

Follow these steps.

Step 1. Add the group of numbers.

$25,436
26,506
25,059
+ 27,275
$104,276

Year	Income	Expenses
1987	$25,436	$10,200
1988	$26,506	$11,600
1989	$25,059	$ 9,072
1990	$27,275	$13,460

Step 2. Divide the answer by the total number of items in the group.

```
      26,069
  4)104,276
   - 8
     24
   - 24
      0 27
   -   24
         36
       - 36
          0
```

The Bergers' average income for 1987 to 1991 was $26,069.

Solve.

1. The chart shows the Bergers' expenses for 1987 to 1990. What was the yearly average for their expenses?

2. The Bergers' gas bills for the last 3 months were $80, $75, and $91. Find their average gas bill.

Answer_____

Answer_____

3. Mr. Berger is an auto mechanic. Last week he worked 10 hours on Monday, 8 hours on Tuesday, 9 hours on Wednesday, 11 hours on Thursday, and 7 hours on Friday. What was the average number of hours he worked each day?

4. Last month Mr. Berger worked 40 hours the first week, 42 hours the second week, 38 hours the third week, and 44 hours the fourth week. What was the average number of hours he worked each week?

Answer_____

Answer_____

5. Mrs. Berger works as a waitress. In tips last week, she made $28 on Monday, $30 on Tuesday, $29 on Wednesday, $33 on Thursday, and $45 on Friday. What was the average amount Mrs. Berger made in tips each day?

6. Last month Mrs. Berger earned $165, $155, $130, and $162 in tips. What was the average amount Mrs. Berger made in tips each week?

Answer_____

Answer_____

7. Mr. and Mrs. Berger are bowling in a 6-game tournament. Mr. Berger's scores were 300, 240, 240, 200, 270, and 280. What was his average score for the tournament?

8. Mrs. Berger bowled 300, 200, 250, 250, 280, and 250. What was her average score for the tournament?

Answer_____

Answer_____

Whole Numbers Skills Inventory

Write each number in words.

1. 32 _____

2. 246 _____

3. 2,316 _____

Compare each set of numbers. Write > or <.

4.
50 ☐ 40

5.
15 ☐ 25

6.
31 ☐ 13

7.
100 ☐ 69

Write the value of the underlined digit in each number.

8.
2̲6 _____

9.
32̲ _____

10.
2̲51 _____

11.
5̲,480 _____

Round each number to the nearest ten.

12.
88 _____

13.
482 _____

14.
3,265 _____

Round each number to the nearest hundred.

15.
328 _____

16.
6,350 _____

17.
45,477 _____

Round each number to the nearest thousand.

18.
4,930 _____

19.
72,001 _____

20.
725,552 _____

Add.

21.
5 + 9 =

22.
8 + 6 + 4 =

23.
$\begin{array}{r} 51 \\ + 20 \\ \hline \end{array}$

24.
6 + 13 + 50 =

25.
$\begin{array}{r} 210 \\ + 483 \\ \hline \end{array}$

26.
$\begin{array}{r} 3,240 \\ 425 \\ + \quad 33 \\ \hline \end{array}$

27.
$\begin{array}{r} 56 \\ + 98 \\ \hline \end{array}$

28.
85 + 22 + 60 =

29.
$\begin{array}{r} 492 \\ + 786 \\ \hline \end{array}$

30.
$\begin{array}{r} 432 \\ 3,297 \\ + 1,565 \\ \hline \end{array}$

31.
13,409 + 359,000 =

32.
$\begin{array}{r} 3,642,000 \\ 3,526 \\ + \quad 15,989 \\ \hline \end{array}$

Subtract.

33.
```
  15
-  7
```

34.
$12 - 4 =$

35.
```
  35
- 24
```

36.
```
  86
-  3
```

37.
$86 - 81 =$

38.
```
  387
-  26
```

39.
```
  5,236
-   102
```

40.
$8,466 - 5,134 =$

41.
```
  46
- 29
```

42.
$73 - 9 =$

43.
```
  30
-  6
```

44.
```
  60
- 35
```

45.
```
  761
- 584
```

46.
$835 - 276 =$

47.
$4,200 - 2,198 =$

48.
```
  15,060
-  3,965
```

49.
```
  240,000
-  86,543
```

Multiply.

50.
$6 \times 7 =$

51.
```
  31
×  3
```

52.
$501 \times 4 =$

53.
```
  2,010
×     9
```

54.
```
  31
× 12
```

55.
$420 \times 43 =$

56.
```
  210
× 231
```

57.
```
  701
× 529
```

58.
```
  7,100
×   100
```

59.
$3,427 \times 1,000 =$

60.
$32 \times 6 =$

61.
```
  467
×   3
```

62.
```
  4,208
×     7
```

63.
$19 \times 27 =$

64.
$9,040 \times 53 =$

65.
```
  438
× 193
```

66.
```
  306
× 700
```

67.
```
  3,460
×   701
```

Divide.

68.
$$14 \div 7 =$$

69.
$$5)\overline{40}$$

70.
$$8)\overline{648}$$

71.
$$6)\overline{366}$$

72.
$$7)\overline{43}$$

73.
$$23 \div 3 =$$

74.
$$366 \div 5 =$$

75.
$$8)\overline{1,744}$$

76.
$$6)\overline{1,507}$$

77.
$$2)\overline{10,480}$$

78.
$$73)\overline{84}$$

79.
$$64)\overline{610}$$

80.
$$1,881 \div 19 =$$

81.
$$50)\overline{40,420}$$

82.
$$436)\overline{3,904}$$

83.
$$841)\overline{85,796}$$

Below is a list of the problems in this Skills Inventory and the pages on which the skills are taught. If you missed any problems, turn to the pages listed and practice the skills. Then correct the problems you missed in the Skills Inventory.

Problem	Practice Page
Unit 1	
1-3	10
4-7	13
8-11	18-19
12-14	20
15-17	21
18-20	22
Unit 2	
21	29-31
22	32
23-24	34-35
25	36
26	37
27-28	41-42
29	43
30	44
31	45
32	48

Problem	Practice Page
Unit 3	
33-34	55-58
35-37	60-61
38-40	62
41-42	66-67
43-44	68-69
45-46	72-73
47-49	75-78
Unit 4	
50	85-87
51	89-90
52-53	91
54	95
55	96
56-57	97-98

Problem	Practice Page
58-59	101-102
60-61	105-106
62	107-108
63-64	110-111
65	112-113
66-67	114-115
Unit 5	
68-69	123-126
70-71	127-128
72-74	129-130
75	134-135
76-77	136-137
78-80	140-142
81	143
82	147-148
83	149-150

Glossary

addend (page 31) - A number that you add in an addition problem.

$$\begin{array}{r} 5 \\ +3 \\ \hline 8 \end{array}$$

addition (page 27) - Putting numbers together to find a total. The symbol + is used in addition.

$$\begin{array}{r} 6 \\ +7 \\ \hline 13 \end{array}$$

average (page 164) - The amount you get when you divide a total by the number of items you added to get that total.

bar graph (page 159) - A graph with bars of different lengths that stand for certain numbers.

borrowing (page 66) - Taking an amount from a top digit in subtraction and adding it to the next digit to the right.

$$\begin{array}{r} {\scriptstyle 1\ 16} \\ \cancel{2}\,\cancel{6} \\ -\ 9 \\ \hline 17 \end{array}$$

carrying (page 44) - Taking an amount from the sum of digits with the same place value and adding it to the next column of digits to the left.

$$\begin{array}{r} {\scriptstyle 1} \\ 18 \\ +\ 7 \\ \hline 25 \end{array}$$

circle graph (page 93) - A circle cut into sections to show the parts that make a total.

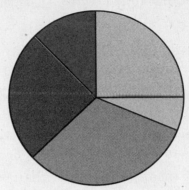

column (page 30) - A vertical line of numbers.

3 2 **9**
5 4 **1**
0 6 **7**

comparing (page 13) - Deciding if a number is equal to, greater than, or less than another number.

difference (page 57) - The answer to a subtraction problem.

$$\begin{array}{r} 15 \\ -\ 10 \\ \hline 5 \end{array}$$

digit (page 12) - One of the ten symbols used to write numbers.

0 1 2 3 4 5 6 7 8 9

dividend (page 125) - The number that you divide into in a division problem.

$$6\overline{)30}^{5}$$

division (page 121) - Splitting an amount into equal groups. The symbols ÷ and $\overline{)}\,$ are used in division.

$$12 \div 2 = 6 \qquad 2\overline{)12}^{6}$$

divisor (page 125) - The number you divide by in a division problem.

$$6\overline{)30}^{5}$$

equal (page 15) - The same in value. The symbol = means *equal*.

$$6 \times 6 = 36$$

estimating (page 38) - Finding an answer by rounding the numbers in a problem. You use estimating when an exact answer is not needed.

greater than (page 13) - More than. The symbol > means *greater than*.

6 > 5 means 6 is greater than 5

horizontal (page 31) - Side-to-side.

hundred (page 10) - The word name for 100.

lead digit (page 49) - The first digit on the left in a number with two or more digits.

1,365

less than (page 13) - Smaller than. The symbol < means *less than*.

7 < 12 means 7 is less than 12

million (page 47) - The word name for 1,000,000.

minuend (page 57) - The number that you subtract from in a subtraction problem.

$$\begin{array}{r} 15 \\ - 10 \\ \hline 5 \end{array}$$

multiplicand (87) - The top number in a multiplication problem.

$$\begin{array}{r} 54 \\ \times\ 3 \\ \hline 162 \end{array}$$

multiplication (page 83) - Combining equal numbers two or more times to get a total. The symbol $\times$ is used in multiplication.

$$\begin{array}{r} 54 \\ \times\ 3 \\ \hline 162 \end{array}$$

multiplier (page 87) - The bottom number in a multiplication problem.

$$\begin{array}{r} 54 \\ \times\ 3 \\ \hline 162 \end{array}$$

number line (page 9) - A line with equally spaced points that are labeled with numbers.

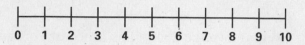

one (page 10) - The word name for 1.

operation (page 155) - The process you use to solve a math problem. The basic operations are addition, subtraction, multiplication, and division.

partial product (page 95) - The total you get when you multiply a number by one digit of another number.

$$\begin{array}{r} 13 \\ \times\ 22 \\ \hline 26 \\ +\ 26 \\ \hline 286 \end{array}$$

perimeter (page 161) - The distance around the outside edges of a figure.

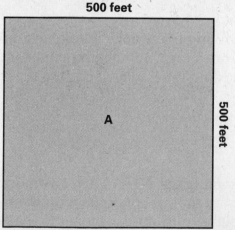

500 feet

A

500 feet

Perimeter of block A is
500 feet x 4 sides = 2000 feet

pictograph (page 104) - A graph that uses symbols or pictures to stand for certain numbers.

A	B	C	D
⚑	⚑		⚑
🎿		🎿	
∩		∩	∩
🚲		🚲	🚲
	🚶🚶	🚶🚶	
	⊼		⊼
	🐟		🐟

place value (page 18) - The value of a digit, based on its place in a number.

The value of 9 in the number 590 is **90**

plus (page 41) - To add. The symbol for plus is +.

product (page 87) - The answer to a multiplication problem.

$$
\begin{array}{r}
54 \\
\times\ 3 \\
\hline
\mathbf{162}
\end{array}
$$

quotient (page 125) - The answer to a division problem.

$$
6\overline{)30}^{\ 5}
$$

rectangle (page 64) - A four-sided figure with equal opposite sides.

remainder (page 129) - The amount left over in a division problem.

$$
\begin{array}{r}
6\ \ \mathbf{R1} \\
6\overline{)37} \\
-36 \\
\hline
1
\end{array}
$$

renaming (page 41) - Carrying or borrowing a number.

$$
\begin{array}{r}
{\scriptstyle 1} \\
26 \\
+\ 9 \\
\hline
35
\end{array}
\qquad
\begin{array}{r}
{\scriptstyle 1\ 16} \\
2\!\!\!/6 \\
-\ 9 \\
\hline
1\,7
\end{array}
$$

rounding (page 20) - Expressing a number to the nearest ten, hundred, thousand, and so on.

row (page 29) - A horizontal line of numbers.

3 2 9
5 4 1
0 6 7

subtraction (page 53) - Taking away a certain amount from another amount to find a difference. The symbol − is used in subtraction.

$$
\begin{array}{r}
15 \\
-\,10 \\
\hline
5
\end{array}
$$

subtrahend (page 57) - The number that you subtract in a subtraction problem.

$$
\begin{array}{r}
15 \\
-\,\mathbf{10} \\
\hline
5
\end{array}
$$

sum (page 31) - The answer to an addition problem.

$$
\begin{array}{r}
5 \\
+\ 3 \\
\hline
8
\end{array}
$$

table (page 23) - Information arranged in rows and columns.

	1980	1990
Pattonville	12,965	13,012
Shoreline	23,312	23,501
Eagle City	11,573	11,416
Benton	24,599	24,467
Hillview	22,207	22,299

ten (page 10) - The word name for 10.

thousand (page 10) - The word name for 1,000.

times (page 85) - To multiply. The symbol for times is ×.

vertical (page 31) - Up-and-down.

zero (page 10) - The word name for 0.

Answers & Explanations

The answer to the problem that was worked out for you in the lesson is written here in color. The next answer has an explanation written beneath it. The answers to the rest of the problems in the lesson follow in order.

Skills Inventory

Page 6

1. twenty-five
2. one hundred seventy-seven
3. three thousand, five hundred eleven
4. 60 < 70
5. 25 > 15
6. 41 > 14
7. 89 < 100
8. 10
9. 7
10. 100
11. 2,000
12. 60
13. 670
14. 1,360
15. 400
16. 7,900
17. 33,800
18. 9,000
19. 45,000
20. 235,000
21. 11
22. 20
23. 77
24. 99
25. 675
26. 5,999
27. 91
28. 169
29. 914
30. 7,861
31. 280,677
32. 2,458,700

Page 7

33. 7
34. 8
35. 24
36. 71
37. 6
38. 662
39. 8,120
40. 3,126
41. 9
42. 73
43. 33
44. 15
45. 148
46. 467
47. 3,814
48. 10,078
49. 30,531
50. 24
51. 104
52. 2,706
53. 12,080
54. 299
55. 16,960
56. 13,530
57. 219,876
58. 610,000
59. 2,409,000
60. 175
61. 1,556
62. 17,545
63. 570
64. 279,220
65. 48,411
66. 305,400
67. 383,540

Page 8

68. 2
69. 6
70. 71
71. 91
72. 7 R3
73. 5 R1
74. 96 R3
75. 328 R2
76. 217 R1
77. 5,115
78. 1 R7
79. 9 R18
80. 77
81. 688 R10
82. 9 R528
83. 103 R1

Unit 1

Page 9

1. 7
2. 15

   If you count each mark until you reach "B," you will have counted to 15.
3. 28
4. 33
5. 49

Page 10

zero	one
two	three
four	five
six	seven
eight	nine
ten	eleven
twelve	thirteen
fourteen	fifteen
sixteen	seventeen
eighteen	nineteen
twenty	twenty-one
twenty-two	twenty-three
twenty-four	twenty-five
thirty	forty
fifty	sixty
seventy	eighty
ninety	one hundred
one thousand	

Page 11

1. 14

   count 3 more
2. 20

   count 5 more

   Each number is 5 more than the last number. The next number would be 20.
3. 20

   count 4 more
4. 7

   count 2 less
5. 0

   count 3 less

   Each number is 3 less than the last number. The next number would be 0.

173

6. 8
count 3 less

7. 30
count 4 more

8. 21
count 2 less

9. 12
count 7 less

10. 22
count 6 more

11. 9
count 5 less

12. 1
count 3 less

Page 12

1. 2 ones

2. 6 ones
The number 6 has six ones.

3. 1 tens 5 ones

4. 8 tens 9 ones
The number 89 has 8 tens and 9 ones.

5. 1 tens 0 ones

6. 2 tens 0 ones

7. 5 tens 0 ones

8. 9 tens 0 ones

9. 2 hundreds
5 tens 4 ones

10. 9 hundreds 7 tens 1 ones
The number 971 has 9 hundreds, 7 tens, and 1 ones.

11. 8 hundreds
5 tens 5 ones

12. 4 hundreds
8 tens 2 ones

13. 1 hundreds
0 tens 6 ones

14. 6 hundreds
0 tens 5 ones

15. 4 hundreds
0 tens 8 ones

16. 3 hundreds
0 tens 2 ones

17. 5 hundreds
0 tens 0 ones

18. 1 hundreds
0 tens 0 ones

19. 7 hundreds
0 tens 0 ones

20. 6 hundreds
0 tens 0 ones

Page 13

1. 50 > 40

2. 10 < 20

3. 80 > 10
80 is to the right of 10 on the number line.

4. 70 > 30

5. 25 < 30

6. 51 > 40

7. 10 < 29

8. 30 < 42

9. 100 > 96

10. 52 > 34

11. 48 < 54

12. 64 < 68

13. 79 < 82

14. 63 < 83

15. 91 > 81

16. 22 < 33

17. 41 > 22

18. 33 < 35

19. 100 > 10

20. 89 < 99

21. 42 > 24

22. 89 < 98

23. 19 < 91

24. 0 < 10

Page 14

Answers may vary.

1. 2 and 3 more is 5
6 and 1 less is 5

2. 4 and 4 more is 8
10 and 2 less is 8

3. 8 and 2 more is 10
15 and 5 less is 10

4. 12 and 2 more is 14
15 and 1 less is 14

Page 15

1. a

2. b

3. a

4. a

5. b

6. a

7. b

8. a

9. a

10. a

11. b

12. b

Page 16

1. 2
count 2 less

2. 9
count 3 less

3. 26
count 5 more

4. 28
count 7 more

5. 6
count 6 less

6. 30
count 7 less

7. 4 ones

8. 2 tens 8 ones

9. 1 hundreds
3 tens 4 ones

10. 6 hundreds
1 tens 4 ones

11. 25 < 31

12. 42 > 22

13. 37 < 41

14. 20 < 50

15. 44 > 39

16. 51 > 15

17.–20. Answers may vary.

17. 3 and 1 more is 4
7 and 3 less is 4

18. 5 and 2 more is 7
10 and 3 less is 7

19. 6 and 5 more is 11
15 and 4 less is 11

20. 9 and 4 more is 13
15 and 2 less is l3

21. b

22. a

Page 17

1. Mary
32 < 36

2. today
Compare 34 and 43. 43 > 34

3. the 10:00 A.M. bus

4. John

5. last Sunday

6. Taylor to Baywater

7. the small box

8. tickets

Page 18

1. 6 tens = 60
7 ones = 7

2. 9 tens = 90
2 ones = 2
The number 92 has 9 tens, or 90; and 2 ones, or 2.

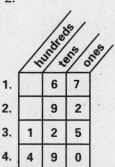

	hundreds	tens	ones
1.		6	7
2.		9	2
3.	1	2	5
4.	4	9	0

3. 1 hundreds = 100
   2 tens = 20
   5 ones = 5
4. 4 hundreds = 400
   9 tens = 90
   0 ones = 0
   The number 490 has 4 hundreds, or 400;
   9 tens, or 90; and 0 ones, or 0.
5. 50
6. 6
   The value of 6 in
   the ones place is 6.
7. 90
8. 100
9. 70
10. 4
11. 200
12. 300
13. 70
14. 9
15. 80
16. 0

Page 19

1. 2 thousands = 2,000
   4 hundreds = 400
   3 tens = 30
   7 ones = 7
2. 3 thousands = 3,000
   0 hundreds = 0
   1 tens = 10
   3 ones = 3
   The number 3,013 has 3 thousands, or
   3,000; 0 hundreds, or 0; 1 tens, or 10; and 3
   ones, or 3.

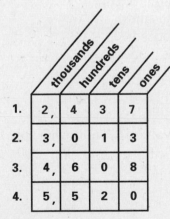

	thousands	hundreds	tens	ones
1.	2,	4	3	7
2.	3,	0	1	3
3.	4,	6	0	8
4.	5,	5	2	0

3. 4 thousands = 4,000
   6 hundreds = 600
   0 tens = 0
   8 ones = 8
4. 5 thousands = 5,000
   5 hundreds = 500
   2 tens = 20
   0 ones = 0
5. 500
6. 90
   The value of 9 in the tens place is 90.

7. 3
8. 30
9. 3,000
10. 8,000
11. 400
12. 2
13. 50

Page 20

1. 50
2. 60
   8 > 5, so 58 rounds up to 60.
3. 50
4. 50
5. 70
6. 60
7. 890
8. 910
   1 < 5, so 911 rounds down to 910.
9. 450
10. 790
11. 390
12. 180
13. 9,550
14. 1,410
   6 > 5, so 1,406 rounds up to 1,410.
15. 6,500
16. 2,000
17. 8,770
18. 1,980
19. 40
20. 220
21. 900
22. 1,890
23. 80
24. 9,990

Page 21

1. 400
2. 500
   4 < 5, so 540 rounds down to 500.
3. 700
4. 600
5. 700
6. 400
7. 1,600
8. 2,600
   4 < 5, so 2,640 rounds down to 2,600.
9. 4,700
10. 1,200
11. 1,100
12. 2,100
13. 16,700
14. 24,400
   4 < 5, so 24,441 rounds down to 24,400.
15. 92,600
16. 18,500
17. 10,400
18. 13,900
19. 800
20. 50,100
21. 9,800
22. 2,600
23. 33,800
24. 600

Page 22

1. 7,000
2. 6,000
   5 = 5, so 5,500 rounds up to 6,000.
3. 4,000
4. 4,000
5. 6,000
6. 5,000
7. 18,000
8. 98,000
   9 > 5, so 97,999 rounds up to 98,000.

9. 37,000　　10. 22,000
11. 14,000　　12. 92,000
13. **112,000**
14. 214,000

　　6 > 5, so 213,649 rounds up to 214,000.

15. 139,000　　16. 265,000
17. 956,000　　18. 231,000
19. 9,000　　20. 149,000
21. 47,000　　22. 561,000
23. 86,000　　24. 7,000

Page 23

1. Eagle City
2. Pattonville, Shoreline, and Hillview
3. Eagle City and Benton
4. Shoreline

Page 24

5. Eagle City　　6. Benton
7. 1990　　8. Eagle City
9. Hillview　　10. 1990
11.

City	1980 Population	Nearest Thousand	1990 Population	Nearest Thousand
Pattonville	12,965	13,000	13,012	13,000
Shoreline	23,312	23,000	23,501	24,000
Eagle City	11,573	12,000	11,416	11,000
Benton	24,599	25,000	24,467	24,000
Hillview	22,207	22,000	22,299	22,000

Unit 1 Review, page 25

1. twenty-five
2. forty-one
3. nine hundred eighty-seven
4. six hundred three
5. one thousand one
6. six thousand, eight hundred fifty-two
7. 65
　　count 10 more
8. 24
　　count 2 more
9. 12
　　count 3 more
10. 9
　　count 2 less
11. 50
　　count 10 more
12. 8
　　count 2 less
13. 20 > 19　　14. 44 < 72
15. 11 > 10　　16. 38 < 98
17. 90 > 70　　18. 64 > 40
19. 44 > 33　　20. 22 < 26

21.–24. Answers may vary.

21. 4 and 2 more is 6
　　7 and 1 less is 6
22. 1 and 1 more is 2
　　4 and 2 less is 2
23. 6 and 6 more is 12
　　15 and 3 less is 12
24. 5 and 4 more is 9
　　12 and 3 less is 9

Page 26

25. a　　26. b
27. b　　28. a
29. 100　　30. 20
31. 900　　32. 8,000
33. 7　　34. 40
35. 80　　36. 20
37. 60　　38. 100
39. 160　　40. 270
41. 1,240　　42. 4,560
43. 500　　44. 900
45. 600　　46. 200
47. 1,200　　48. 5,900
49. 33,500　　50. 58,500
51. 7,000　　52. 4,000
53. 9,000　　54. 11,000
55. 35,000　　56. 99,000
57. 168,000　　58. 133,000

Unit 2

Page 27

1. 3 tens 7 ones
2. 5 hundreds
　　5 tens 0 ones
　　The number 550 has 5 hundreds, 5 tens, and 0 ones.
3. 3 thousands
　　9 hundreds
　　0 tens 1 ones

Page 28

4. **2,000**
5. 5
　　The value of 5 in the ones place is 5.
6. 40　　7. 800
8. 200　　9. 50
10. 9　　11. 0
12. 9,000　　13. 8
14. 40
15. 120
　　2 < 5, so 122 rounds down to 120.
16. 310　　17. 2,450
18. **100**
19. 4,600
　　5 = 5, so 4,559 rounds up to 4,600.
20. 16,600　　21. 100
22. **1,000**
23. 16,000
　　9 > 5, so 15,987 rounds up to 16,000.
24. 234,000　　25. 1,000

1.	0	1	2	3	4	5	6	7	8	9
2.	1	2	3	4	5	6	7	8	9	10
3.	2	3	4	5	6	7	8	9	10	11
4.	3	4	5	6	7	8	9	10	11	12
5.	4	5	6	7	8	9	10	11	12	13
6.	5	6	7	8	9	10	11	12	13	14
7.	6	7	8	9	10	11	12	13	14	15
8.	7	8	9	10	11	12	13	14	15	16
9.	8	9	10	11	12	13	14	15	16	17
10.	9	10	11	12	13	14	15	16	17	18

Page 30

+	0	1	2	3	4	5	6	7	8	9
0	0	1	2	3	4	5	6	7	8	9
1	1	2	3	4	5	6	7	8	9	10
2	2	3	4	5	6	7	8	9	10	11
3	3	4	5	6	7	8	9	10	11	12
4	4	5	6	7	8	9	10	11	12	13
5	5	6	7	8	9	10	11	12	13	14
6	6	7	8	9	10	11	12	13	14	15
7	7	8	9	10	11	12	13	14	15	16
8	8	9	10	11	12	13	14	15	16	17
9	9	10	11	12	13	14	15	16	17	18

1. 9
2. 12
Find 3 in the column along the top. Find the row beginning with 9. Move right on the row until it meets the column with 3. The place where the row and column meet is the sum of 3 + 9, or 12.

3.	12	4.	2
5.	13	6.	11
7.	12	8.	14
9.	2	10.	10
11.	13	12.	11
13.	9	14.	14
15.	9	16.	5
17.	16	18.	10
19.	18	20.	10

Page 31

1.	14	2.	10
3.	16	4.	9
5.	1	6.	2
7.	6	8.	6
9.	0	10.	3
11.	8	12.	6
13.	12	14.	9
15.	0	16.	11
17.	6	18.	16

19.	1	20.	9
21.	10	22.	5
23.	4	24.	5

25.–40. Answers may vary.

25.
5 + 4 = 9
8 + 1 = 9
7 + 2 = 9
6 + 3 = 9

26.
6 + 9 = 15
7 + 8 = 15
8 + 7 = 15
9 + 6 = 15

27.
9 + 9 = 18
12 + 6 = 18
10 + 8 = 18
11 + 7 = 18

28.
5 + 7 = 12
6 + 6 = 12
7 + 5 = 12
8 + 4 = 12

29.
4 + 1 = 5
3 + 2 = 5
2 + 3 = 5
1 + 4 = 5

30.
6 + 7 = 13
7 + 6 = 13
8 + 5 = 13
9 + 4 = 13

31.
5 + 2 = 7
4 + 3 = 7
3 + 4 = 7
2 + 5 = 7

32.
4 + 0 = 4
3 + 1 = 4
2 + 2 = 4
1 + 3 = 4

33.
7 + 9 = 16
9 + 7 = 16
8 + 8 = 16
10 + 6 = 16

34.
5 + 5 = 10
3 + 7 = 10
4 + 6 = 10
8 + 2 = 10

35.
6 + 8 = 14
7 + 7 = 14
8 + 6 = 14
9 + 5 = 14

36.
9 + 2 = 11
8 + 3 = 11
7 + 4 = 11
6 + 5 = 11

37.
9 + 8 = 17
8 + 9 = 17
10 + 7 = 17
7 + 10 = 17

38.
7 + 1 = 8
6 + 2 = 8
5 + 3 = 8
4 + 4 = 8

39.
5 + 1 = 6
4 + 2 = 6
3 + 3 = 6
2 + 4 = 6

40.
2 + 1 = 3
0 + 3 = 3
1 + 2 = 3
3 + 0 = 3

Page 32

1. 11
2. 10
Add the first two digits. 6 + 2 = 8.
Then add the last digit to the 8. 2 + 8 = 10.

```
  6
  2
+ 2
────
 10
```

3.	9	4.	10
5.	13	6.	11
7.	11		
8.	6		

Line up the digits in a column. Add the first two digits. 3 + 2 = 5. Then add the 1 to 5. 1 + 5 = 6.

$$\begin{array}{r} 3 \\ 2 \\ +1 \\ \hline 6 \end{array}$$

9. 12   **10.** 13
11. 18
12. 21

Line up the digits. Add the first two digits. 7 + 3 = 10. Add the last 2 digits. 9 + 2 = 11. Add the two sums. 10 + 11 = 21.

$$\begin{array}{r} 7 \\ 3 \\ 9 \\ +2 \\ \hline 21 \end{array}$$

13. 17   **14.** 21
15. 15 hours

Add to find the total hours Roy worked.

$$\begin{array}{r} 4 \\ 6 \\ +5 \\ \hline 15 \end{array} \text{ hours}$$

16. 18 clients

Add to find how many clients Jean prepared taxes for in all.

$$\begin{array}{r} 3 \\ 6 \\ 4 \\ +5 \\ \hline 18 \end{array} \text{ clients}$$

Page 33

1. c

The beach umbrella costs $8. The T-shirt costs $4. These two amounts added together, 8 + 4 = 12, will be less than the $15 Harry has to spend. He will get change from $15.

2. b

From the sign, you can see that a beach towel costs $5. If she buys a towel and a skirt, the cost will be greater than $10. If she buys a towel and cutoffs, the cost will also be greater than $10.

3. a

The total bill for the three items Jasmine plans to buy would be $15. 7 + 5 + 3 = 15. 15 > 10.

4. a

The two items Carl bought cost $9 each. 9 + 9 = 18. The four items Kai bought cost $16 all together. 18 > 16.

5. c

The cost of the two items Chris wants to buy is $16. 7 + 9 = 16. The only item he would have enough money to buy is the sandals. 16 + 3 = 19. 19 < 20.

6. b

The two items Sue bought cost $11. 4 + 7 = 11. The only other two items that equal $11 would be the skirt, $6, and a beach towel, $5. 6 + 5 = 11.

Page 34

1. 84
2. 77

Add the ones. 5 + 2 = 7. Then add the tens. 6 + 1 = 7.

$$\begin{array}{r} 65 \\ +12 \\ \hline 77 \end{array}$$

3. 99   **4.** 67
5. 92   **6.** 48
7. 96
8. 48

Add the ones. 5 + 3 = 8. Then add the tens. 4 + 0 = 4.

$$\begin{array}{r} 45 \\ +\ 3 \\ \hline 48 \end{array}$$

9. 18   **10.** 58
11. 39   **12.** 18
13. 99   **14.** 91
15. 89   **16.** 64
17. 38   **18.** 67
19. 87   **20.** 29
21. 35   **22.** 88
23. 78   **24.** 45
25. 81   **26.** 69
27. 79   **28.** 58
29. 95   **30.** 77

Page 35

1. 69
2. 28

Line up the digits. Then add the ones. 5 + 3 = 8. Add the tens. 1 + 1 = 2.

$$\begin{array}{r} 15 \\ +13 \\ \hline 28 \end{array}$$

3. 95   **4.** 84
5. 68   **6.** 49
7. 77   **8.** 44
9. 49   **10.** 78

11. 67　　　　　　　**12.** 48

Line up the digits. Then add the ones.
2 + 4 + 1 = 7. Add the tens. 3 + 2 + 1 = 6.

```
  32
  24
+ 11
  67
```

13. 69　　　　　　**14.** 19 vacations
15. $13

```
  $13            10
  $ 1             5
+ 12           + 4
  $13            19
```

Page 36

1. 129
2. 899

Add the ones. 4 + 5 = 9. Add the tens.
9 + 0 = 9. Then add the hundreds. 7 + 1 = 8.

```
  794
+ 105
  899
```

3. 174　　　　　**4.** 997
5. 435　　　　　**6.** 799
7. 538　　　　　**8.** 379
9. 398　　　　　**10.** 218
11. 589
12. 899

First add the ones. 2 + 0 + 7 = 9. Add the
tens. 2 + 0 + 7 = 9. Add the hundreds.
6 + 1 + 1 = 8.

```
  622
  100
+ 177
  899
```

13. 368　　　　　**14.** 597
15. 367　　　　　**16.** 469
17. 895　　　　　**18.** 888

Add the ones. 1 + 3 + 0 + 1 = 5. Add the
tens. 0 + 8 + 1 + 0 = 9. Add the hundreds.
2 + 3 + 3 = 8.

```
  201
  383
   10
+ 301
  895
```

19. 738　　　　　**20.** 684

Page 37

1. 1,589
2. 3,800

Line up the digits. Add the ones.
0 + 0 = 0. Add the tens. 0 + 0 = 0. Add the
hundreds. 3 + 5 = 8. Add the thousands.
3 + 0 = 3.

```
  3,300
+   500
  3,800
```

3. 5,995　　　　**4.** 6,936
5. 1,755　　　　**6.** 2,589
7. 7,054　　　　**8.** 5,367
9. 2,569　　　　**10.** 5,979
11. 9,967　　　　**12.** 7,885

Page 38

1. $80　　　　　**2.** $50

$13 rounds to $10　　$10 + $10 + $10
$22 rounds to $20　　+ $20 = $50
$49 rounds to $50
$10 + $20 + $50 = $80

Page 39

3. $80
$10 + $20 + $40 + $10 = $80
4. Clothes
$80 > $50
5. Food
$230 > $80
6. $780
$500 + $230 + $50 = $780
7. $1,080
$1,000 + $80 = $1,080
8. $70
$50 + $20 = $70
9. $260　　　　　　**10.** No
$240 + $20 = $260　　$250 < $260

Page 40

1. 5　　　　　　**2.** 70
3. 9　　　　　　**4.** 50
5. 700　　　　　**6.** 900
7. 1,000　　　　**8.** 700
9. 9,000　　　　**10.** 60
11. 40　　　　　**12.** 80
13. 150　　　　　**14.** 980
15. 820　　　　　**16.** 2,470
17. 5,310　　　　**18.** 4,990
19. 68　　　　　**20.** 34
21. 78　　　　　**22.** 89
23. 99　　　　　**24.** 99
25. 66　　　　　**26.** 74
27. 79　　　　　**28.** 97
29. 4,875　　　　**30.** 4,867
31. 9,978　　　　**32.** 9,889
33. 4,798　　　　**34.** 9,963
35. 9,579

Page 41

1. 42

2. 54
Line up the digits. Add the ones. 7 + 7 = 14.
Rename 14 ones as 1 ten and 4 ones. Write 4
in the ones column. Carry 1 ten. Add the
tens. 1 + 2 + 2 = 5.

$$\begin{array}{r} 1 \\ 27 \\ +\ 27 \\ \hline 54 \end{array}$$

3.	90	**4.**	90
5.	80	**6.**	65
7.	80	**8.**	92
9.	30	**10.**	70
11.	97	**12.**	75
13.	92	**14.**	95
15.	85	**16.**	44
17.	83	**18.**	33
19.	43	**20.**	76

Page 42

1. 115
2. 103
Add the ones. 4 + 9 = 13. Rename. Write 3
in the ones column. Carry 1 ten. Add the
tens. 1 + 7 + 2 = 10. Write 0 in the tens
column. Write 1 in the hundreds column.

$$\begin{array}{r} 1 \\ 74 \\ +\ 29 \\ \hline 103 \end{array}$$

3.	120	**4.**	171
5.	144	**6.**	143
7.	129	**8.**	142
9.	152	**10.**	166
11.	174	**12.**	124
13.	200	**14.**	198
15.	157	**16.**	123
17.	139	**18.**	96

Page 43

1. 901
2. 903
Add the ones. 8 + 5 = 13. Carry 1 ten. Add
the tens. 1 + 7 + 2 = 10. Carry 1 hundred.
Add the hundreds. 1 + 8 = 9.

$$\begin{array}{r} 11 \\ 878 \\ +\ \ 25 \\ \hline 903 \end{array}$$

3.	1,012	**4.**	1,020
5.	1,000	**6.**	916
7.	915	**8.**	1,106
9.	451	**10.**	1,192

11. 1,592
Add the ones. 1 + 8 + 3 = 12. Carry 1 ten.
Add the tens. 1 + 3 + 2 + 3 = 9. Add the
hundreds. 3 + 8 + 4 = 15.

$$\begin{array}{r} 1 \\ 331 \\ 828 \\ +\ 433 \\ \hline 1,592 \end{array}$$

12.	2,641	**13.**	888
14.	2,434	**15.**	2,409
16.	1,014	**17.**	1,005
18.	1,633		

Page 44

1. 2,227
2. 2,743
Add the ones. 9 + 4 = 13. Carry 1 ten.
Add the tens. 1 + 7 + 6 = 14. Carry
1 hundred. Add the hundreds. 1 + 5 + 1 = 7.
Add the thousands. 2 + 0 = 2

$$\begin{array}{r} 11 \\ 2,579 \\ +\ \ \ 164 \\ \hline 2,743 \end{array}$$

3.	1,202	**4.**	1,220
5.	3,542	**6.**	5,477
7.	2,224	**8.**	9,909
9.	16,121	**10.**	19,434
11.	18,199	**12.**	17,987
13.	30,510	**14.**	51,221
15.	18,558	**16.**	71,519

Page 45

1. 410
2. 710
Add the ones. 9 + 1 = 10. Carry 1 ten. Add
the tens. 1 + 0 + 0 = 1. Add the hundreds.
4 + 3 = 7.

$$\begin{array}{r} 1 \\ 409 \\ +\ 301 \\ \hline 710 \end{array}$$

3.	1,311	**4.**	1,912
5.	6,710	**6.**	5,164
7.	6,213	**8.**	992
9.	7,012	**10.**	9,817
11.	18,118	**12.**	26,917
13.	10,210	**14.**	14,610
15.	23,414	**16.**	48,514

Page 46

1. 29

2. 27

Add groups of digits in the ones column.
7 + 8 = 15. 5 + 5 + 2 = 12. 15 + 12 = 27.

```
      7
      8
      5
      5
   +  2
     27
```

3. 240   **4.** 223
5. 1,746   **6.** 1,092
7. 8,108   **8.** 15,788
9. 22,023   **10.** 14,722
11. 5,385   **12.** 69,320

Page 47

1.
3 millions	3,000,000
4 hundred thousands	400,000
7 ten thousands	70,000
2 thousands	2,000
4 hundreds	400
0 tens	00
0 ones	0

2.
6 millions	6,000,000
4 hundred thousands	400,000
8 ten thousands	80,000
0 thousands	0,000
6 hundreds	600
0 tens	00
3 ones	3

3. 40
4. 3

The value of 3 ones in 103 is 3.

5. 4,000   **6.** 900
7. 20,000   **8.** 6,000
9. 200,000   **10.** 3,000
11. 3,000,000

Page 48

1. 119,541
2. 145,278

Add, beginning with the ones place.

```
    11
   38,468
 + 106,810
  145,278
```

3. 157,142   **4.** 1,823,032
5. 1,499,000   **6.** 796,846
7. 63,340   **8.** 2,160,614
9. 3,049,382   **10.** 2,267,541
11. 7,834,034   **12.** 1,372,497
13. 61,421   **14.** 149,403
15. 347,710

Page 50

1. 600 miles   **2.** 800 miles

```
180 miles rounds to       100
200 miles                 100
193 miles rounds to       200
200 miles                 200
245 miles rounds to     + 200
200 miles                 800 miles
```
200 + 200 + 200
= 600 miles

3. 80 gallons
10 + 10 + 20 + 20 + 20 = 80 gallons

4. $390
$60 + $80 + $90 + $100 + $60 = $390

5. less   **6.** 2,000 miles
$390 < $500   1,927 miles rounds
                     to 2,000 miles

7. two months ago   **8.** 3,000 miles
2,000 > 800   2,794 miles rounds
                     to 3,000 miles

9. 6,000 miles
3,000 + 3,000 = 6,000 miles

10. the one she'll take next month
800 < 6,000

Unit 2 Review, page 51

1. 11   **2.** 10
3. 11   **4.** 12
5. 18   **6.** 10
7. 99   **8.** 95
9. 95   **10.** 99
11. 89   **12.** 99
13. 64   **14.** 97
15. 68   **16.** 89
17. 349   **18.** 899
19. 449   **20.** 1,997
21. 6,898   **22.** 6,297
23. 5,899   **24.** 2,555
25. 90   **26.** 95
27. 140   **28.** 95
29. 105   **30.** 120
31. 107   **32.** 54
33. 145   **34.** 163

Page 52

35. 315   **36.** 10,003
37. 10,120   **38.** 1,100
39. 1,384   **40.** 943
41. 4,029   **42.** 2,163
43. 9,817   **44.** 18,118
45. 26,917   **46.** 1,746
47. 1,092   **48.** 106,056
49. 1,088,033   **50.** 7,745,811

51. 12,173,634   **52.** 2,435,355
53. 58,767   **54.** 601,175

Unit 3

Page 53

1. 9 ten thousands
3 thousands
4 hundreds
2 tens
7 ones

2. 4 ten thousands
2 thousands
0 hundreds
7 tens
6 ones

Page 54

3. 498

4. 375
1
346
+ 29
375

5. 5,281   **6.** 9,934
7. 2,533   **8.** 8,731
9. 1,529   **10.** 2,024
11. 30   **12.** 160
5 = 5, so 155
rounds up to 160
13. 410   **14.** 1,300
15. 400   **16.** 800
17. 1,000   **18.** 5,400
19. 6,000   **20.** 9,000
21. 15,000   **22.** 100,000
23. 300   **24.** 28
28 >18
25. 73   **26.** 297
27. 860   **28.** 4,000

Page 55

1.	0	1	2	3	4	5	6	7	8	9
2.	0	1	2	3	4	5	6	7	8	9
3.	0	1	2	3	4	5	6	7	8	9
4.	0	1	2	3	4	5	6	7	8	9
5.	0	1	2	3	4	5	6	7	8	9
6.	0	1	2	3	4	5	6	7	8	9
7.	0	1	2	3	4	5	6	7	8	9
8.	0	1	2	3	4	5	6	7	8	9
9.	0	1	2	3	4	5	6	7	8	9
10.	0	1	2	3	4	5	6	7	8	9

Page 56

1. 6
2. 7
Find 8 in the farthest column on the left.
Move right on the row to 15. Move up from
15 to the top of the column to find 7.
3. 8   **4.** 4
5. 9   **6.** 5
7. 5   **8.** 3

9. 6   **10.** 3
11. 9   **12.** 9
13. 2   **14.** 8
15. 5   **16.** 8
17. 16   **18.** 0

Page 57

1. 8   **2.** 4
3. 4   **4.** 6
5. 4   **6.** 8
7. 7   **8.** 0
9. 11   **10.** 11
11. 10   **12.** 10
13. 4   **14.** 5
15. 5   **16.** 6
17. 15   **18.** 9
19. 7   **20.** 7
21. 5   **22.** 2
23. 9   **24.** 8
25. 8   **26.** 1
27. 0   **28.** 7
29. 10   **30.** 9
31. 0   **32.** 5

33.–41. Answers may vary.

33. $9 - 2 = 7$ **34.** $10 - 1 = 9$
35. $7 - 2 = 5$ **36.** $4 - 4 = 0$
37. $6 - 2 = 4$ **38.** $16 - 8 = 8$
39. $8 - 7 = 1$ **40.** $10 - 4 = 6$
41. $2 - 0 = 2$

Page 58

1. 9
2. 1
Use addition to check your answer.
8   1
− 7   + 7
1   8
3. 6   **4.** 8
5. 8   **6.** 4
7. 9   **8.** 8
9. 9   **10.** 3
11. 8   **12.** 2
13. 5   **14.** 7
15. 11   **16.** 7
17. 9   **18.** 6

Page 59

1. 11 degrees
62
− 51
11 degrees

2. 26 degrees
69
− 42
27 degrees

3. 37 degrees

$$\begin{array}{r}97\\-\ 60\\\hline 37\end{array}\ \text{degrees}$$

4. 13 degrees

$$\begin{array}{r}49\\-\ 36\\\hline 13\end{array}\ \text{degrees}$$

5. 44 degrees

$$\begin{array}{r}88\\-\ 44\\\hline 44\end{array}\ \text{degrees}$$

6. 40 degrees

$$\begin{array}{r}81\\-\ 41\\\hline 40\end{array}\ \text{degrees}$$

Page 60

1. 44

2. 17

Subtract the ones. Use the subtraction facts. $9 - 2 = 7$. Then subtract the tens. $8 - 7 = 1$.

$$\begin{array}{r}89\\-\ 72\\\hline 17\end{array}\qquad\begin{array}{r}72\\+\ 17\\\hline 89\end{array}$$

3. 21 **4.** 53
5. 43 **6.** 12
7. 21 **8.** 45
9. 28 **10.** 12
11. 67 **12.** 21
13. 50
14. 40

Subtract the ones. $9 - 9 = 0$. Subtract the tens. $7 - 3 = 4$.

$$\begin{array}{r}79\\-\ 39\\\hline 40\end{array}$$

15. 10 **16.** 5
17. 31 **18.** 32
19. 23 **20.** 40

Page 61

1. 31

2. 73

Subtract the ones. $7 - 4 = 3$. Then subtract the tens. $7 - 0 = 7$.

$$\begin{array}{r}77\\-\ 4\\\hline 73\end{array}\qquad\begin{array}{r}73\\+\ 4\\\hline 77\end{array}$$

3. 93 **4.** 81
5. 12 **6.** 22
7. 54 **8.** 94
9. 21 goldfish

$$\begin{array}{r}29\\-\ 8\\\hline 21\end{array}\ \text{goldfish}$$

10. 42 guppies

$$\begin{array}{r}46\\-\ 4\\\hline 42\end{array}\ \text{guppies}$$

Page 62

1. 420

2. 115

Subtract the ones. $6 - 1 = 5$. Then subtract the tens. $7 - 6 = 1$. Then subtract the

hundreds. $8 - 7 = 1$.

$$\begin{array}{r}876\\-\ 761\\\hline 115\end{array}\qquad\begin{array}{r}115\\+\ 761\\\hline 876\end{array}$$

3. 1,165 **4.** 201
5. 100 **6.** 435
7. 7,060 **8.** 5,871
9. 2,121
10. 4,663

Line up the digits. Subtract the ones, tens, and hundreds.

$$\begin{array}{r}4,899\\-\ \ \ 236\\\hline 4,663\end{array}\qquad\begin{array}{r}4,663\\+\ \ \ 236\\\hline 4,899\end{array}$$

11. 2,712 **12.** 56 feet

$$\begin{array}{r}1,456\\-\ 1,400\\\hline 56\end{array}\ \text{more feet}$$

13. $321

$$\begin{array}{r}\$786\\-\ \ 465\\\hline \$321\end{array}\ \text{more on Sunday}$$

Page 63

1. 3 **2.** 8
3. 8 **4.** 14
5. 17 **6.** 7
7. 11 **8.** 7
9. 15 **10.** 9
11. 13 **12.** 99
13. 3 **14.** 94
15. 20 **16.** 49
17. 23 **18.** 60
19. 34 **20.** 146
21. 433 **22.** 8,999
23. 1,984 **24.** 4,431
25. 2,899 **26.** 5,125
27. $30 **28.** $10
$15 + $15 = $30 $40 - $30 = $10

Page 65

1. **Step 1.**
$1,850 can save
$730 money spent
Step 2. Since you need a difference, subtract.
Step 3. $1,850 - $730
Step 4. $1,850 - $730 = $1,120
Step 5. Carolyn will save $1,120.

2. **Step 1.**
36 cats in 1989
52 cats in 1990
72 cats in 1991
41 cats in 1992

Step 2. You need to add to find out how many cats were sold all together.
Step 3. 36 + 52 + 72 + 41
Step 4. 36 + 52 + 72 + 41 = 201
Step 5. Della sold 201 cats in four years.

Page 66
1. 18
2. 19

Since you can't subtract 3 from 2, borrow 1 ten. Rename the borrowed ten as 10 ones and add it to the 2 ones. 12 − 3 = 9 ones. Then subtract the tens. 8 − 7 = 1 ten.

$$\begin{array}{r} {}^{8}\,{}^{12} \\ 9\!\!\!/\,2\!\!\!/ \\ -\ 7\ 3 \\ \hline 1\ 9 \end{array} \qquad \begin{array}{r} {}^{1} \\ 19 \\ +\ 73 \\ \hline 92 \end{array}$$

3. 18   4. 38
5. 45   6. 25
7. 17   8. 75
9. 8   10. 3
11. 9   12. 8
13. 25   14. 28
15. 48   16. 6
17. 39   18. 7
19. 65   20. 68

Page 67
1. 18
2. 19

Borrow 1 ten and rename. Subtract the ones. 13 − 4 = 9. Subtract the tens. 4 − 3 = 1 ten.

$$\begin{array}{r} {}^{4}\,{}^{13} \\ 5\!\!\!/\,3\!\!\!/ \\ -\ 3\ 4 \\ \hline 1\ 9 \end{array} \qquad \begin{array}{r} {}^{1} \\ 19 \\ +\ 34 \\ \hline 53 \end{array}$$

3. 15   4. 34
5. 9   6. 13
7. 8   8. 4
9. 73   10. 59
11. 39   12. 29
13. $17   14. $28

$$\begin{array}{r} {}^{3}\,{}^{15} \\ \$4\!\!\!/\,5\!\!\!/ \\ -\ 2\ 8 \\ \hline \$1\ 7 \end{array} \qquad \begin{array}{r} {}^{6}\,{}^{14} \\ \$7\!\!\!/\,4\!\!\!/ \\ -\ 4\ 6 \\ \hline \$2\ 8 \end{array}$$

Page 68
1. 17
2. 24

Borrow 1 ten and rename as 10 ones. Subtract the ones. 10 − 6 = 4 ones. Then subtract the tens. 4 − 2 = 2 tens.

$$\begin{array}{r} {}^{4}\,{}^{10} \\ 5\!\!\!/\,0\!\!\!/ \\ -\ 2\ 6 \\ \hline 2\ 4 \end{array} \qquad \begin{array}{r} {}^{1} \\ 24 \\ +\ 26 \\ \hline 50 \end{array}$$

3. 31   4. 26
5. 6   6. 7
7. 2   8. 9
9. 26   10. 43
11. 68   12. 81
13. 37   14. 75
15. 19   16. 4
17. 15   18. 62
19. 21   20. 41

Page 69
1. 45
2. 23

Rename 1 ten as 10 ones. Subtract the ones. 10 − 7 = 3 ones. Subtract the tens. 2 − 0 = 2 tens.

$$\begin{array}{r} {}^{2}\,{}^{10} \\ 3\!\!\!/\,0\!\!\!/ \\ -\ \ 7 \\ \hline 2\ 3 \end{array} \qquad \begin{array}{r} 23 \\ +\ 7 \\ \hline 30 \end{array}$$

3. 31   4. 4
5. 40   6. 59
7. 74   8. 1
9. 7   10. 10
11. 3   12. 50
13. 18   14. $11

$$\begin{array}{r} {}^{8}\,{}^{10} \\ 9\!\!\!/\,0\!\!\!/ \\ -\ 7\ 2 \\ \hline 1\ 8 \end{array} \qquad \begin{array}{r} {}^{2}\,{}^{11} \\ \$3\!\!\!/\,0\!\!\!/ \\ -\ 1\ 9 \\ \hline \$1\ 1 \end{array}$$

Page 70
1. 8   2. 7
3. 14   4. 38
5. 31   6. 111
7. 160   8. 235
9. 2,810   10. 1,595
11. 35   12. 104
13. 8   14. 91
15. 65   16. 35
17. 78   18. 9
19. 23   20. 25
21. 42   22. 72
23. 46   24. 9
25. 20   26. 3
27. 14 hours   28. 42 hours

$$\begin{array}{r} {}^{2}\,{}^{10} \\ 3\!\!\!/\,0\!\!\!/ \\ -\ 1\ 6 \\ \hline 1\ 4\ \ \text{hours} \end{array} \qquad \begin{array}{r} 22 \\ +\ 20 \\ \hline 42\ \ \text{hours} \end{array}$$

Page 71

1.

	Nails	Screws	Washers	Nuts
Amount needed in stock	80	74	60	45
In stock at end of the month	78	65	52	39
Amount Brenda should order	2	9	8	6

2.

	Monday	Tuesday	Wednesday	Thursday	Friday	Saturday
Beginning Count	87	80	66	54	47	38
Cans Sold	7	14	12	7	9	28
Ending Count	80	66	54	47	38	10

Page 72

1. 177

2. 188

Rename 1 ten as 10 ones. Subtract the ones 11 − 3 = 8 ones. Rename 1 hundred as 10 tens. Subtract the tens. 15 − 7 = 8 tens. Subtract the hundreds. 4 − 3 = 1 hundred.

$$
\begin{array}{r} 15 \\ 4\ \cancel{5}\ 11 \\ \cancel{5}\,\cancel{6}\,1 \\ -\ 3\,7\,3 \\ \hline 1\,8\,8 \end{array}
\qquad
\begin{array}{r} 11 \\ 188 \\ +\,373 \\ \hline 561 \end{array}
$$

3. 759   **4.** 229

5. 108   **6.** 28

7. 207   **8.** 195

9. 84   **10.** 75

11. 190   **12.** 176

13. 389   **14.** 209

15. 299   **16.** 357

Page 73

1. 1,657

2. 2,907

Rename 1 ten as 10 ones. 14 − 7 = 7 ones. Subtract tens. 8 − 8 = 0 tens. To subtract hundreds, rename 1 thousand as 10 hundreds. 17 − 8 = 9 hundreds. Subtract the thousands. 3 − 1 = 2 thousands.

$$
\begin{array}{r} 3\ 17\ 8\ 14 \\ \cancel{4},\cancel{7}\cancel{9}\cancel{4} \\ -\,1,8\,8\,7 \\ \hline 2,9\,0\,7 \end{array}
\qquad
\begin{array}{r} 1\ \ 1 \\ 2,907 \\ +\,1,887 \\ \hline 4,794 \end{array}
$$

3. 3,092   **4.** 7,173

5. 10,908   **6.** 35,748

7. 75,726   **8.** 178,612

9. 887,018

Page 74

1. 89   **2.** 579

3. 1,506   **4.** 253

5. 183   **6.** 683

7. 2,340   **8.** 10,838

9. 12,126   **10.** 97,334

11. 2,355   **12.** 6,011

13. 51,373 **14.** 98,738

15. 950,153 **16.** 75,169

17. 87,220 miles   **18.** 855,101 miles

$$
\begin{array}{r} 88,640 \\ -\ 1,420 \\ \hline 87,220 \ \text{miles} \end{array}
\qquad
\begin{array}{r} 5\ 1210 \\ 8\,\cancel{6}\,3,\cancel{0}\,2\,7 \\ -\ \ \ 7,9\,2\,6 \\ \hline 8\,5\,5,1\,0\,1 \ \text{miles} \end{array}
$$

Page 75

1. 237

2. 202

To subtract ones, rename. There are no tens. Rename 1 hun-dred as 10 tens. Rename 1 ten as 10 ones. Now you have 2 hundreds, 9 tens, and 10 ones. Subtract. 10 − 8 = 2 ones. 9 − 9 = 0 tens. 2 − 0 = 2 hundreds.

$$
\begin{array}{r} 2\ 9\ 10 \\ \cancel{3}\cancel{0}\cancel{0} \\ -\ \ 9\,8 \\ \hline 2\,0\,2 \end{array}
\qquad
\begin{array}{r} 11 \\ 202 \\ +\ 98 \\ \hline 300 \end{array}
$$

3. 344   **4.** 502

5. 1,458   **6.** 3,193

7. 2,007   **8.** 8,223

9. 844   **10.** 17,441

11. 53,550 **12.** 85,478

13. 3,859   **14.** 21,852

15. 65,994 **16.** 40,818

Page 76

1. 3,505

2. 297

There are no ones, tens, or hundreds. Rename 1 thousand as 10 hundreds, rename 1 hundred as 10 tens, and rename 1 ten as 10 ones. Now you have 6 thousands, 9 hundreds, 9 tens, and 10 ones. Subtract. 10 − 3 = 7 ones. 9 − 0 = 9 tens. 9 − 7 = 2 hundreds. 6 − 6 = 0 thousands.

```
      9 9
   6 10 10 10
   7,0 0 0              1 11
   - 6,7 0 3             297
   ─────────          + 6,703
     2 9 7              ─────
                        7,000
```

3. 15 **4.** 2,230
5. 23,109 **6.** 26,593
7. 96,604 **8.** 180,070
9. 5,074 **10.** 18,328
11. 536,341 **12.** 257,381
13. 243,968

There are no ones, tens, hundreds, thousands, or ten thousands. Rename to get 2 hundred thousands, 9 ten thousands, 9 thousands, 9 hundreds, 9 tens, and 10 ones. Subtract. $10 - 2 = 8$ ones. $9 - 3 = 6$ tens. $9 - 0 = 9$ hundreds. $9 - 6 = 3$ thousands. $9 - 5 = 4$ ten thousands. $2 - 0 = 2$ hundred thousands.

```
      9 9 9 9
2 10 10 10 10 10
3 0 0,0 0 0          1 1 1 1 1
-   5 6,0 3 2        2 4 3,9 6 8
─────────────       + 5 6,0 3 2
  2 4 3,9 6 8       ───────────
                     3 0 0,0 0 0
```

14. 663,725

Page 77

1. 449
2. 102

To subtract ones, rename. There are no tens. Rename 1 hundred as 10 tens. Rename 1 ten as 10 ones. Now you have 2 hundreds, 9 tens, and 11 ones. Subtract $11 - 9 = 2$ ones. $9 - 9 = 0$ tens. $2 - 1 = 1$ hundred.

```
        9
   2 10 11
   3 0 1              1 1
   - 1 9 9            102
   ─────            + 199
   1 0 2             ─────
                      301
```

3. 139 **4.** 479
5. 129 **6.** 347
7. 415 **8.** 608
9. 1,255 **10.** 3,529
11. 5,369 **12.** 4,706
13. 157 **14.** 208
15. 1,067

Page 78

1. 2,516
2. 2,109

Rename to get 3 thousands, 9 hundreds, 9 tens, and 11 ones. Subtract.
$11 - 2 = 9$ ones. $9 - 9 = 0$ tens. $9 - 8 = 1$

```
      9 9
   3 10 10 11
   4,0 0 1            1 11
   - 1,8 9 2          2,109
   ─────────        + 1,892
     2,1 0 9          ─────
                      4,001
```

3. 9 **4.** 1,659
5. 6,317 **6.** 10,857
7. 17,351 **8.** 9,267
9. 88,533 **10.** 114,086
11. 2,076 **12.** 18,452
13. 25,407

Page 79

1. 19,000 feet $3 < 5$, so 19,340 rounds down to 19,000.
2. 23,000 feet
$8 > 5$, so 22,831 rounds up to 23,000.

Page 80

3. 14,000 feet $4 < 5$, so 14,410 rounds down to 14,000.
4. 14,000 feet
$6 > 5$, so 13,677 rounds up to 14,000.
5. 12,000 feet
$3 < 5$, so 12,388 rounds down to 12,000.
6. Kilimanjaro
$19,000 > 14,000$
7. Mount McKinley
$12,000 < 20,000$

8.
```
   2,000 feet
     14,000
   - 12,000
   ────────
      2,000
```

9.
```
   9,000 feet
     23,000
   - 14,000
   ────────
      9,000
```

10.
```
   9,000 feet
     29,000
   - 20,000
   ────────
      9,000
```

11.
```
   3,000 feet
     20,000
   - 17,000
   ────────
      3,000
```

12.
```
   3,000 feet
     19,000
   - 16,000
   ────────
      3,000
```

Unit 3 Review, page 81

1. 9 **2.** 6
3. 8 **4.** 14
5. 11 **6.** 70
7. 7 **8.** 2
9. 32 **10.** 62
11. 124 **12.** 910
13. 314 **14.** 105
15. 52 **16.** 140
17. 1,023 **18.** 36
19. 17 **20.** 9
21. 7 **22.** 9
23. 35 **24.** 10

25.	43	26.	5
27.	1	28.	34
29.	47	30.	54
31.	75	32.	14
33.	8		

Page 82

34.	69	35.	207
36.	2,059	37.	1,055
38.	3,696	39.	1,897
40.	16,003	41.	107
42.	46	43.	373
44.	1,538	45.	1,448
46.	62,346	47.	88,943
48.	11,373	49.	206,726
50.	665,099		

Unit 4

Page 83

1. 2 ones
2. 5 hundreds
   The 5 is in the third place to the left, the hundreds place.

3.	6 tens	4.	1 thousand
5.	6 thousands	6.	0 tens

Page 84

7. 353

8. 1,397
   Line up the digits and add.
   ```
     1,365
   +    32
     1,397
   ```

9.	16,572	10.	345

11. 2,010
    Line up the digits and add.
    ```
       1 11
       1,619
    +    391
       2,010
    ```

12. 103,000

13. 791

14. 1,712
    Line up the digits and add.
    ```
          1
        1,709
    +       3
        1,712
    ```

15.	543	16.	15,912
17.	56,313	18.	348
19.	3,121	20.	5,900
21.	32,513	22.	14,020

Page 85

1.	0	1	2	3	4	5	6	7	8	9
2.	0	2	4	6	8	10	12	14	16	18
3.	0	3	6	9	12	15	18	21	24	27
4.	0	4	8	12	16	20	24	28	32	36
5.	0	5	10	15	20	25	30	35	40	45
6.	0	6	12	18	24	30	36	42	48	54
7.	0	7	14	21	28	35	42	49	56	63
8.	0	8	16	24	32	40	48	56	64	72
9.	0	9	18	27	36	45	54	63	72	81

Page 86

×	0	1	2	3	4	5	6	7	8	9
0	0	0	0	0	0	0	0	0	0	0
1	0	1	2	3	4	5	6	7	8	9
2	0	2	4	6	8	10	12	14	16	18
3	0	3	6	9	12	15	18	21	24	27
4	0	4	8	12	16	20	24	28	32	36
5	0	5	10	15	20	25	30	35	40	45
6	0	6	12	18	24	30	36	42	48	54
7	0	7	14	21	28	35	42	49	56	63
8	0	8	16	24	32	40	48	56	64	72
9	0	9	18	27	36	45	54	63	72	81

1. 42

2. 27
   Find the number 3 in farthest column on the left. Move across that row until you reach the column with the number 9 at the top. The number in the box is 27.

3.	35	4.	0
5.	81	6.	32
7.	30	8.	12
9.	56	10.	12
11.	36	12.	6
13.	16	14.	0
15.	5	16.	72
17.	4	18.	21
19.	54	20.	40
21.	8	22.	9
23.	0	24.	10

Page 87

1.	25	2.	16
3.	21	4.	36
5.	8	6.	0
7.	1	8.	5
9.	4	10.	3
11.	6	12.	9
13.	0	14.	45
15.	3	16.	4
17.	5	18.	3
19.	56	20.	30

21.–40. Answers may vary.

21. $5 \times 4 = 20$
$4 \times 5 = 20$

22. $2 \times 8 = 16$
$8 \times 2 = 16$
$4 \times 4 = 16$

23. $3 \times 9 = 27$
$9 \times 3 = 27$

24. $4 \times 8 = 32$
$8 \times 4 = 32$

25. $6 \times 7 = 42$
$7 \times 6 = 42$

26. $2 \times 6 = 12$
$6 \times 2 = 12$
$3 \times 4 = 12$
$4 \times 3 = 12$

27. $1 \times 9 = 9$
$3 \times 3 = 9$
$9 \times 1 = 9$

28. $0 \times 0 = 0$
$5 \times 0 = 0$
$1 \times 0 = 0$
$6 \times 0 = 0$
$2 \times 0 = 0$
$7 \times 0 = 0$
$3 \times 0 = 0$
$8 \times 0 = 0$
$4 \times 0 = 0$
$9 \times 0 = 0$

29. $1 \times 8 = 8$
$8 \times 1 = 8$
$2 \times 4 = 8$
$4 \times 2 = 8$

30. $6 \times 9 = 54$
$9 \times 6 = 54$

31. $5 \times 9 = 45$
$9 \times 5 = 45$

32. $8 \times 8 = 64$

33. $3 \times 5 = 15$
$5 \times 3 = 15$

34. $3 \times 7 = 21$
$7 \times 3 = 21$

35. $4 \times 9 = 36$
$9 \times 4 = 36$
$6 \times 6 = 36$

36. $8 \times 9 = 72$
$9 \times 8 = 72$

37. $3 \times 8 = 24$
$8 \times 3 = 24$
$4 \times 6 = 24$
$6 \times 4 = 24$

38. $5 \times 5 = 25$

39. $2 \times 5 = 10$
$5 \times 2 = 10$

40. $2 \times 9 = 18$
$9 \times 2 = 18$
$3 \times 6 = 18$
$6 \times 3 = 18$

Page 88

1. b
6 boxes of pens at \$2 per box = $6 \times \$2 = \$12$

2. a
$\$12 < \$20$

3. b
$9 \times 6 = 54$

4. c

5. b
$8 \times \$2 = \$16$

6. a
$5 \times \$3 = \$15$
$$\begin{array}{r} 1 \\ \$15 \\ + \ 16 \\ \hline \$31 \end{array}$$
$\$31 < \$40$

Page 89

1. 69

2. 22
Line up the digits. Multiply the ones.
$2 \times 1 = 2$ ones. Multiply the tens.
$2 \times 1 = 2$ tens.
$$\begin{array}{r} 11 \\ \times \ \ 2 \\ \hline 22 \end{array}$$

3. 39 **4.** 48
5. 63 **6.** 33
7. 32 **8.** 82
9. 84 **10.** 84
11. 66 **12.** 88
13. 153 **14.** 486
15. 699 **16.** 864
17. 936 **18.** 844
19. 369 **20.** 462
21. 562 **22.** 806
23. 990 **24.** 480
25. 36
26. 69
Line up the digits. Multiply the ones.
$3 \times 3 = 9$ ones. Multiply the tens.
$3 \times 2 = 6$ tens.
$$\begin{array}{r} 23 \\ \times \ \ 3 \\ \hline 69 \end{array}$$

27. 408 **28.** 688

Page 90

1. 106

2. 123
Multiply the ones. $3 \times 1 = 3$ ones. Multiply the tens. $3 \times 4 = 12$ ones. Since the answer is more than 10, put the 2 in the tens column and the 1 in the hundreds column.
$$\begin{array}{r} 41 \\ \times \ \ 3 \\ \hline 123 \end{array}$$

3. 128 **4.** 1,055
5. 1,648 **6.** 1,266
7. 2,177 **8.** 2,088
9. 21,336 **10.** 12,226
11. 248 **12.** 249
13. 497 **14.** 3,248
15. 156 packages **16.** \$105
$$\begin{array}{r} 52 \\ \times \ \ 3 \\ \hline 156 \end{array} \text{ packages}$$
$$\begin{array}{r} 21 \\ \times \$ \ 5 \\ \hline \$105 \end{array}$$

Page 91

1. 1,509

2. 240

Multiply the ones. $4 \times 0 = 0$ ones. Multiply the tens. $4 \times 6 = 24$ tens. Put the 4 in the tens column and the 2 in the hundreds column.

$$\begin{array}{r} 60 \\ \times\ \ 4 \\ \hline 240 \end{array}$$

3. 1,809   **4.** 120
5. 1,408   **6.** 12,008
7. 10,046   **8.** 56,008
9. 18,060   **10.** 16,008
11. 14,007   **12.** 18,039
13. 20,408   **14.** 48,080
15. $1,206

Since 2 weeks $\times$ 2 = 4 weeks, multiply $603 $\times$ 2.

$$\begin{array}{r} \$603 \\ \times\ \ 2 \\ \hline \$1,206 \end{array}$$

16. $906

$$\begin{array}{r} \$302 \\ \times\ \ 3 \\ \hline \$906 \end{array}$$

Page 92

1. 12   **2.** 42
3. 32   **4.** 3
5. 9   **6.** 17
7. 30   **8.** 41
9. 69   **10.** 84
11. 19   **12.** 93
13. 50   **14.** 99
15. 80   **16.** 19
17. 48   **18.** 61
19. 60   **20.** 80
21. 99   **22.** 90
23. 840   **24.** 866
25. 537   **26.** 1,980
27. 6,306   **28.** 6,409
29. 150   **30.** 357
31. 100   **32.** 3,099
33. 18,009   **34.** 1,408
35. 159   **36.** 91
37. 169   **38.** 2,800
39. 24,800   **40.** 9,910
41. 8,575   **42.** 63,000

Page 93

1. 220 pounds   **2.** 800 pounds

Page 94

3. 400 pounds   **4.**
$$\begin{array}{r} 800\ \text{pounds} \\ 400\ \text{pounds} \\ \times\ \ 2 \\ \hline 800\ \text{pounds} \end{array}$$

5.
$$\begin{array}{r} 1{,}600\ \text{pounds} \\ 400\ \text{pounds} \\ \times\ \ 4 \\ \hline 1{,}600\ \text{pounds} \end{array}$$

6.
$$\begin{array}{r} 2{,}400\ \text{pounds} \\ 800\ \text{pounds} \\ \times\ \ 3 \\ \hline 2{,}400\ \text{pounds} \end{array}$$

7.
$$\begin{array}{r} 6{,}400\ \text{pounds} \\ 800\ \text{pounds} \\ \times\ \ 8 \\ \hline 6{,}400\ \text{pounds} \end{array}$$

8.
$$\begin{array}{r} 880\ \text{pounds} \\ 220\ \text{pounds} \\ \times\ \ 4 \\ \hline 880\ \text{pounds} \end{array}$$

9.
$$\begin{array}{r} 1{,}200\ \text{pounds} \\ 400\ \text{pounds} \\ +\ 800\ \text{pounds} \\ \hline 1{,}200\ \text{pounds} \end{array}$$

10.
$$\begin{array}{r} 4{,}800\ \text{pounds} \\ 1{,}200\ \text{pounds} \\ \times\ \ 4\ \text{pounds} \\ \hline 4{,}800\ \text{pounds} \end{array}$$

11.
$$\begin{array}{r} 1{,}020\ \text{pounds} \\ 220\ \text{pounds} \\ +\ 800\ \text{pounds} \\ \hline 1{,}020\ \text{pounds} \end{array}$$

12.
$$\begin{array}{r} 4{,}080\ \text{pounds} \\ 1{,}020\ \text{pounds} \\ \times\ \ 4 \\ \hline 4{,}080\ \text{pounds} \end{array}$$

Page 95

1. 682
2. 408

Multiply by 4 ones. $4 \times 2 = 8$ ones. $4 \times 1 = 4$ tens. Write 48. Multiply by 3 tens. $3 \times 2 = 6$ tens. $3 \times 1 = 3$ hundreds. Write 36. Add the partial products.

$$\begin{array}{r} 12 \\ \times\ 34 \\ \hline 48 \\ +\ 36\ \ \\ \hline 408 \end{array}$$

3. 299   **4.** 616
5. 504   **6.** 483
7. 168   **8.** 924
9. 890   **10.** 516
11. 990   **12.** 840
13. 750   **14.** 880
15. 660

Page 96

1. 1,092
2. 949

Multiply by 3 ones. $3 \times 3 = 9$ ones. $3 \times 7 = 21$ tens. Write 219. Multiply by 1 ten. $1 \times 3 = 3$ tens. $1 \times 7 = 7$ hundreds. Write 73. Add the partial products.

$$\begin{array}{r} 73 \\ \times\ 13 \\ \hline 219 \\ +\ 73\ \ \\ \hline 949 \end{array}$$

3. 1,400   **4.** 3,165
5. 21,600   **6.** 25,886
7. 10,880   **8.** 50,400
9. 19,866   **10.** 170,714
11. 137,148   **12.** 1,333,031
13. 965,052   **14.** 132,528

15. 2,240,704   **16.**   4,947,000
17. 1,986,622

Page 97

1.   97,344
2.   48,160

Multiply by 2 ones. 2 × 0 = 0 ones. 2 × 3 = 6 tens. 2 × 4 = 8 hundreds Write 860. Multiply by 1 ten. 1 × 0 = 0 tens. 1 × 3 = 3 hundreds. 1 × 4 = 4 thousands. Write 4,300. Multiply by 1 hundred. 1 × 0 = 0 hundreds. 1 × 3 = 3 thousands. 1 × 4 = 4 ten thousands. Write 43,000. Add the partial products.

```
        430
     × 112
        860
      4 30
   + 43 0
     48,160
```

3. 26,866   **4.** 66,521
5. 85,012   **6.** 29,040
7. 70,503   **8.** 43,400
9. 66,822   **10.** 84,400
11. 97,546   **12.** 82,600

Page 98

1.   122,430
2.   195,000

Multiply by 5 ones. 5 × 0 = 0 ones. 5 × 0 = 0 tens. 5 × 6 = 30 hundreds. Write 3,000. Multiply by 2 tens. 2 × 0 = 0 tens. 2 × 0 = 0 hundreds. 2 × 6 = 12 thousands. Write 12,000. Multiply by 3 hundreds. 3 × 0 = 0 hundreds. 3 × 0 = 0 thousands. 3 × 6 = 18 ten thousands. Write 180,000. Add the partial products.

```
        600
     × 325
      3 000
     12 00
   + 180 0
    196,000
```

3. 511,128   **4.** 68,523,000
5. 113,364   **6.** 2,574,800
7. 22,917,129   **8.** 55,436,120
9. 12,432 pages **10.** $224

```
    112  pages              $112
  × 111                   ×    2
    112                    $ 224
  1 12
+ 11 2
  12,432  pages
```

Page 99

1.   75,025 boxes   **2.**   180,450 packages
          3,001 cases   4,010 cases

```
     ×     25  boxes           ×      45  packages of
        15 005                     20 050  paper plates
      + 60 02                     + 160 40
        75,025  boxes             180,450  packages
```

3.   360 rolls   **4.**   1,206
           10 shelves   402 boxes

```
     × 36  rolls               ×     3  shelves
        60                        1,206  boxes
      + 30
       360  rolls
```

Page 100

1. 420   **2.** 13
3. 48   **4.** 1
5. 660   **6.** 41
7. 389   **8.** 488
9. 1,284   **10.** 21,229
11. 466   **12.** 610
13. 1,134   **14.** 127,920
15. 10,000   **16.** 6,900
17. 39,249   **18.** 28,800
19. 13,000   **20.** 500
21. 20,408   **22.** 300
23. 7,000   **24.** 68,000
25. 307,622   **26.** 1,580
27. 114   **28.** 1,532,599

Page 101

1.   960
2.   5,200

Multiply by 0 ones. Write the zero in the ones column. Multiply by 1. Write the answer to the left of the zero. The answer is the same as the top number, 520, plus 1 zero.

```
      520
   ×   10
    5,200
```

3. 10,850   **4.** 78,310
5. 763,000   **6.** 46,100
7. 98,200

Multiply by 0 ones. Write the zero in the ones column. Multiply by 0 tens. Write the 0 in the tens column. Multiply by 1 hundred. Write the answer to the left of the 2 zeros. The answer is the same as the top number, 982, plus 2 zeros.

```
      982
   × 100
   98,200
```

8. 330,500
9. 4,672,000   **10.** 3,990,000
11. 3,382,000
12. 1,590,000

Multiply by 0 ones. Write the zero in the ones column. Multiply by 0 tens. Write the 0 in the tens column. Multiply by 0 hundreds. Write the 0 in the hundreds column. Multiply by 1 thousand. Write the answer to the left of the 3 zeros. The answer is the same as the top number, 1,590, plus 3 zeros.

$$\begin{array}{r} 1{,}590 \\ \times\ 1{,}000 \\ \hline 1{,}590{,}000 \end{array}$$

13. 2,706,000   **14.** 25,400,000
15. 17,000,000   **16.** 5,460
17. 23,890   **18.** 47,700
19. 1,290,300   **20.** 2,900
21. 36,000   **22.** 1,109,000
23. 20,000,000

Page 102

1. 270
2. 1,950

Write the number you started with, 195. Since there is 1 zero in 10, put 0 after 195.

3. 34,020   **4.** 3,100
5. 28,600

Write the number you started with, 286. Since there are 2 zeros in 100, put 2 zeros after 286.

6. 1,502,900
7. 490,000
8. 1,830,000

Write the number you started with, 1,830. Since there are 3 zeros in 1,000, put 3 zeros after 1,830.

9. 27,600,000   **10.** 2,101,000
11. 13,300   **12.** 69,970
13. 410   **14.** 20,100
15. 33,032,000   **16.** 2,000
17. 310,000   **18.** 21,000,000
19. 890   **20.** 4,200
21. 51,000   **22.** 36,000
23. 500,000   **24.** 9,900

Page 103

1. 600 million bags of potatoes
200 million × 3 = 600 million bags of potatoes
2. 800 million bags of potatoes
200 million × 4 = 800 million bags of potatoes

3. 200 million bags of potatoes
200 million × 1 = 200 million bags of potatoes
4. 800 million bags of potatoes
400 million × 2 years = 800 million bags of potatoes.

Page 104

1. 120 million tons
20 million × 6 = 120 million tons
2. 40 million tons
20 million × 2 = 40 million tons
3. 60 million tons
20 million × 3 = 60 million tons
4. 40,000 million pounds
20 million × 2,000 = 40,000 million pounds
5. 120 million tons
60 million × 2 years = 120 million tons
6. 600 million tons
120 million × 5 years = 600 million tons

Page 105

1. 141
2. 256

Multiply the 2 by 8 ones. 8 × 2 = 16 ones. Rename 16 ones as 1 ten and 6 ones. Write the 6, and carry the 1 ten. Multiply the 3 by 8 ones. 8 × 3 = 24 tens. Add the carried 1 ten. 24 + 1 = 25 tens. Write 25.

$$\begin{array}{r} 1 \\ 32 \\ \times\ 8 \\ \hline 256 \end{array}$$

3. 651   **4.** 180
5. 702   **6.** 324
7. 310   **8.** 282
9. 399   **10.** 738
11. 1,000   **12.** 1,050
13. 1,700   **14.** 2,500
15. 7,875   **16.** 6,412
17. 3,456   **18.** 2,600
19. 2,697   **20.** 1,540

Page 106

1. 48,744
2. 43,968

Multiply by 6 ones. Add the carried numbers.

$$\begin{array}{r} 1\ 1\ 4 \\ 7{,}3\ 2\ 8 \\ \times\ \ \ \ 6 \\ \hline 4\ 3{,}9\ 6\ 8 \end{array}$$

3. 17,860   **4.** 27,810
5. 52,694   **6.** 260,900

7.	275,800	8.	828,000
9.	13,448	10.	95,200
11.	153,086	12.	41,934
13.	$73,500	14.	$51,400

13.
$24,500
× 3
$73,500

14.
$51,400
$24,500
+ 1,200
$25,700
1
$25,700
× 2
$51,400

Page 107

1. 3,054
2. 1,535
   Multiply by 5 ones. Add the carried numbers.
   3
   307
   × 5
   1,535

3.	7,248	4.	1,435
5.	1,616	6.	6,318
7.	2,721	8.	3,045
9.	3,036	10.	2,416
11.	2,812	12.	1,872
13.	6,440	14.	3,025
15.	6,464	16.	5,418
17.	4,949	18.	2,781
19.	1,008	20.	1,803
21.	3,236	22.	872

Page 108

1. 28,242
2. 27,219
   Multiply by 3 ones. Add the carried numbers.
   2
   9,073
   × 3
   27,219

3.	40,445	4.	25,235
5.	85,616	6.	264,380
7.	160,192	8.	818,181
9.	210,040	10.	213,542
11.	180,045	12.	$2,430

12.
3
$405
× 6
$2,430

13.
$24,300
$2,430
× 10
$24,300

Page 109

1.	42	2.	20
3.	72	4.	393
5.	259	6.	590
7.	1,206	8.	472
9.	936	10.	36,064
11.	630,045	12.	100
13.	496	14.	65
15.	90	16.	86
17.	37	18.	744
19.	140	20.	44
21.	616	22.	1,239
23.	2	24.	510
25.	8,336	26.	693
27.	86,940	28.	5,790
29.	388	30.	342,664
31.	90	32.	1,290,499
33.	1,800	34.	2,200
35.	305,624	36.	1,104
37.	503,200	38.	1,482,103

Page 110

1. 1,610
2. 1,416
   Multiply by 4 ones. 4 × 9 = 36 ones. Write 6, and carry the 3. 4 × 5 = 20 tens. Add 3 tens. Write 23. Multiply by 2 tens. 2 × 9 = 18 tens. Write 8, and carry the 1. 2 × 5 = 10 hundreds. Add the carried 1. Write 11. Add the partial products.
   59
   × 24
   236
   + 1 18
   1,416

3.	3,975	4.	3,038
5.	6,450	6.	13,338
7.	47,034	8.	22,386
9.	27,812	10.	17,825
11.	79,398	12.	27,500
13.	20,502	14.	14,616
15.	6,831		

Page 111

1. 132,900
2. 73,242
   Line up the digits. Multiply by 8 ones. Multiply by 1 ten. Carry when needed. Add the partial products.
   4,069
   × 18
   32 552
   + 40 69
   73,242

3. 414,360 **4.** 1,082,664

5. 888,185 **6.** 7,446,231

7. 1,120,590 miles **8.** 2,388,600 miles

$$
\begin{array}{r}
24{,}902 \text{ miles} \\
\times 45 \\
\hline
124\ 510 \\
+ 996\ 08 \\
\hline
1{,}120{,}590 \text{ miles}
\end{array}
$$

$$
\begin{array}{r}
477{,}720 \text{ miles} \\
\times 5 \\
\hline
2{,}388{,}600 \text{ miles}
\end{array}
$$

Page 112

1. 130,410

2. 64,152

Multiply by 2 ones. Multiply by 3 tens. Multiply by 1 hundred. Carry when needed. Add the partial products.

$$
\begin{array}{r}
486 \\
\times\ 132 \\
\hline
972 \\
14\ 58 \\
+\ 48\ 6 \\
\hline
64{,}152
\end{array}
$$

3. 488,670 **4.** 292,274

5. 338,469 **6.** 366,014

7. 2,684,478 **8.** 11,966,589

9. 14,907,298 **10.** 29,522,932

11. 83,250 **12.** 528,768

13. 544,260 **14.** 13,288,582

Page 113

1. 218,592

2. 123,344

Multiply by 3 ones. Multiply by 9 tens. Multiply by 5 hundreds. Carry when needed. Add the partial products.

$$
\begin{array}{r}
208 \\
\times\ 593 \\
\hline
624 \\
18\ 72 \\
+\ 104\ 0 \\
\hline
123{,}344
\end{array}
$$

3. 670,714 **4.** 51,435

5. 84,258 **6.** 803,926

7. 3,189,030 **8.** 4,800,474

9. 837,753 **10.** 1,978,880

11. 1,499,300 **12.** 15,554,354

13. 12,853,162 **14.** 30,592,185

15. 38,563,200

Page 114

1. 175,821

2. 387,200

Multiply by 5 ones. Multiply by 0 tens. Put a 0 in the tens column. Multiply by 6 hundreds, and put the partial product to the left of the zero. Add the partial products.

$$
\begin{array}{r}
640 \\
\times\ 605 \\
\hline
3\ 200 \\
0\ 00 \\
+\ 384\ 0 \\
\hline
387{,}200
\end{array}
$$

3. 439,488 **4.** 233,640

5. 122,800 **6.** 2,736,000

7. 2,920,000 **8.** 1,706,400

9. 981,400 **10.** 5,400,000

11. 6,512,500 **12.** 45,513,816

13. 29,016,000 **14.** 5,023,012

Page 115

1. 189,958

2. 291,500

Multiply by 0 ones. Write one zero in the ones column. Multiply by 0 tens. Write one 0 in the tens column. Multiply by 5 hundreds. $5 \times 3 = 15$ hundreds. $5 \times 8 = 40$ thousands. $5 \times 5 = 25$ ten thousands. Write 291,500 to the left of the two zeros.

$$
\begin{array}{r}
583 \\
\times\ 500 \\
\hline
291{,}500
\end{array}
$$

3. 67,946 **4.** 348,870

5. 281,800 **6.** 3,987,456

7. 6,644,800 **8.** 8,344,400

9. 4,396,098 **10.** 16,296,000

11. 62,747,115 **12.** 6,800,000

Page 116

1.
$$
\begin{array}{r}
\$20{,}000 \\
\$400 \\
\times\ \ 50 \\
\hline
\$20{,}000
\end{array}
$$

2.
$$
\begin{array}{r}
\$4{,}000 \\
\$400 \\
\times\ \ 10 \\
\hline
\$4{,}000
\end{array}
$$

3.
$$
\begin{array}{r}
\$1{,}000 \\
\$100 \\
\times\ \ 10 \\
\hline
\$1{,}000
\end{array}
$$

4.
$$
\begin{array}{r}
\$700 \\
\$70 \\
\times\ \ 10 \\
\hline
\$700
\end{array}
$$

Page 117

5.
$$
\begin{array}{r}
\$500 \\
\$50 \\
\times\ 10 \\
\hline
\$500
\end{array}
$$

6.
$$
\begin{array}{r}
\$500 \\
\$10 \\
\times\ 50 \\
\hline
\$500
\end{array}
$$

7.
$$
\begin{array}{r}
\$40 \\
\$10 \\
\times\ \ 4 \\
\hline
\$40
\end{array}
$$

8.
$$
\begin{array}{r}
\$2{,}500 \\
\$50 \\
\times\ 50 \\
\hline
\$2{,}500
\end{array}
$$

9.
$$
\begin{array}{r}
\$1{,}000 \\
\$100 \\
\times\ \ 10 \\
\hline
\$1{,}000
\end{array}
$$

10. No.
$$
\begin{array}{r}
\$20 \\
\times\ 20 \\
\hline
\$400 \\
\$400 < \$600
\end{array}
$$

Unit 4 Review, page 118

1.	81	**2.**	35
3.	72	**4.**	24
5.	24	**6.**	21
7.	40	**8.**	0
9.	46	**10.**	80
11.	328	**12.**	48
13.	189	**14.**	663
15.	2,877	**16.**	426
17.	180	**18.**	2,109
19.	2,010	**20.**	63,009
21.	24,800	**22.**	6,028
23.	504	**24.**	680
25.	5,061	**26.**	4,228
27.	19,500	**28.**	387,903
29.	274,296	**30.**	96,960
31.	745,984	**32.**	4,480,056

Page 119

33.	41,480	**34.**	56,700
35.	209,916	**36.**	2,962,862
37.	46,299,000	**38.**	470
39.	1,890	**40.**	15,700
41.	289,000	**42.**	2,586,000
43.	10,000,000	**44.**	3,600
45.	295,000	**46.**	250
47.	340,600	**48.**	267
49.	2,043	**50.**	44,940
51.	46,600	**52.**	6,814
53.	90,054	**54.**	320,616
55.	42,140	**56.**	138,402
57.	891,810	**58.**	1,875
59.	1,794	**60.**	24,752
61.	26,708	**62.**	343,246
63.	362,970		

Page 120

64.	321,245	**65.**	842,022
66.	1,645,494	**67.**	1,786,173
68.	560,700	**69.**	1,166,388
70.	13,383,500	**71.**	403,088
72.	749,997	**73.**	105,763
74.	99,770	**75.**	607,221
76.	79,184	**77.**	81,200
78.	737,836	**79.**	8,112,936
80.	19,734,000		

Unit 5

Page 121

1. 10

2. 30

7 > 5, so 27 rounds up to 30.

3.	50	**4.**	70

5. 200

6. 600

5 = 5, so 550 rounds up to 600.

7.	600	**8.**	400

Page 122

9. 2

10. 114

Line up the digits.
Subtract.

```
  468
− 354
  114
```

11. 0

12. 109

13. 103

14. 3,343

```
         9  9
     4 10 10 10
     5, 0  0  0
   − 1, 6  5  7
     3, 3  4  3
```

15.	5,065	**16.**	126
17.	5	**18.**	8
19.	7	**20.**	8
21.	192	**22.**	3,243

```
     47
   × 69
    423
 + 2 82
  3,243
```

23.	28,250	**24.**	35,224
25.	8	**26.**	3
27.	9	**28.**	8
29.	29,385	**30.**	3,626
31.	575,946	**32.**	156,624

Page 123

1.	0	1	2	3	4	5	6	7	8	9
2.	0	1	2	3	4	5	6	7	8	9
3.	0	1	2	3	4	5	6	7	8	9
4.	0	1	2	3	4	5	6	7	8	9
5.	0	1	2	3	4	5	6	7	8	9
6.	0	1	2	3	4	5	6	7	8	9
7.	0	1	2	3	4	5	6	7	8	9
8.	0	1	2	3	4	5	6	7	8	9
9.	0	1	2	3	4	5	6	7	8	9

Page 124

1. 4

2. 2

Find the smaller number, 7, in the farthest row on the left. Then move to the right along the row until you find the larger number, 14. Move to the top of the column to find the answer, 2.

3.	4	**4.**	3
5.	5	**6.**	6

7. 2   8. 7
9. 7   10. 5
11. 9   12. 9
13. 8   14. 6
15. 8   16. 7
17. 3   18. 8

Page 125

1. 2
2. 3

Find the smaller number, 4 in the farthest row on the left. Then move to the right along the row until you find the larger number, 12. Move to the top of the column to findthe answer, 3.

3. 0   4. 2
5. 5   6. 6
7. 6   8. 9
9. 35   10. 42
11. 45   12. 0
13. 9   14. 9
15. 8   16. 5
17. 14   18. 4
19. 21   20. 5
21. 9   22. 6
23. 4   24. 36
25. 40   26. 7
27. 5   28. 6
29. 8   30. 64
31. 2   32. 7

33.–41. Answers may vary.

33. $6 \div 2 = 3$ 34. $2 \div 1 = 2$
$3 \div 1 = 3$ $4 \div 2 = 2$
$9 \div 3 = 3$ $6 \div 3 = 2$
$12 \div 4 = 3$ $8 \div 4 = 2$
$15 \div 5 = 3$ $10 \div 5 = 2$
$18 \div 6 = 3$ $12 \div 6 = 2$
$21 \div 7 = 3$ $14 \div 7 = 2$
$24 \div 8 = 3$ $16 \div 8 = 2$
$27 \div 9 = 3$ $18 \div 9 = 2$

35. $4 \div 1 = 4$ 36. $0 \div 0 = 0$
$8 \div 2 = 4$ $0 \div 1 = 0$
$12 \div 3 = 4$ $0 \div 2 = 0$
$16 \div 4 = 4$ $0 \div 3 = 0$
$20 \div 5 = 4$ $0 \div 4 = 0$
$24 \div 6 = 4$ $0 \div 5 = 0$
$28 \div 7 = 4$ $0 \div 6 = 0$
$32 \div 8 = 4$ $0 \div 7 = 0$
$36 \div 9 = 4$ $0 \div 8 = 0$
    $0 \div 9 = 0$

37. $8 \div 1 = 8$ 38. $7 \div 1 = 7$
$16 \div 2 = 8$ $14 \div 2 = 7$
$24 \div 3 = 8$ $21 \div 3 = 7$
$32 \div 4 = 8$ $28 \div 4 = 7$
$40 \div 5 = 8$ $35 \div 5 = 7$
$48 \div 6 = 8$ $42 \div 6 = 7$
$56 \div 7 = 8$ $49 \div 7 = 7$
$64 \div 8 = 8$ $56 \div 8 = 7$
$72 \div 9 = 8$ $63 \div 9 = 7$

39. $5 \div 1 = 5$ 40. $9 \div 1 = 9$
$10 \div 2 = 5$ $18 \div 2 = 9$
$15 \div 3 = 5$ $27 \div 3 = 9$
$20 \div 4 = 5$ $36 \div 4 = 9$
$25 \div 5 = 5$ $45 \div 5 = 9$
$30 \div 6 = 5$ $54 \div 6 = 9$
$35 \div 7 = 5$ $63 \div 7 = 9$
$40 \div 8 = 5$ $72 \div 8 = 9$
$45 \div 9 = 5$ $81 \div 9 = 9$

41. $6 \div 1 = 6$
$12 \div 2 = 6$
$18 \div 3 = 6$
$24 \div 4 = 6$
$30 \div 5 = 6$
$36 \div 6 = 6$
$42 \div 7 = 6$
$48 \div 8 = 6$
$54 \div 9 = 6$

Page 126

1. 5
2. 6

Check division by multiplying the answer, 6, by the number you divided by, 6.

$$\begin{array}{r} 6 \\ \times\, 6 \\ \hline 36 \end{array}$$

3. 9   4. 9
5. 5   6. 7
7. 9   8. 8
9. 0   10. 7
11. 7   12. 8
13. 5   14. 7
15. 8   16. 9

Page 127

1. 4
2. 9

Divide. Since you can't divide 4 by 5 evenly, divide 45 by 5. $45 \div 5 = 9$. Check division by multiplying the answer, 9, by the number you divided by, 5.

$$5\overline{)45}^{\,9} \qquad \begin{array}{r} 9 \\ \times\, 5 \\ \hline 45 \end{array}$$

3. 9   4. 6
5. 21   6. 32

195

7. 72   **8.** 61
9. 21   **10.** 21
11. 71   **12.** 51
13. 93   **14.** 42
15. 63   **16.** 71
17. 91   **18.** 71
19. 61   **20.** 64

Page 128

1. 42
2. 64

Divide. Since you can't divide 3 by 6 evenly, divide 38 by 6. $38 \div 6$ isn't a basic fact, so use the closest fact, $36 \div 6 = 6$. Multiply. $6 \times 6 = 36$. Subtract. $38 - 36 = 2$. Bring down the 4. $24 \div 6 = 4$. Check by multiplying.

$$
\begin{array}{r}
64 \\
6\overline{)384} \\
-36 \\
\hline
24 \\
-24 \\
\hline
0
\end{array}
\qquad
\begin{array}{r}
64 \\
\times 6 \\
\hline
384
\end{array}
$$

3. 55   **4.** 46
5. 82   **6.** 94
7. 86   **8.** 54
9. 86   **10.** 95
11. 56   **12.** 48
13. 32   **14.** 53
15. 67   **16.** 52

Page 129

1. 5 R2
2. 3 R1

Use the basic facts. $10 \div 3 = 3$, with an amount left over. Multiply $3 \times 3 = 9$. Subtract. $10 - 9 = 1$. The remainder is 1. Check by multiplying and adding the remainder.

$$
\begin{array}{r}
3 \;\; R1 \\
3\overline{)10} \\
-9 \\
\hline
1
\end{array}
\qquad
\begin{array}{r}
3 \\
\times 3 \\
\hline
9 \\
+1 \\
\hline
10
\end{array}
$$

3. 3 R3   **4.** 8 R3
5. 3 R2   **6.** 5 R4
7. 5 R1   **8.** 8 R2
9. 5 R1   **10.** 7 R1
11. 9 R7   **12.** 7 R1
13. 7 R3   **14.** 8 R1
15. 5 R4   **16.** 5 R2

Page 130

1. 29 R5
2. 38 R2

Divide. $19 \div 5 = 3$, with an amount left over. Multiply. $3 \times 5 = 15$. Subtract. $19 - 15 = 4$. Bring down 2. Divide. $42 \div 5 = 8$ and an amount left over. Multiply. $5 \times 8 = 40$. Subtract. $42 - 40 = 2$. 2 is the remainder. Check by multiplying and adding the remainder.

$$
\begin{array}{r}
38 \;\; R2 \\
5\overline{)192} \\
-15 \\
\hline
42 \\
-40 \\
\hline
2
\end{array}
\qquad
\begin{array}{r}
38 \\
\times 5 \\
\hline
190 \\
+2 \\
\hline
192
\end{array}
$$

3. 45 R2   **4.** 47 R1
5. 63 R2   **6.** 98 R3
7. 82 R1   **8.** 72 R4
9. 77 R2   **10.** 59 R1
11. 69 R1   **12.** 94 R2

Page 131

1. 214 R1
2. 224 R2

Divide. $6 \div 3 = 2$. Multiply. $2 \times 3 = 6$. Subtract. $6 - 6 = 0$. Bring down the 7. $7 \div 3 = 2$, plus an amount left over. Multiply. $2 \times 3 = 6$. Subtract. $7 - 6 = 1$. Bring down the 4. $14 \div 3 = 4$, plus an amount left over. Multiply. $4 \times 3 = 12$. Subtract. $14 - 12 = 2$. The remainder is 2.

$$
\begin{array}{r}
224 \;\; R2 \\
3\overline{)674} \\
-6 \\
\hline
07 \\
-6 \\
\hline
14 \\
-12 \\
\hline
2
\end{array}
\qquad
\begin{array}{r}
224 \\
\times 3 \\
\hline
672 \\
+2 \\
\hline
674
\end{array}
$$

3. 239 R1   **4.** 218 R3
5. 2,371 R2   **6.** 2,663 R2
7. 1,131 R3   **8.** 1,122 R3
9. 1,337 R2   **10.** 1,347 R3
11. 1,763 R1   **12.** 1,294 R5

Page 132

1. $36

Divide the total, $144, by 4.

$$
\begin{array}{r}
\$\,36 \\
4\overline{)\$144} \\
-12 \\
\hline
24 \\
-24 \\
\hline
0
\end{array}
$$

Divide. 14 ÷ 4 = 3, plus an amount left over. Multiply. 3 × 4 = 12. Subtract. 14 − 12 = 2. Bring down the 4. Divide. 24 ÷ 4 = 6. Multiply. 6 × 4 = 24. Subtract. 24 − 24 = 0. There is no remainder. Each person paid $36.

2. $6

```
    $ 6
4 )$24
   − 24
      0
```

3. $145

```
        $145
4 )$580
   − 4
     18
   − 16
     20
   − 20
      0
```

4. $116

```
        $116
5 )$580
   − 5
     08
   − 5
     30
   − 30
      0
```

Page 133

1.	8	**2.**	30
3.	9	**4.**	8
5.	7	**6.**	17
7.	4	**8.**	8
9.	41	**10.**	128
11.	72	**12.**	69
13.	609	**14.**	91
15.	350	**16.**	21
17.	2 R4	**18.**	7 R2
19.	66	**20.**	7 R2
21.	250	**22.**	3 R5
23.	364	**24.**	8 R1
25.	17	**26.**	1,980
27.	98	**28.**	37 R3
29.	662	**30.**	65
31.	522	**32.**	556
33.	88 R1		

Page 134

1. 438 R5

2. 269

Divide. 16 ÷ 6 = 2, with an amount left over. Multiply. 2 × 6 = 12. Subtract. 16 − 12 = 4. Bring down the 1. Divide. 41 ÷ 6 = 6, plus an amount left over. Multiply. 6 × 6 = 36. Subtract. 41 − 36 = 5. Bring down the 4. Divide. 54 ÷ 6 = 9. Multiply. 9 × 6 = 54. Subtract. 54 − 54 = 0. There is no remainder.

```
        269
6 )1,614             269
   − 1 2            ×    6
      41            1,614
   − 36
      54
    − 54
       0
```

3.	427 R2	**4.**	644 R2
5.	733 R3	**6.**	728 R4
7.	243	**8.**	368 R3
9.	889 R1	**10.**	469 R3
11.	633 R1	**12.**	424 R2

Page 135

1. 361 R8

2. 861

Divide. 68 ÷ 8 = 8, plus an amount left over. Multiply. 8 × 8 = 64. Subtract. 68 − 64 = 4. Bring down the 8. Divide. 48 ÷ 8 = 6. Multiply. 6 × 8 = 48. Subtract. 48 − 48 = 0. Bring down the 8. Divide. 8 ÷ 8 = 1. Multiply. 1 × 8 = 8. Subtract. 8 − 8 = 0. There is no remainder.

```
        861
8 )6,888             861
   − 6 4            ×    8
      48            6,888
    − 48
      08
     − 8
       0
```

3.	6,122 R5	**4.**	9,581
5.	6,314	**6.**	5,295 R1
7.	16,897 R1	**8.**	7,158 R5
9.	9,215 R1	**10.**	9,126 R2

Page 136

1. 15

2. 26 R1

Divide. 20 ÷ 8 = 2, plus an amount left over. Multiply. 2 × 8 = 16. Subtract. 20 − 16 = 4. Bring down the 9. Divide. 49 ÷ 8 = 6, plus an amount left over. Multiply 6 × 8 = 48. Subtract 49 − 48 = 1. There is a remainder of 1.

```
      26 R1
8 )209               26
   − 16            ×    8
     49               208
   − 48             +    1
      1               209
```

3.	84	**4.**	81 R1
5.	751		

6. 286 R6

Divide. 20 ÷ 7 = 2, plus an amount left over.
Multiply. 2 × 7 = 14. Subtract. 20 − 14 = 6.
Bring down the 0. Divide. 60 ÷ 7 = 8, plus
an amount left over. Multiply. 8 × 7 = 56.
Subtract. 60 − 56 = 4. Bring down the 8.
Divide. 48 ÷ 7 = 6. Multiply. 6 × 7 = 42.
Subtract. The remainder is 6.

$$
\begin{array}{r}
286\ \text{R6} \\
7)\overline{2{,}008} \\
-14 \\
\hline
60 \\
-56 \\
\hline
48 \\
-42 \\
\hline
6
\end{array}
\qquad
\begin{array}{r}
286 \\
\times\ 7 \\
\hline
2{,}002 \\
+\ 6 \\
\hline
2{,}008
\end{array}
$$

7. 833 R5   **8.** 1,625 R7

9. 5,358 R2   **10.** 1,667 R4

Page 137

1. 400

2. 600

Divide. 30 ÷ 5 = 6. Multiply, subtract, and
bring down 0. 6 × 5 = 30. 30 − 30 = 0.
Divide. 0 ÷ 5 = 0. Multiply, subtract, and
bring down the last 0. Multiply and
subtract. There is no remainder.

$$
\begin{array}{r}
600 \\
5)\overline{3{,}000} \\
-30 \\
\hline
00 \\
-0 \\
\hline
00 \\
-0 \\
\hline
0
\end{array}
\qquad
\begin{array}{r}
600 \\
\times\ 5 \\
\hline
3{,}000
\end{array}
$$

3. 400   **4.** 2,000

5. 8,000   **6.** 6,000

7. 6,000   **8.** 4,000

9. 8,000   **10.** 9,000

11. 7,000   **12.** 8,000

Page 138

1. $40

Round $209 to the nearest hundred. $209
rounds to $200. To split $200 into 5 equal
amounts, divide by 5.

$$
\begin{array}{r}
\$40 \\
5)\overline{\$200} \\
-20 \\
\hline
00 \\
-0 \\
\hline
0
\end{array}
\qquad
\begin{array}{r}
\$40 \\
\times\ 5 \\
\hline
\$200
\end{array}
$$

They will pay about $40 each month.

2. $50

$$
\begin{array}{r}
\$50 \\
8)\overline{\$400} \\
-40 \\
\hline
00 \\
-0 \\
\hline
0
\end{array}
\qquad
\begin{array}{r}
\$50 \\
\times\ 8 \\
\hline
\$400
\end{array}
$$

They will pay about $50 each month.

3. $120

$$
\begin{array}{r}
\$120 \\
5)\overline{\$600} \\
-5 \\
\hline
10 \\
-10 \\
\hline
00 \\
-0 \\
\hline
0
\end{array}
\qquad
\begin{array}{r}
\$120 \\
\times\ 5 \\
\hline
\$600
\end{array}
$$

He will pay about $120 each month.

4. $75

$$
\begin{array}{r}
\$75 \\
8)\overline{\$600} \\
-56 \\
\hline
40 \\
-40 \\
\hline
0
\end{array}
\qquad
\begin{array}{r}
\$75 \\
\times\ 8 \\
\hline
\$600
\end{array}
$$

He will pay about $75 each month.

Page 139

5. $2,400

$$
\begin{array}{r}
\$2{,}400 \\
2)\overline{\$4{,}800} \\
-4 \\
\hline
08 \\
-8 \\
\hline
00 \\
-0 \\
\hline
00 \\
-0 \\
\hline
0
\end{array}
\qquad
\begin{array}{r}
\$2{,}400 \\
\times\ 2 \\
\hline
\$4{,}800
\end{array}
$$

Each payment will be about $2,400.

6. $800

$$
\begin{array}{r}
\$800 \\
6)\overline{\$4{,}800} \\
-48 \\
\hline
00 \\
-0 \\
\hline
00 \\
-0 \\
\hline
0
\end{array}
\qquad
\begin{array}{r}
\$800 \\
\times\ 6 \\
\hline
\$4{,}800
\end{array}
$$

He will pay about $800 each month.

7. $1,200

$$4 \overline{)\$4,800}$$
$$\frac{-\ 4}{\ \ 0\ 8}$$
$$\frac{-\ 8}{\ \ \ 00}$$
$$\frac{-\ 0}{\ \ \ \ 00}$$
$$\frac{-\ 0}{\ \ \ \ \ 0}$$

$1,200
$$\begin{array}{r} \$1,200 \\ \times\ \ \ \ 4 \\ \hline \$4,800 \end{array}$$

He will pay about $1,200 each month.

8. $1,025

$$8 \overline{)\$8,200}$$
$$\frac{-\ 8}{\ \ 0\ 20}$$
$$\frac{-\ 16}{\ \ \ \ 40}$$
$$\frac{-\ 40}{\ \ \ \ \ 0}$$

$1,025
$$\begin{array}{r} \$1,025 \\ \times\ \ \ \ 8 \\ \hline \$8,200 \end{array}$$

Each payment will be about $1,025.

9. $300

$$2 \overline{)\$600}$$
$$\frac{-\ 6}{\ \ 00}$$
$$\frac{-\ 0}{\ \ \ 00}$$
$$\frac{-\ 0}{\ \ \ \ 0}$$

$300
$$\begin{array}{r} \$300 \\ \times\ \ \ 2 \\ \hline \$600 \end{array}$$

Each payment will be about $300.

10. $50

$$12 \overline{)\$600}$$
$$\frac{-\ 60}{\ \ \ 00}$$
$$\frac{-\ 0}{\ \ \ \ 0}$$

$50
$$\begin{array}{r} \$50 \\ \times\ \ 12 \\ \hline 100 \\ +\ 50 \\ \hline \$600 \end{array}$$

Each payment will be about $50.

11. $200

$$2 \overline{)\$400}$$
$$\frac{-\ 4}{\ \ 00}$$
$$\frac{-\ 0}{\ \ \ 00}$$
$$\frac{-\ 0}{\ \ \ \ 0}$$

$200
$$\begin{array}{r} \$200 \\ \times\ \ \ 2 \\ \hline \$400 \end{array}$$

Each department will pay about $200 a month.

12. $50

$$4 \overline{)\$200}$$
$$\frac{-\ 20}{\ \ \ 00}$$
$$\frac{-\ 0}{\ \ \ \ 0}$$

$50
$$\begin{array}{r} \$50 \\ \times\ \ 4 \\ \hline \$200 \end{array}$$

Each payment will be about $50.

Page 140

1. 3 R2

2. 4 R2

Estimate how many times 12 goes into 50 by dividing 5 by 1. $5 \div 1 = 5$. Write 5 above the 0 and multiply. $5 \times 12 = 60$, which is too large. Try 4. Multiply. $4 \times 12 = 48$. Subtract. $50 - 48 = 2$. The answer is 4, plus a remainder of 2.

$$12 \overline{)50} \quad \overset{4\ R2}{}$$
$$\frac{-\ 48}{\ \ \ 2}$$

$$\begin{array}{r} 12 \\ \times\ \ 4 \\ \hline 48 \\ +\ 2 \\ \hline 50 \end{array}$$

3. 3   **4.** 2
5. 15   **6.** 16 R2
7. 12 R5   **8.** 13 R3
9. 29 R15   **10.** 12
11. 14 R30   **12.** 13 R7

Page 141

1. 3 R24

2. 7 R8

Estimate how many times 22 goes into 162 by dividing 16 by 2. $16 \div 2 = 8$. Write 8 above the 2. Multiply. $8 \times 22 = 176$, which is too large. Try 7. $7 \times 22 = 154$. Subtract. $162 - 154 = 8$. The answer is 7, plus a remainder of 8.

$$22 \overline{)162} \quad \overset{7\ R8}{}$$
$$\frac{-\ 154}{\ \ \ 8}$$

$$\begin{array}{r} 22 \\ \times\ \ 7 \\ \hline 154 \\ +\ 8 \\ \hline 162 \end{array}$$

3. 7 R29   **4.** 6 R3
5. 45   **6.** 29 R26
7. 52 R28   **8.** 86 R28
9. 87 R25   **10.** 71 R18
11. 77 R60

Page 142

1. 169 R18

2. 96

Divide. 51 rounds down to 50. Estimate how many times 51 goes into 4,896 by dividing 48 by 5. $48 \div 5 = 9$. Put 9 above the 9. Multiply. $9 \times 51 = 459$. Subtract, and bring down. $489 - 459 = 30$. Estimate how many times 51 goes into 306 by dividing 30 by 5. $30 \div 5 = 6$. Multiply. $6 \times 51 = 306$. Subtract. $306 - 306 = 0$. There is no remainder.

$$\begin{array}{r} 96 \\ 51\overline{)4{,}896} \\ -4\,59 \\ \hline 306 \\ -306 \\ \hline 0 \end{array} \qquad \begin{array}{r} 96 \\ \times 51 \\ \hline 96 \\ +480 \\ \hline 4{,}896 \end{array}$$

3.	51 R56	**4.**	114 R20
5.	1,121	**6.**	751 R21
7.	566 R10	**8.**	1,159
9.	812 R16	**10.**	1,124 R8
11.	1,912		

Page 143

1. 35

2. 31

Divide, multiply, subtract, and bring down.

$$\begin{array}{r} 31 \\ 30\overline{)930} \\ -90 \\ \hline 30 \\ -30 \\ \hline 0 \end{array} \qquad \begin{array}{r} 31 \\ \times 30 \\ \hline 930 \end{array}$$

3.	84 R25	**4.**	59 R2
5.	65	**6.**	1,821
7.	2,934	**8.**	988
9.	625 R7	**10.**	1,911
11.	8,631	**12.**	852
13.	466	**14.**	1,312 R36

Page 144

1.	82	**2.**	9
3.	98	**4.**	7
5.	2,623	**6.**	12
7.	13	**8.**	3 R1
9.	100	**10.**	9
11.	2,970	**12.**	49
13.	4,900	**14.**	70
15.	130	**16.**	16,290
17.	182 R32	**18.**	304
19.	26	**20.**	562 R9
21.	45,888	**22.**	48
23.	86		

Page 145

24.	2,722	**25.**	76 R3
26.	388,800	**27.**	721 R2
28.	684,432	**29.**	2,943
30.	16,413	**31.**	8,327
32.	117 R20	**33.**	4,862,053
34.	1,570	**35.**	5,837
36.	8,878	**37.**	2,376 R8
38.	818,000	**39.**	629
40.	755 R5	**41.**	926,480
42.	66,572		

Page 146

1. Bunty

Find the unit price of Diva paper towels. 94 cents $\div$ 2 = 47 cents. Compare the prices. 49 cents > 47 cents. Bunty costs more.

2. Meaty Chow

80 cents $\div$ 4 = 20 cents. $85 \div 5 = 17$ cents. 20 > 17. Meaty Chow costs more.

3. Italia

63 cents $\div$ 8 = 7 cents R7. 90 cents $\div$ 10 = 9 cents. 9 > 7 R7. Italia costs more.

4. 3 cents

Find how much one pound of onions costs. 57 cents $\div$ 3 = 19 cents. 20 cents − 19 cents = 1 cent. You will save 1 cent per pound or 3 cents.

Page 147

1. 13

2. 12

Divide 8,304 by 692 by estimating how many times 6 goes into 8. $8 \div 6 = 1$, plus an amount left over. Multiply. $692 \times 1 = 692$. Subtract. $830 - 692 = 138$. Bring down the 4. Divide 1384 by 692 by estimating how many times 6 goes into 13. $13 \div 6 = 2$, plus an amount left over. Multiply. $692 \times 2 = 1384$. Subtract. $1384 - 1384 = 0$. There is no remainder.

$$\begin{array}{r} 12 \\ 692\overline{)8{,}304} \\ -6\,92 \\ \hline 1\,384 \\ -1\,384 \\ \hline 0 \end{array} \qquad \begin{array}{r} 692 \\ \times\ 12 \\ \hline 1\,384 \\ +6\,92 \\ \hline 8{,}304 \end{array}$$

3.	14 R5	**4.**	11 R143
5.	18	**6.**	57
7.	92 R5	**8.**	17
9.	7 R6		

Page 148

1. 318
2. 911 R30
   Divide, multiply, subtract, and bring down.

$$
\begin{array}{r}
911\ \text{R30} \\
653\overline{)594{,}913} \\
-587\ 7 \\
\hline
7\ 21 \\
-6\ 53 \\
\hline
683 \\
-653 \\
\hline
30
\end{array}
\qquad
\begin{array}{r}
911 \\
\times\ 653 \\
\hline
2\ 733 \\
45\ 55 \\
+546\ 6 \\
\hline
594{,}883 \\
+\qquad 30 \\
\hline
594{,}913
\end{array}
$$

3. 68
4. 242 R214
5. 157
6. 867 R49
7. 817 R151
8. 118 R278
9. 479

Page 149

1. 203
2. 1,002
   Divide, multiply, subtract, and bring down.
   7 is larger than zero, so you can't divide.
   Put 0 in the answer, and bring down the 1.
   7 > 1, so put another zero in the answer and
   bring down the 4. Divide. 14 ÷ 7 = 2.
   Multiply. 2 × 7 = 14. Subtract. 14 − 14 = 0.
   There is no remainder.

$$
\begin{array}{r}
1{,}002 \\
7\overline{)7{,}014} \\
-7 \\
\hline
0\ 0 \\
-\ 0 \\
\hline
01 \\
-\ 0 \\
\hline
14 \\
-14 \\
\hline
0
\end{array}
\qquad
\begin{array}{r}
1{,}002 \\
\times\qquad 7 \\
\hline
7{,}014
\end{array}
$$

3. 506
4. 806
5. 402
6. 803 R37
7. 506 R3
8. 103
9. 902 R1

Page 150

1. 306 R2
2. 6,002 R5
   Divide, multiply, subtract, and bring down.
   Repeat as many times as necessary to solve
   the problem.

$$
\begin{array}{r}
6{,}002\ \text{R5} \\
9\overline{)54{,}023} \\
-54 \\
\hline
0\ 0 \\
-\ 0 \\
\hline
02 \\
-\ 0 \\
\hline
23 \\
-18 \\
\hline
5
\end{array}
\qquad
\begin{array}{r}
6{,}002 \\
\times\qquad 9 \\
\hline
54{,}018 \\
+\qquad 5 \\
\hline
54{,}023
\end{array}
$$

3. 5,090 R2
4. 808 R1
5. 5,020
6. 900 R14
7. 750 R19
8. 601
9. 100

Page 151

1. 156 stands

$$
\begin{array}{r}
156 \\
100\overline{)15{,}600} \\
-10\ 0 \\
\hline
5\ 60 \\
-5\ 00 \\
\hline
600 \\
-600 \\
\hline
0
\end{array}
$$

   She delivered to 156 stands.

2. 19,665 papers

$$
\begin{array}{r}
19{,}665 \\
3\overline{)58{,}995} \\
-3 \\
\hline
28 \\
-27 \\
\hline
1\ 9 \\
-1\ 8 \\
\hline
19 \\
-18 \\
\hline
15 \\
-15 \\
\hline
0
\end{array}
$$

   She delivered 19,665 papers each day.

3. 806 bundles

$$
\begin{array}{r}
806 \\
25\overline{)20{,}150} \\
-20\ 0 \\
\hline
150 \\
-150 \\
\hline
0
\end{array}
$$

   She delivered 806 bundles.

4. $2

$$
\begin{array}{r}
\$2 \\
150\overline{)300} \\
-300 \\
\hline
0
\end{array}
$$

   He charged $2 for each paper.

Unit 5 Review, page 152

1.	3	**2.**	3
3.	8	**4.**	9
5.	6	**6.**	5
7.	5	**8.**	5
9.	4	**10.**	0
11.	12	**12.**	132
13.	111	**14.**	41
15.	71	**16.**	231
17.	241	**18.**	91
19.	29	**20.**	54
21.	233	**22.**	53 R6
23.	39 R3	**24.**	358 R7
25.	5,579 R1	**26.**	125
27.	432	**28.**	15,141
29.	3,341		

Page 153

30.	2	**31.**	3
32.	3	**33.**	2
34.	9	**35.**	26 R5
36.	77 R45	**37.**	211
38.	72 R5	**39.**	442 R20
40.	937	**41.**	65 R50
42.	216 R5	**43.**	312
44.	329	**45.**	356 R27
46.	1,181 R4	**47.**	4,751

Page 154

48.	2 R163	**49.**	1 R69
50.	1 R70	**51.**	1 R332
52.	7 R177	**53.**	1 R726
54.	36 R26	**55.**	51
56.	10,994 R1	**57.**	20 R120
58.	50	**59.**	60
60.	190	**61.**	250

Unit 6

Page 155

1. 47

2. 72

Line up the digits. Add the ones. $5 + 7 = 12$. Carry 1 ten. Add the tens. $1 + 2 + 4 = 7$

$$\begin{array}{r} 1 \\ 25 \\ + 47 \\ \hline 72 \end{array}$$

3.	251	**4.**	150
5.	885	**6.**	2,100
7.	7,305	**8.**	10,993
9.	41,100	**10.**	112,037

Page 156

11. 53

12. 10

Line up the digits. Subtract the ones. $4 - 4 = 0$. Subtract the tens. $8 - 7 = 1$.

$$\begin{array}{r} 84 \\ - 74 \\ \hline 10 \end{array}$$

13.	47	**14.**	158
15.	79	**16.**	2,488
17.	3,277	**18.**	4,358
19.	5,830	**20.**	10,359
21.	128		
22.	600		

Multiply by 0 ones. Multiply by 3 tens. Add the partial products.

$$\begin{array}{r} 20 \\ \times 30 \\ \hline 00 \\ + 60 \\ \hline 600 \end{array}$$

23.	1,476	**24.**	267
25.	3,240	**26.**	4,140
27.	26,871	**28.**	278,388
29.	128,940	**30.**	206,500
31.	51		
32.	61 R5		

Divide. $43 \div 7 = 6$, plus an amount left over. Multiply. $7 \times 6 = 42$. Subtract. $43 - 42 = 1$. Bring down 1. Divide. $12 \div 7 = 1$, plus an amount left over. Multiply $7 \times 1 = 7$. Subtract. $12 - 7 = 5$. There is a remainder of five.

$$\begin{array}{r} 61 \ R5 \\ 7\overline{)432} \\ - 42 \\ \hline 12 \\ - 7 \\ \hline 5 \end{array}$$

33.	104	**34.**	70
35.	92		

Page 157

1. 255

$5 + 250 = 255$ milligrams. There were 255 total milligrams of cholesterol in his breakfast.

2. 150

$75 \times 2 = 150$ milligrams. She will take in 150 milligrams of cholesterol.

3. b, 134

$67 \times 2 = 134$ milligrams of cholesterol in 6 ounces of chicken.

4. c, 8

$75 - 67 = 8$. There are 8 more milligrams of cholesterol in 3 ounces of beef.

Page 158

1. 72

$6 \times 12 = 72$. The cord is 72 inches long.

2. 3,520

$2 \times 1,760 = 3,520$. There are 3,520 yards in 2 miles.

3. c, 108

$9 \times 12 = 108$. Each board is 108 inches long.

4. b, 3

$9 \div 3 = 3$. Each board is 3 yards long.

Page 159

1. 30

$80 - 50 = 30$ inches. Thirty more inches of rain fell in July.

2. July $40 \times 2 = 80$

The rainfall for August was half the rainfall for July.

3. d, 5

$10 - 5 = 5$. Five more inches of rain fell in April.

4. a, 120

$80 + 40 = 120$. 120 total inches of rain fell in July and August.

Page 160

1. 3,240

$500 + 1,120 + 1,120 + 500 = 3,240$. Carolyn walks 3,240 feet in one round trip.

2. 1,620

$500 + 1,120 = 1,620$. She walked 1,620 feet.

Page 161

3. 2,000 feet

$500 + 500 + 500 + 500 = 2,000$. She walked 2,000 feet in all.

4. 3,620 feet

$1,120 + 1,000 + 500 + 500 + 500 = 3,620$. Brad drove a total of 3,620 feet.

5. B, C, H, G

6. 3,000 feet

$500 + 500 + 500 + 500 + 500 + 500 = 3,000$ feet (or $500 \times 6 = 3,000$)

7. No

$500 + 500 + 500 + 500 + 500 + 500 = 3,000$ (or $500 \times 6 = 3,000$). The perimeter of the park is the same as the distance Bob walked.

8. 5,500 feet

$500 \times 11 = 5,500$. The length of the shortest path would be 5,500 feet.

Page 162

1. $40

$2 \times \$100 = \$200$. $2 \times \$10 = \$20$. $\$20 \times 12 = \$240$. $\$240 - \$200 = \$40$. They will save $40.

2. $168

$4 \times \$7 = \$28$. $\$28 \times 6 = \$168$. The grandparents spend $168 for the 6 concerts.

Page 163

3. 302

$1,595 + 100 + 530 = 2,225$. $2,527 - 2,225 = 302$. They sold 302 senior citizens' tickets.

4. 2,750

$100 + 150 = 250$. $3,000 - 250 = 2,750$. 2,750 seats are not reserved.

5. $22,920

$1,926 \times \$10 = \$19,260$. $732 \times \$5 = \$3,660$ $\$19,260 + \$3,660 = \$22,920$. The concert hall made $22,920.

6. $5,320

$342 + 418 = 760$. $760 \times \$7 = \$5,320$. The concert hall made $5,320.

7. $6,315

$1,263 \times \$5 = \$6,315$. $1,263 \times \$10 = \$12,630$ $\$12,630 - \$6,315 = \$6,315$. They would have made $6,315 more.

8. 175

$1,900 + 925 = 2,825$. $3,000 - 2,825 = 175$. They sold 175 senior citizens' tickets.

Page 164

1. $11,083

$\$10,200 + \$11,600 + \$9,072 + \$13,460 = \$44,332$. $\$44,332 \div 4 = \$11,083$. The average of their expenses was $11,083.

2. $82

$\$80 + \$75 + \$91 = \$246$. $\$246 \div 3 = \$82$. The average was $82.

Page 165

3. 9

$10 + 8 + 9 + 11 + 7 = 45$. $45 \div 5 = 9$. He worked an average of 9 hours each day.

4. 41

$40 + 42 + 38 + 44 = 164$. $164 \div 4 = 41$. He worked an average of 41 hours each week.

5. $33

$\$28 + \$30 + \$29 + \$33 + \$45 = \$165$. $\$165 \div 5 = \$33$. She made an average of $33 each day.

6. $153

$165 + $155 + $130 + $162 = $612. $612 ÷ 4 = $153. She made an average of $153 each week.

7. 255

300 + 240 + 240 + 200 + 270 + 280 = 1,530. 1,530 ÷ 6 = 255. His average score was 255.

8. 255

300 + 200 + 250 + 250 + 280 + 250 = 1,530. 1,530 ÷ 6 = 255. Her average score was 255.

Skills Inventory

Page 166

1. thirty-two
2. two hundred forty-six
3. two thousand, three hundred sixteen
4. 50 > 40
5. 15 < 25
6. 31 > 13
7. 100 > 69
8. 20
9. 2
10. 200
11. 5,000
12. 90
13. 480
14. 3,270
15. 300
16. 6,400
17. 45,500
18. 5,000
19. 72,000
20. 726,000
21. 14
22. 18
23. 71
24. 69
25. 693
26. 3,698
27. 154
28. 167
29. 1,278
30. 5,294
31. 372,409
32. 3,661,515

Page 167

33. 8
34. 8
35. 11
36. 83
37. 5
38. 361
39. 5,134
40. 3,332
41. 17
42. 64
43. 24
44. 25
45. 177
46. 559
47. 2,002
48. 11,095
49. 153,457
50. 42
51. 93
52. 2,004
53. 18,090
54. 372
55. 18,060
56. 48,510
57. 370,829
58. 710,000
59. 3,427,000
60. 192
61. 1,401
62. 29,456
63. 513
64. 479,120
65. 84,534
66. 214,200
67. 2,425,460

Page 168

68. 2
69. 8
70. 81
71. 61
72. 6 R1
73. 7 R2
74. 73 R1
75. 218
76. 251 R1
77. 5,240
78. 1 R11
79. 9 R34
80. 99
81. 808 R20
82. 8 R416
83. 102 R14

KEY OPERATION WORDS

Word problems often contain clue words that help you solve the problem. These words tell you whether you need to add, subtract, multiply, or divide. The lists of words below will help you decide which operation to use when solving word problems.

Addition

add
all together
and
both
combined
in all
increase
more
plus
sum
total

Subtraction

change (money)
decrease
difference
left
less than
more than
reduce
remain or remaining
smaller, larger, farther,
   nearer, and so on

Multiplication

in all
of
multiply
product
times (as much)
total
twice
whole

Division

average
cut
divide
each
equal pieces
every
one
split

TABLE OF MEASUREMENTS

Time

60 seconds = 1 minute
60 minutes = 1 hour
24 hours = 1 day
7 days = 1 week
52 weeks = 1 year
12 months = 1 year
365 days = 1 year

Weight

16 ounces = 1 pound
2,000 pounds = 1 ton

Length

12 inches = 1 foot
36 inches = 1 yard
3 feet = 1 yard
5,280 feet = 1 mile
1,760 yards = 1 mile

Capacity

8 ounces = 1 cup
2 cups = 1 pint
4 cups = 1 quart
2 pints = 1 quart
4 quarts = 1 gallon
8 pints = 1 gallon
16 cups = 1 gallon